# Building on
# Foundations for Eternal Life

## Embracing Truth over Deception

By Thomas G. Edel

*...like a tree planted by streams of water...*

*Psalm 1*

# *Building on*
# Foundations for
# Eternal Life
## *Embracing Truth over Deception*
### By *Thomas G. Edel*

A free download of this book may be available at
ShalomKoinonia.org

Please send comments & suggestions for revision to:
Thomas@ShalomKoinonia.org

# Table of Contents

Greed / Money
Fear
Free Will?

Gain is Godliness
Godliness Is a Means of Gain
A New-Covenant Perspective
Godliness with Contentment
A Living Hope

Hard and Soft Science
Naturalism
Microevolution and Macroevolution
Creation or Evolution?
Science, Philosophy, or Religion?

What Is Unity Based On?
One Body
Disputable Matters
Secondary Issues
Heresy
Our Way Is the Only Way!
Division or Love?

Right Distinctions
We Condemn Ourselves
Don't Judge Motives
Only Judge Actions
Discern Evil and Avoid Evil
Jesus Will Judge
Don't Take Revenge

Receive the Holy Spirit
Filled with the Holy Spirit
"Baptize"
Jewish Baptisms

Baptized in the Holy Spirit
Spiritual Gifts
Speaking in Tongues
Controlling or Empowering?
A Second Blessing?
Benefits of the Holy Spirit

Ways God Has Spoken
Has God Stopped Speaking?
What Is Normal and Common?
Clarity and Certainty
Thoughts and Impressions
Consider Other Possible Sources
Discerning the Difference
Learning from History
Growing Up
My Experience

Knowledge, Understanding, or Wisdom?
God's Viewpoint
By Example or Teaching?
Is It Applicable?
Context and Culture
Scripture or Tradition?
Translation Problems
Compare Scripture with Scripture
Reading into Scripture
Don't Oversimplify

What Is "the Kingdom of God"?
Other Kingdoms and Governments
Living Under Existing Governments
Entering the Kingdom
Living in the Kingdom

# Preface

*And he said to all, "If anyone would come after me, let him deny himself and take up his cross daily and follow me."*
*Luke 9:23 ESV*

---

Have you chosen to follow Jesus? If so, may these pages help you on your journey as we walk the narrow path.

Are you not yet a follower of Jesus? If not yet, I encourage you to consider reading *"Beneath Foundations for Eternal Life."* That book explores self-evident truths that are independent of scripture and that direct us to look to scripture for truth. Free ebook versions of that book (as well as this book) should be available at: ShalomKoinonia.org.

This present book is a sequel to another book titled *"Foundations for Eternal Life."* That book deals with foundational topics that have clear scriptural support. I encourage you to read that book before reading this book. It should be available at the same website indicated above.

This present book deals with many topics that are less foundational, including some topics that aren't so clear in scripture. Even so, these topics are important, and should not be ignored. They have a strong impact on how we live, how we serve our Lord Jesus and serve one another.

Keep in mind that salvation is primarily about coming to Jesus, trusting in Jesus, and following Jesus. He is the Christ, the Son of God, Lord of all. The previous book, *"Foundations for Eternal Life,"* focuses on the more-important aspects of following Jesus. Please understand the subjects in that book before reading this book. This book, which deals more with secondary issues, runs the risk of overcomplicating things for some people. If you don't sense a need for greater understanding regarding some of the topics discussed in this book, prayerfully consider skipping those topics for now. However, many people stumble in their spiritual lives due to lack of understanding in these areas. It is my hope that this book will help many people understand spiritual things better, and live better as a result.

This book turned out to be rather long. If you don't have time to read all of it, I think it would be profitable to read Parts 1, 2 , and 3, and then consider reading any subjects in Part 4 that are of particular interest to you (Part 4, *"Common Deceptions,"* is about 60% of the book). Also, many people may choose to skim or skip most of chapter 5 (a long chapter in Part 1). However, I encourage you to read the first two sections in that chapter (through the *"Chapter Summary"* section). Those changes reduce the page count from about 398 printed pages to about 130 printed pages.

For those interested, this book can be used to facilitate **small group discussion or study.** Pick topics that interest the group for as many meetings as seems beneficial. The discussion could revolve around a simple ongoing question: **"What about you? How should this affect you?"** Per the copyright notice at the front of this book, **this book may be freely copied and freely distributed.** Ebook versions of this book, and versions of this book that are configured for printing, may be available at: ShalomKoinonia.org.

I am indebted to the many people who have helped me in my own search for truth (which is still ongoing). Some of you I know personally; some I know only through your writings or audio-visual works; some lived before my time. Thank you for speaking truth into my life. Thanks also to those who reviewed draft versions of this book and gave valuable feedback. It is a better book because of you.

How great and good is our God! May these pages help you walk closely with him day by day.

> *Oh, magnify the LORD with me, and let us exalt his name together!*         *Psalm 34:3 ESV*

\*\*\*\*\*\*\*\*\*\*\*\*

# Introduction

*Blessed are those who find wisdom,*
*those who gain understanding,*
*for she is more profitable than silver*
*and yields better returns than gold.*
*She is more precious than rubies;*
*nothing you desire can compare with her.*
*Proverbs 3:13-15 NIV*

---

*"Nothing you desire can compare with her."* Do you have it? Is it really that valuable? Do you have *wisdom* and *understanding*? Consider how some people seem to approach this subject:

- Some people seem to prefer ignorance over understanding and wisdom. They seem to think that being ignorant will somehow protect them from truth that they suspect they won't like.

- Others believe that good intentions are enough; that somehow good intentions will protect them from deception or harm. They think their intentions are always good, so they don't pursue wisdom and understanding.

- Some believe that the devil and his angels have no influence on them. They have been taught that the devil "cannot touch them," so these people are slow to discern his deceptions.

- Some people expect the Holy Spirit to continually tell them what to do, when to do it, where to do it, and how to do it. They think they are being spiritual to hold such a viewpoint. They avoid using their own ability to reason.

- Others think that pursuing knowledge, understanding, and wisdom is not being spiritual. They think all those things have been superseded by the coming of the Holy Spirit.

- Others pursue knowledge, understanding, and wisdom through academic study, but obtain only knowledge.

- Still others think that wisdom and understanding is primarily about knowing right doctrines and obeying religious rules, rather than knowing God, loving God, and loving others.

- Some people are tired of being deceived. They want to know truth and live by truth. They want to grow in understanding and wisdom. Some people are ready to put deception behind them.

What about you?

Do you want to live by truth and overcome deception? Do you want *wisdom* and *understanding*? If so, I invite you to join me in exploring how to embrace truth and reject what is false; how to grow in *wisdom* and *understanding*. This is an important key to spiritual strength and spiritual growth.

Most of the concepts discussed in this book go back hundreds of years, if not thousands of years. However, the way these ideas are presented is new, to some degree at least. It is my hope that by addressing these subjects from a somewhat new perspective that you will arrive at a deeper understanding of truth, and that your life will benefit from that. May God bless you with such understanding as you explore these pages.

*Oh, taste and see that the LORD is good!*
*Blessed is the man who takes refuge in him!*
*Psalm 34:8 ESV*

\*\*\*\*\*\*\*\*\*\*\*\*

# PART 1
# From Truth to Wisdom

In Part 1 we'll explore some general principles regarding *truth, knowledge, understanding,* and *wisdom.*

Some people debate whether or not *truth* really exists. However, that is not our concern in this book. This book is built upon the simple premise that *truth* does exist, and that it is to our advantage to embrace *truth* and reject *error.* We should live our lives based on *truth,* and we should reject things that are *false.* If you don't agree with this premise, I recommend that you first read the book *"Beneath Foundations for Eternal Life"* (by the same author as this book).

The existence of truth is not dependent on whether people know it, or are ignorant of it, or reject it. However, truth that is not known or accepted by people is usually of little benefit to them. So, we'll quickly move on to discuss the importance of *knowing* truth, *understanding* truth, and *wisdom* (living according to truth).

Please note that I'll be giving fairly narrow definitions to words like *truth, knowledge, understanding,* and *wisdom.* It is not my intent to claim that my definitions should apply to all the various uses of these words throughout scripture and elsewhere. Rather, it is my intent to look at how scripture deals with the concepts associated with these definitions.

A primary goal in exploring *truth, knowledge, understanding,* and *wisdom* is to live better: to know God better, to love God better, and to love others better. We should all aim to be growing in the areas Paul prayed about:

*And it is my prayer that your love may abound more and more, with knowledge and all discernment, so that you may approve what is excellent, and so be pure and blameless for the day of Christ, filled with the fruit of righteousness that comes through Jesus Christ, to the glory and praise of God.* *Philippians 1:9-11 ESV*

\*\*\*\*\*\*\*\*\*\*\*\*

# Chapter 1
# Truth

*Jesus answered, "You say that I am a king. In fact, the reason I was born and came into the world is to testify to the truth. Everyone on the side of truth listens to me."*

*"What is truth?" retorted Pilate.*　　　　*John 18:37-38 NIV*

---

What is *truth*?

Let me propose a simple definition of *truth* based on common usage of the word:

> **Truth:** Accurate information about how things actually are.

This definition is probably incomplete in many ways, but I hope you agree that this definition is at least consistent with how the word *truth* is often used.

To get a deeper understanding of *truth*, let's look at a few verses in scripture that relate to *truth*, all from the New Testament book of John:

> *For the law was given through Moses; grace and truth came through Jesus Christ.*　　　*John 1:17 ESV*

> *Jesus said to him, "I am the way, and the truth, and the life."*　　　*John 14:6 ESV*

> *"But when he, the Spirit of truth, comes, he will guide you into all the truth."*　　　*John 16:13 NIV*

> *"Sanctify them in the truth; your word is truth."*
> 　　　*John 17:17 ESV*

> *"In fact, the reason I was born and came into the world is to testify to the truth. Everyone on the side of truth listens to me."*　　　*John 18:37 NIV*

Those verses broaden our understanding of the nature of

truth. In some sense:

- *Truth* came through Jesus.
- Jesus is the *truth*.
- The Spirit of *truth* will guide Jesus' disciples into *truth*.
- Jesus prayed for his disciples to be sanctified in the *truth*.
- The word of the Father is *truth*.
- Jesus came into the world to testify to the *truth*.
- Everyone on the side of *truth* listens to Jesus.

John also records these words of Jesus written to the believers in Philadelphia:

> **"These are the words of him who is holy and true..."**
> *Revelation 3:7 NIV*

The apostle John claims twice that what he wrote about Jesus is true:

> **The man who saw it has given testimony, and his testimony is true. He knows that he tells the truth, and he testifies so that you also may believe.** *John 19:35 NIV*

> **This is the disciple who testifies to these things and who wrote them down. We know that his testimony is true.**
> *John 21:24 NIV*

While Jesus is closely aligned with truth, he indicates that the opposite is true of the devil. Jesus said this to some of the religious people of his day:

> **"You are of your father the devil, and your will is to do your father's desires. He was a murderer from the beginning, and does not stand in the truth, because there is no truth in him. When he lies, he speaks out of his own character, for he is a liar and the father of lies."**
> *John 8:44 ESV*

*Truth* is often understood as being the opposite of deception, falsehood, error, and lies. Deception, falsehood, error, and lies generally involve **wrong** *information about how things actually are.* If deception, falsehood, error, and lies didn't exist, then the concept of truth would, perhaps, be meaningless.

*Truth* can be divided into different categories, such as scientific truth, historical truth, financial truth, political truth, and spiritual truth. Of course, people often disagree about what is true or not true in each of these categories. Some people may try to publicize truth about a particular subject, while other people may try to suppress truth about such things. This book is primarily concerned with spiritual truth, though it may touch on some other areas of truth, such as historical truth and scientific truth. A primary goal of this book is to make spiritual truth more widely known and understood.

Knowing *truth* is important. It should be self-evident that if we live our lives based on deception, error, and lies—rather than truth—then it is more likely that bad things will happen to us, or that we will do things we will later regret. Living our lives based on truth helps us to avoid many problems, and to do good, rather than bad.

So, we begin with the understanding that truth exists, truth is important to Jesus, knowing truth is important, and we should aim to live our lives based on truth.

## For Further Reflection

- Read the gospel of John, keeping an eye out for the importance and nature of **truth**, and things that are **true.**

\*\*\*\*\*\*\*\*\*\*\*\*

# Chapter 2
# Knowledge

*"My people are destroyed for lack of knowledge."*
*Hosea 4:6 WEB*

*We know that we all have knowledge.*
*Knowledge puffs up, but love builds up.*
*1Corinthians 8:1 WEB*

---

Let's continue clarifying the intended meanings of some important words. It is difficult to communicate *truth* in a book if the meanings of various words are not clear.

Recall a simple definition of *truth* from chapter 1:

**Truth:** Accurate information about how things actually are.

It should be clear that truth exists whether anyone acknowledges it or not. Truth is not dependent on anyone knowing it or agreeing with it. For example, the existence of gravity is a truth we are all acquainted with to varying degrees. We all experience the earth's gravity pulling us down toward the earth. Apart from a miracle happening, a person cannot claim that gravity doesn't exist and then be able to float away, free from gravity. Gravity exists whether we acknowledge it or not, or whether we understand it or not. It does not cease to exist if we don't believe in it or know about it. Truth about gravity is not dependent on our personal knowledge or beliefs about it.

It is like this with all kinds of truths. They exist whether or not we believe in them. Many truths are not as clear as the existence of gravity, but they still exist, whether we know about them or not, whether we acknowledge them or not.

Now let's look at the word *Knowledge*. *Knowledge* has to do with people learning and knowing different kinds of *truth*.

Knowledge exists only to the extent that various truths are known by various people.

A distinction is necessary here. The word *knowledge* can be used to refer to all truth known by all people. In this sense knowledge can be preserved and increased by various truths being written down in books and journals (in physical or electronic form) and being made accessible to people through libraries or electronic means (such as the Internet). However, in this book I want to focus on the personal *knowledge* we each individually have, which is comprised of the various *truths* we each know. This personal knowledge will vary from day to day, as we learn some truths we had not previously known, and forget some truths we had previously learned. On this basis, I propose this simple definition of knowledge:

**Knowledge:** Various truths known by an individual.

I want to distinguish *knowledge* from *skill, understanding,* and *wisdom*. Knowledge, the way I am intending the word, is a first level of embracing truth. It is simply a matter of knowing facts (or "truths"). *Skill, understanding, and wisdom* are deeper levels of embracing or using truth, and will be discussed more in the following chapters.

We all have at least some knowledge about many things. Having knowledge is associated with a common problem: ***"Knowledge puffs up"*** (1 Corinthians 8:1). We tend to be proud about what we know. Some forms of pride are condemned in the New Testament (Romans 12:16, 1 Corinthians 13:4, 2 Timothy 3:2, 1 Peter 5:5). So, having knowledge can be detrimental if it is not combined rightly with understanding, wisdom, humility, and love.

## For Further Reflection

- What kinds of truths do you know?

\*\*\*\*\*\*\*\*\*\*\*

# Chapter 3
# Understanding

*Now as for these four youths, God gave them knowledge and skill in all learning and wisdom; and Daniel had understanding in all visions and dreams.*    Daniel 1:17 WEB

---

Do you have a favorite sport?  If so, you probably know the rules about how to play it pretty well.  But how good are you at playing it?  It's one thing to have *knowledge* about how to play, but it's quite another thing to play with *skill*.  Acquiring skill generally involves a great deal of practice.  Knowing how to play is often relatively easy; but acquiring skill in playing is usually much more difficult.

So it is in many areas of life.  Learning the facts about how to do something is usually much easier than acquiring skill to actually do it.

There is a similar relationship between *knowledge* and *understanding*.  Just having knowledge about various things is not enough.  Just as it takes practice to become skillful at physical tasks, one must practice using *knowledge* to develop *understanding*.

You probably know people who seem to have a lot of *knowledge*; they know a lot of facts.  Yet they may not be very good at applying their *knowledge* to real-life situations.  It's one thing to have *knowledge*, but it's quite another thing to have *understanding*.

Recall the simple definitions of *truth* and *knowledge* from previous chapters:

> **Truth:**  Accurate information about how things actually are.

> **Knowledge:**  Various truths known by an individual.

Having *understanding* about a particular subject is more than just having *knowledge* about that subject; it is more than just knowing various *truths*. Having *understanding* is knowing how to apply *truths* in such a way as to solve or prevent problems; or to facilitate a positive outcome.

Based on this, I propose a simple definition of *understanding*:

> **Understanding:** Knowing how to use knowledge effectively.

Consider a common example. To enter many professions it is generally required that a person do more than just gain *knowledge* through classroom learning or from self-study. Usually practical experience related to the profession is required. Just having lots of knowledge is usually not adequate. It generally takes some kind of practical experience to gain the *understanding* necessary to properly practice the profession.

So it is with many areas of life. There is not much of a limit to the amount of *knowledge* one can obtain through study, but study alone often does not result in much *understanding*. Deep understanding is usually gained by processes different than simply acquiring knowledge through study. *Understanding* generally comes through experience, not just by knowing *truth*, not just by having *knowledge*.

I think most of us make it our goal to have *skill* regarding the things we do. We aren't satisfied just having *knowledge* about how to do something; we want to be able to do it well. Likewise, we should make it our goal to have *understanding* about various things that affect our lives, and not settle for just having *knowledge*.

## For Further Reflection

- Is there an area of life you have a lot of knowledge about, but not much understanding?

\*\*\*\*\*\*\*\*\*\*\*\*

# Chapter 4
# Wisdom & Faith

*How much better it is to get wisdom than gold!*
*Yes, to get understanding is to be chosen rather than silver.*
Proverbs 16:16 WEB

---

Before we discuss wisdom, let's remember some important context. A primary goal in exploring truth, knowledge, understanding, and wisdom is to ultimately live better: to know God better, to love God better, and to love others better. As Paul said:

> *If I speak with the languages of men and of angels, but don't have love, I have become sounding brass, or a clanging cymbal. If I have the gift of prophecy, and know all mysteries and all knowledge; and if I have all faith, so as to remove mountains, but don't have love, I am nothing. If I give away all my goods to feed the poor, and if I give my body to be burned, but don't have love, it profits me nothing.* 1Corinthians 13:1-3 WEB

Is there someone near you who needs you to demonstrate Christ's love to them right now? If so, please put this book down and go tend to that. It's okay; this book can wait. Go show someone the love of God working through you. Putting right beliefs into right actions is what wisdom is about.

*****(Really, it's okay, this marks the spot)******

## Wisdom

Now, please continue with me as I define another important word. Please keep in mind that the definitions I make in this book are for the purpose of communicating truths in the context of this book. Other people may use the same words with different meanings for other purposes. I am not claiming that my definitions should apply to other contexts. The contexts in which words are used often affects their intended meaning.

We have seen how *understanding* is a deeper application of truth than just having *knowledge*. In a similar way, *wisdom* is a deeper application of truth than *understanding* is.

It is one thing to know various truths; I call that *knowledge*. It is another thing to have knowledge and know how to use it effectively; I call that *understanding*. It is still another thing to have knowledge and understanding, and to actually put them into practice for right living; I call that *wisdom*.

Consider an example. The teachers of the law and the Pharisees of Jesus' day were considered by many to be experts in their culture's religious system. However, Jesus condemned them, saying *"they do not practice what they preach"* (Matthew 23:3 NIV). Apparently, they had knowledge about what was right and wrong, and apparently had at least some understanding to be able to *"preach"* to others, but they didn't put their understanding into practice in their own lives. Jesus called them *"hypocrites"* (Matthew 23:13, 15, 23, 25, 27, 29).

So, I propose this definition for the word *wisdom*:

**Wisdom:**  Having knowledge and understanding, and putting them into practice for right living.

Our goal should be to have *wisdom*, to consistently live according to good knowledge and understanding. Just having *knowledge* and *understanding* about various *truths* is not enough, we must put our knowledge and understanding into practice if we are to experience spiritual success, if we are to have *wisdom*.

Now, since I am promoting *wisdom* (as I have defined it) as an important goal, it is important to see that scripture also emphasizes the importance of *wisdom* (as I have defined it). However, scripture will usually phrase this concept somewhat differently, using phrases like:

- Walk in wisdom.
- Walk in understanding.
- Walk in righteousness.
- Keep God's word.
- Obey God's commands.
- Bear good fruit.

Please consider for a moment how each of those phrases is related to *having knowledge and understanding, and putting them into practice for right living* (my definition of *wisdom*).

Now let's look at some verses that associate *"wisdom"* as used in scripture (or being *"wise"*), with *wisdom* as I have defined it. My intent here is to show that spiritual *"wisdom"* in scripture (not worldly *"wisdom"*) is often associated with *putting knowledge and understanding into practice for right living* (per my definition of *wisdom*).

> *"See, I have taught you statutes and rules, as the LORD my God commanded me, that you should do them in the land that you are entering to take possession of it. Keep them and do them, for that will be your wisdom and your understanding in the sight of the peoples, who, when they hear all these statutes, will say, 'Surely this great nation is a wise and understanding people.'"*
> *Deuteronomy 4:5-6 ESV*

> *Then you will understand righteousness and justice and equity, every good path; for wisdom will come into your heart, and knowledge will be pleasant to your soul; discretion will watch over you, understanding will guard you... So you will walk in the way of the good and keep to the paths of the righteous.*      *Proverbs 2:9-11, 20 ESV*

> *Doesn't wisdom cry out? Doesn't understanding raise her voice? ... "I walk in the way of righteousness, in the midst of the paths of justice ... Now therefore, my sons,*

*listen to me, for blessed are those who keep my ways. Hear instruction, and be wise. Don't refuse it."*

*Proverbs 8:1, 20, 32-33 WEB*

*Wisdom has built her house. She has carved out her seven pillars. ... She cries from the highest places of the city: ... "Leave your simple ways, and live. Walk in the way of understanding."*

*Proverbs 9:1, 3, 6 WEB*

*"Everyone then who hears these words of mine and does them will be like a wise man who built his house on the rock. And the rain fell, and the floods came, and the winds blew and beat on that house, but it did not fall, because it had been founded on the rock. And everyone who hears these words of mine and does not do them will be like a foolish man who built his house on the sand. And the rain fell, and the floods came, and the winds blew and beat against that house, and it fell, and great was the fall of it."*

*Matthew 7:24-27 ESV*

*"Who then is the faithful and wise servant, whom his lord has set over his household, to give them their food in due season? Blessed is that servant whom his lord finds doing so when he comes. Most certainly I tell you that he will set him over all that he has."*

*Matthew 24:45-47 WEB*

*"Those who were foolish, when they took their lamps, took no oil with them, but the wise took oil in their vessels with their lamps."*

*Matthew 25:3-4 WEB*

*Therefore watch carefully how you walk, not as unwise, but as wise; redeeming the time, because the days are evil.*

*Ephesians 5:15-16 WEB*

*For this cause, we also, since the day we heard this, don't cease praying and making requests for you, that you may be filled with the knowledge of his will in all spiritual wisdom and understanding, that you may walk worthily of the Lord, to please him in all respects, bearing fruit in every good work...*  Colossians 1:9-10 WEB

*Let the word of Christ dwell in you richly; in all wisdom teaching and admonishing one another with psalms, hymns, and spiritual songs, singing with grace in your heart to the Lord.*  Colossians 3:16 WEB

*Walk in wisdom toward those who are outside, redeeming the time.*  Colossians 4:5 WEB

*Who is wise and understanding among you?  Let them show it by their good life, by deeds done in the humility that comes from wisdom.*  James 3:13 NIV

*But the wisdom that is from above is first pure, then peaceful, gentle, reasonable, full of mercy and good fruits, without partiality, and without hypocrisy.*  James 3:17 WEB

Here are some verses that emphasize the importance of doing what we understand, without directly associating it with **wisdom**:

*"Not everyone who says to me, 'Lord, Lord,' will enter into the Kingdom of Heaven; but he who does the will of my Father who is in heaven."*  Matthew 7:21 WEB

*But be doers of the word, and not hearers only, deceiving yourselves.*  James 1:22 ESV

And here is a passage that I find sums up the importance of *knowledge, understanding,* and *wisdom*:

*And it is my prayer that your love may abound more and more, with knowledge and all discernment, so that you may approve what is excellent, and so be pure and blameless for the day of Christ, filled with the fruit of righteousness that comes through Jesus Christ, to the glory and praise of God.*  Philippians 1:9-11 ESV

In those verses I hear Paul praying that people's **love** would **abound** with the things we have been discussing:

- *"with knowledge"* roughly correlates with having *knowledge* as I have defined it.

- *"all discernment, so that you may approve what is excellent"* roughly correlates with having *understanding*, per my definition of that word.

- *"and so be pure and blameless for the day of Christ, filled with the fruit of righteousness"* roughly correlates with right living (based on applying knowledge and understanding), which correlates with how I have defined *wisdom*.

And the final part of those verses clarifies the source of these good things: *"that comes through Jesus Christ, to the glory and praise of God."*

So, we see the importance of actually applying our knowledge and understanding to how we live. It is not enough to know and understand various truths; wisdom involves putting our knowledge and understanding into practice.

## Faith

Now let's consider how *wisdom* relates to *spiritual truth* and *faith*. *Faith* appears to me to be similar to *wisdom* in many respects. Faith involves *knowing, understanding,* and *acting* on spiritual truth, similar to how wisdom involves *knowing, understanding,* and *acting* on truth in general. Let's briefly consider those three aspects of faith.

First, faith involves *knowing* about spiritual truth, in accord with this verse:

> *Now faith is confidence in what we hope for and assurance about what we do not see.*     Hebrews 11:1 NIV

From this we see that faith involves at least some *knowledge* about present spiritual reality (*"what we do not see"*) and about things that will happen in the future (*"what we hope for"*).

*Knowledge* related to faith is often learned through other people. Consider what Paul wrote:

> *How then will they call on him in whom they have not believed? How will they believe in him whom they have not heard? How will they hear without a preacher? And how will they preach unless they are sent? As it is written: "How beautiful are the feet of those who preach the Good News of peace, who bring glad tidings of good things!" But they didn't all listen to the glad news. For Isaiah says, "Lord, who has believed our report?" So faith comes by hearing, and hearing by the word of God.*
> *Romans 10:14-17 WEB*

*Hearing the word of God* communicates *knowledge* about salvation to people. Faith in Jesus can happen only with some level of *knowledge* about Jesus. We see from those verses the important role that *knowledge* has in building faith.

Second, *faith* involves *understanding* spiritual truth. This is a rather tricky subject, as *understanding* associated with spiritual truth may take the form of spiritual conviction, rather than reasoned understanding. Per Hebrews 11:1 (above), faith involves **confidence** and **assurance**, not just intellectual knowledge. *Understanding* associated with *faith* involves having **confidence** and **assurance** about things that aren't visible and things we hope for in the future.

This may be clarified by an example. Consider two people who hear a salvation message about Jesus (per Romans 10:14-17 above). The first person may view their new knowledge merely as doctrines of a religion, and have little conviction as to its truth. However, the second person may acquire the same knowledge, but additionally may be convinced of its truth, and believes that what was shared is truly the path to life. Only the second person *understands* the message in the sense I am meaning.

Third, *faith* involves acting on what we know and understand, similar to how *wisdom* involves *"having knowledge and understanding, and putting them into practice for right living."* In our example, the first person will likely NOT repent and have faith in Jesus, since the first person does not really *understand* the message. This correlates with what Jesus said regarding the parable of the sower and the seed:

> *"When anyone hears the word of the kingdom and does not understand it, the evil one comes and snatches away what has been sown in his heart. This is what was sown along the path."*
> *Matthew 13:19 ESV*

However, the second person in our example does understand the message, and has opportunity to act on it and be saved. This also correlates with what Jesus said regarding the parable of the sower and the seed:

> *"As for what was sown on good soil, this is the one who hears the word and understands it. He indeed bears fruit and yields, in one case a hundredfold, in another sixty, and in another thirty."*
> *Matthew 13:23 ESV*

The *fruit* is the result of putting into practice *the word* that was heard and understood.

James also addresses the importance of faith being associated with action:

> *You foolish person, do you want evidence that faith without deeds is useless? Was not our father Abraham considered righteous for what he did when he offered his son Isaac on the altar? You see that his faith and his actions were working together, and his faith was made complete by what he did. And the scripture was fulfilled that says, "Abraham believed God, and it was credited to him as righteousness," and he was called God's friend.*
> *James 2:20-23 NIV*

Consider also how the people of faith mentioned in Hebrews

11 are characterized by their actions that resulted from their faith. For example:

> *By faith Moses' parents hid him for three months after he was born, because they saw he was no ordinary child, and they were not afraid of the king's edict.*
>
> *By faith Moses, when he had grown up, refused to be known as the son of Pharaoh's daughter. He chose to be mistreated along with the people of God rather than to enjoy the fleeting pleasures of sin.*
>
> *Hebrews 11:23-25 NIV*

To better understand that faith involves *knowing*, *understanding*, and *acting* on spiritual truth, let's look at some examples of people who were said to have little or no faith, and people who had great faith. First, let's look at what happened with the twelve disciples early in Jesus' ministry:

> *That day when evening came, he said to his disciples, "Let us go over to the other side." Leaving the crowd behind, they took him along, just as he was, in the boat. There were also other boats with him. A furious squall came up, and the waves broke over the boat, so that it was nearly swamped. Jesus was in the stern, sleeping on a cushion. The disciples woke him and said to him, "Teacher, don't you care if we drown?"*
>
> *He got up, rebuked the wind and said to the waves, "Quiet! Be still!" Then the wind died down and it was completely calm.*
>
> *He said to his disciples, "Why are you so afraid? Do you still have no faith?"*
>
> *They were terrified and asked each other, "Who is this? Even the wind and the waves obey him!"*
>
> *Mark 4:35-41 NIV*

Here we see that the disciples lacked *knowledge* about who

Jesus is, and about his power, since they asked ***"Who is this? Even the wind and the waves obey him!"*** They clearly didn't *understand* that Jesus is Lord of all, and didn't understand that they were safe with Jesus in their boat. This lack of knowledge and understanding led them to *act* out of fear. Jesus questioned them: ***"Do you still have no faith?"***

Now let's look at a person who Jesus said had "great faith":

> ***When Jesus had entered Capernaum, a centurion came to him, asking for help. "Lord," he said, "my servant lies at home paralyzed, suffering terribly."***
>
> ***Jesus said to him, "Shall I come and heal him?"***
>
> ***The centurion replied, "Lord, I do not deserve to have you come under my roof. But just say the word, and my servant will be healed. For I myself am a man under authority, with soldiers under me. I tell this one, 'Go,' and he goes; and that one, 'Come,' and he comes. I say to my servant, 'Do this,' and he does it."***
>
> ***When Jesus heard this, he was amazed and said to those following him, "Truly I tell you, I have not found anyone in Israel with such great faith. I say to you that many will come from the east and the west, and will take their places at the feast with Abraham, Isaac and Jacob in the kingdom of heaven. But the subjects of the kingdom will be thrown outside, into the darkness, where there will be weeping and gnashing of teeth."***
>
> ***Then Jesus said to the centurion, "Go! Let it be done just as you believed it would." And his servant was healed at that moment.*** *Matthew 8:5-13 NIV*

I don't think it is reading too much into these verses to understand that the centurion had heard about Jesus, and had at least some *knowledge* about Jesus, especially about the miracles of healing that he was doing. The centurion *understood* that Jesus could also heal his servant. He *acted* on that understanding by going to Jesus and asking for help.

He also *understood* that Jesus must have great authority in order to do such miracles, and that Jesus didn't need to come in person to heal his servant, so he *acted* in faith by saying: ***"But just say the word, and my servant will be healed."*** Jesus referred to all of this as ***"great faith."***

Let's look at another example of **great faith:**

> *Leaving that place, Jesus withdrew to the region of Tyre and Sidon. A Canaanite woman from that vicinity came to him, crying out, "Lord, Son of David, have mercy on me! My daughter is demon-possessed and suffering terribly."*
>
> *Jesus did not answer a word. So his disciples came to him and urged him, "Send her away, for she keeps crying out after us."*
>
> *He answered, "I was sent only to the lost sheep of Israel."*
>
> *The woman came and knelt before him. "Lord, help me!" she said.*
>
> *He replied, "It is not right to take the children's bread and toss it to the dogs."*
>
> *"Yes it is, Lord," she said. "Even the dogs eat the crumbs that fall from their master's table."*
>
> *Then Jesus said to her, "Woman, you have great faith! Your request is granted." And her daughter was healed at that moment.*                    Matthew 15:21-28 NIV

Again, I don't think it is reading too much into these verses to understand that the woman had heard about Jesus, and had at least some *knowledge* about Jesus, especially about miracles of healing and deliverance from evil spirits. She appears to *understand* that Jesus is the promised Messiah, since she calls him "Son of David." She also *understands* that Jesus is able to drive the demon out of her daughter. She likely also *understands* that her non-Jewish background may be a hindrance to getting the healing she seeks. She *acts* on her understanding by going to Jesus and persistently crying out for help. When Jesus initially is slow to answer, and then answers rather harshly, she does not answer back harshly, but acknowledges her situation and still persists in asking for help. Jesus calls this **"great faith,"** and the woman's daughter is healed.

So, we see that faith involves *knowing*, *understanding*, and *acting* on spiritual truth.

For clarity, let's summarize some important points:

**Truth** is accurate information about how things actually are. **Truth** exists independent of our knowledge of it, and is not affected by whether or not we agree with it.

**Knowledge** involves learning and knowing various *truths*.

**Understanding** involves having knowledge and knowing how to use *knowledge* effectively.

**Wisdom** involves having knowledge and understanding, and putting them into practice for right living.

**Faith** involves *knowing*, *understanding*, and *acting* on spiritual truth, similar to how wisdom involves *knowing*, *understanding*, and *acting* on truth in general.

## For Further Reflection

- Have you ever **not** done what you knew you should do?

- Do you have faith that affects how you live?

\*\*\*\*\*\*\*\*\*\*\*

# Chapter 5
# Growing in Understanding & Wisdom

*Blessed is the one who finds wisdom, and the one who gets understanding, for the gain from her is better than gain from silver and her profit better than gold.*
*She is more precious than jewels,*
*and nothing you desire can compare with her.*
*Proverbs 3:13-15 ESV*

---

Growing in understanding and wisdom is a key aspect of growing spiritually. Consider your own salvation. How did it happen? I suspect it followed this pattern:

- You learned various *truths* about Jesus and about salvation through faith in Jesus. You learned that he is the Christ, the Son of God, Lord of all; that he died on the cross to pay the penalty for your sins; that eternal life is given to all who follow him. Stated somewhat differently, you gained *knowledge* about Jesus and salvation.

- You *understood* that those *truths* applied to you. You were lost apart from Jesus, and you *understood* that you needed to follow Jesus in order to be forgiven of your sins and be saved.

- You chose to act on that understanding, and chose to follow Jesus. Putting understanding into practice is roughly how I have defined *wisdom*. You acted with *wisdom* when you chose to follow Jesus.

- You *experienced* new life in Jesus; you were born again!

A similar process is usually involved in spiritual growth after salvation. An improvement in spiritual *experience* generally follows an increase in *knowledge*, *understanding*, and *wisdom* (putting new understanding into practice).

Regarding spiritual growth, it should be apparent that *faith* is an important component of spiritual growth. We have already discussed how faith is closely associated with spiritual *knowledge, understanding,* and *wisdom. Faith* involves *knowing, understanding,* and *acting* on spiritual truth, similar to how wisdom involves *knowing, understanding,* and *acting* on truth in general. Faith is not just having intellectual knowledge and understanding about spiritual truth. Faith involves a strong belief that affects how we live.

Many people look for spiritual experiences to happen ahead of, or independent of, faith and wisdom, but that is not usually how it happens. Improved spiritual *experience* usually comes *after we act* in faith on new understanding. Sometimes this involves new grace from God, but usually it involves new understanding of grace that God has already given all believers through Jesus. Consider Peter's words:

> *His divine power has granted to us all things that pertain to life and godliness, through the knowledge of him who called us to his own glory and excellence, by which he has granted to us his precious and very great promises, so that through them you may become partakers of the divine nature, having escaped from the corruption that is in the world because of sinful desire.*
>
> *2Peter 1:3-4 ESV*

God has already given us **all things that pertain to life and godliness.** If we find we are lacking in this area, it is not because God is withholding something we need. Rather, our lack is likely due to not understanding and applying grace that God has already made available to us.

For example, many believers may not experience deliverance from the power of sin when they are first saved. They usually know that their sins have been forgiven through the sacrifice of Jesus, but they may not experience freedom from the power sin. Experiencing freedom from sin does not normally involve new grace from God, but rather involves understanding and applying grace that has already been given. Freedom from the power of sin often involves deeper *knowledge* and *understanding* about how we each died with Jesus, counting his death as our own death to sin, and learning to walk in that truth (*wisdom*). This topic will be discussed more in Chapter 20 *"Spirit and Flesh in Conflict."*

So, we see that spiritual growth is often associated with an increase in *knowledge, understanding,* and *wisdom.* Failure to grow in these areas may seriously hinder spiritual growth.

## Chapter Summary

We now turn our attention to how we can grow in the areas of *knowledge, understanding,* and *wisdom.* We'll be looking at various scriptures to see the many ways we can grow in these areas.

While, in a theoretical sense, God is the source of all knowledge and understanding, in a practical sense God calls us to cooperate with him in growing in these areas. We need to depend on God, while actively being involved, similar to the situations mentioned in this verse:

> **Unless the LORD builds the house, those who build it labor in vain. Unless the LORD watches over the city, the watchman stays awake in vain.** *Psalm 127:1 ESV*

This verse is not saying we should expect God to build us a house without our active involvement, or to trust God to watch over the city without posting a watchman, but rather to depend on God for success while we actively participate. Likewise, scripture calls us to actively participate in growing in knowledge, understanding, and wisdom, as the following pages will show.

This is a long chapter. Depending on how well you already know scripture, how mature in faith you are, and how much time you have to read this book, you may want to skim parts of this chapter, or maybe even skip the rest of it for now (maybe come back to it later, if you have time). To help you make that decision, here is an outline of the rest of this chapter (this is simply a list of all the subheadings):

- Please Understand
- Knowledge Is Just a Starting Point
- Acknowledge and Respect God
- Know You Can Be Deceived
- Know your Need
- Be Honest with God
- Understanding Comes from God
- Ask God for Understanding
- The Holy Spirit
- Look to Scripture
- Do It, and Know
- Delight in Understanding & Wisdom
- Gifted Teachers
- Good Relationships
- Listen to Advice
- Different Viewpoints
- Observation and Reason
- Not by Worldly Learning and Philosophy
- Don't Reject Truth
- Don't Be Proud
- Affliction and Suffering
- Wisdom Makes Right Choices
- Wisdom Chooses God's Way
- Jesus

It seems rather sobering how many aspects there are to growing in understanding and wisdom. Perhaps this subject is not as simple as we first thought!

## Please Understand

Before we look at the many ways we can grow in *knowledge*,

*understanding*, and *wisdom*, I need to address a problem that requires your *understanding*. Let me try to explain.

I have defined *knowledge, understanding*, and *wisdom* as:

- **Knowledge:** Various truths known by an individual.

- **Understanding:** Knowing how to use *knowledge* effectively.

- **Wisdom:** Having *knowledge* and *understanding*, and putting them into practice for right living.

However, it appears to me that where the Bible uses the words "knowledge," "understanding," and "wisdom," it often does not adhere to my narrow definitions for those words. There seems to be more overlap in how these words are used in the Bible than how I have defined them in this book. I think this issue goes beyond Bible translations and is inherent in the original writings in the original languages. I'm pretty sure this is not just a translation problem (though translations likely contribute to the problem). It goes deeper than that. It is a problem with language itself.

In particular, the words "wisdom" and "understanding" often seem to be used somewhat interchangeably in scripture. The word "wisdom" in scripture often is used with a meaning that is close to my definition of "*understanding*." Likewise, the word "understanding" in scripture sometimes seems to be used in a way that is close to my definition of "*wisdom*."

Using imperfect languages to communicate truth is difficult, partly because the meanings of many words are partly dependent on the context they are used in. Also, words may have somewhat different meanings or connotations to different people. Then there is the problem of translating from one language and culture to another language and culture. Things can get very messy very quickly!

Even though my definitions of *knowledge, understanding*, and *wisdom* are not always the intended meanings of those words as used in scripture, I hope you agree with me that scripture does often discuss the concepts associated with my definitions of those words. In this chapter I hope to show the many ways scripture indicates we can grow in *knowledge, understanding*, and *wisdom*, and to show the importance of doing so.

I won't be concerned about whether particular usages of words like "wisdom" and "understanding" in scripture correlate completely with my definitions. That's not the point. The point is to see the importance of acquiring those kinds of things, and how to grow in those kinds of things, regardless of the specific words used.

## Knowledge Is Just a Starting Point

Before we dig into scripture, let's look at some practical aspects of how *knowledge, understanding* and *wisdom* relate to each other.

While it is possible to have *knowledge* without *understanding*, it is normally not possible to have *understanding* without at least some *knowledge,* since *understanding* involves knowing how to apply *knowledge* effectively. Likewise, it is possible to have *understanding* without *wisdom*, but it is not normally possible to have *wisdom* without at least some *understanding,* since *wisdom* involves putting *knowledge* and *understanding* into practice for right living.

As already mentioned, our goal should be to have *wisdom*, to consistently live according to good *knowledge* and *understanding*. However, we can't skip acquiring *knowledge* and *understanding* and go directly to having *wisdom*. *Understanding* must be built on a foundation of *knowledge*, and *wisdom* must be supported by *understanding*.

However, don't be discouraged if you think you have little knowledge. While knowledge is necessary to grow in understanding and wisdom, knowledge is not usually the weak link in the process of gaining wisdom. It seems to me that most people have much more knowledge than understanding and wisdom. A little knowledge, understood well and put into practice, is much more valuable than lots of knowledge not understood well, or not put into practice. So don't be discouraged if you think you have little knowledge. Rather focus on understanding what you do know, and put it into practice. Doing so will make you much wiser than many people who have lots of education and scholarly degrees, but who don't put their knowledge and understanding into practice.

Now, let's look at scripture for various ways we can grow in *knowledge, understanding*, and *wisdom*.

## Acknowledge and Respect God

Scripture says:

*"To man he said, 'Behold, the fear of the Lord, that is wisdom. To depart from evil is understanding.'"*
*Job 28:28 WEB*

*The fear of Yahweh is the beginning of wisdom. All those who do his work have a good understanding.*
*Psalm 111:10 WEB*

*The fear of the LORD is the beginning of knowledge; fools despise wisdom and instruction.* *Proverbs 1:7 ESV*

*The fear of the LORD is the beginning of wisdom, and knowledge of the Holy One is understanding.*
*Proverbs 9:10 NIV*

*The fear of Yahweh teaches wisdom. Before honor is humility.* *Proverbs 15:33 WEB*

A proper respect for God is foundational to knowledge, understanding, and wisdom. Do not expect success in growing in these areas without this key perspective in your life.

# Know You Can Be Deceived

We can be deceived both in our *knowledge* and in our *understanding*. Consider Solomon's words:

> *There is a way that seems right to a man, but its end is the way to death.*     *Proverbs 14:12, 16:25 ESV*

People following *the way to death* generally don't have a proper *understanding* of key spiritual principles. They think they are on a path to life. They may know many spiritual truths, but they fail to *understand* them in a way that leads to salvation, rather than *to death*.

This is not a matter of failing to exercise *wisdom* (failing to do what we *understand* we should do). Rather, it is a failure of *understanding*, for it is *"a way that seems right."* People following the *way that seems right* think they are on the right path, but they aren't. They are deceived. They lack true *understanding*.

Deception will be discussed in more detail in Part 2 of this book.

# Know Your Need

An important step toward acquiring true *knowledge* and *understanding* of a subject is to know our own lack, to realize our need for more, and to seek after *knowledge* and *understanding*. Consider these verses:

> *My son, if you receive my words and treasure up my commandments with you, making your ear attentive to wisdom and inclining your heart to understanding; yes, if you call out for insight and raise your voice for understanding, if you seek it like silver and search for it as for hidden treasures, then you will understand the fear of the LORD and find the knowledge of God.*
> *Proverbs 2:1-5 ESV*

> *Get wisdom. Get understanding. Don't forget, and*

*don't deviate from the words of my mouth. Don't forsake her, and she will preserve you. Love her, and she will keep you. Wisdom is supreme. Get wisdom. Yes, though it costs all your possessions, get understanding. Esteem her, and she will exalt you. She will bring you to honor, when you embrace her.*
*Proverbs 4:5-8 WEB*

Fools tend to do the opposite:

*A fool takes no pleasure in understanding, but only in expressing his opinion.*
*Proverbs 18:2 ESV*

## Be Honest with God

Part of walking in *wisdom* is having right relationship with God. Scripture often speaks of how God helps us to grow in *understanding* and *wisdom* as we walk in right relationship with him. One of the keys to right relationship with God is being honest with God. God values honesty; he is not impressed when we aren't truthful with him.

Most of us understand that God sees everything. We can't hide anything from him. As David wrote:

*You have searched me, LORD, and you know me. You know when I sit and when I rise; you perceive my thoughts from afar. You discern my going out and my lying down; you are familiar with all my ways. Before a word is on my tongue you, LORD, know it completely.*
*Psalm 139:1-4 NIV*

A lack of honesty with God simply hurts your relationship with God. Being honest with God shows we trust him with our problems and builds relationship. Consider these verses:

*Kings take pleasure in honest lips; they value the one who speaks what is right.*
*Proverbs 16:13 NIV*

*LORD, who may dwell in your sacred tent? Who may live on your holy mountain? The one ... who speaks the*

*truth from their heart...* *Psalm 15:1-2 NIV*

**The LORD is near to all who call on him, to all who call on him in truth.** *Psalm 145:18 ESV*

**I acknowledged my sin to you. I didn't hide my iniquity. I said, I will confess my transgressions to Yahweh, and you forgave the iniquity of my sin.** *Psalm 32:5 WEB*

Consider especially that last verse: *"I acknowledged my sin to you. I didn't hide my iniquity."* Are you having trouble with sin in some area of life? (Who of us doesn't have some weakness we deal with?) Don't try to hide this from God. Confess it to him whenever it comes up. Whenever that weakness surfaces, use it as a reminder that it's time to speak to God truthfully about it. Do it as often as it comes up. You can start each time by saying something like "O God, here's that problem I need help with again..." And remember:

**If we say we have no sin, we deceive ourselves, and the truth is not in us. If we confess our sins, he is faithful and just to forgive us our sins and to cleanse us from all unrighteousness.** *1John 1:8-9 ESV*

## Understanding Comes from God

Do you recall how Jesus' disciples seemed to be slow to understand things before Jesus' death and resurrection? For example, when Jesus spoke of his upcoming death and resurrection, Luke records this:

**The disciples did not understand any of this. Its meaning was hidden from them, and they did not know what he was talking about.** *Luke 18:34 NIV*

But, after Jesus rose, that's a different story. What was the difference? Many would say the difference is the coming of the Holy Spirit, and that is true in many ways. However, Luke records something that happened before they were filled with the Holy Spirit at Pentecost (in Acts 2):

> *Then he opened their minds, that they might understand the Scriptures.*  *Luke 24:45 WEB*

Jesus *"opened their minds, that they might understand."* That is a critical key to understanding. In this case, the ability to understand clearly comes from God, and apparently that ability is not given to everyone.

Consider some more verses which indicate that understanding comes from God:

> *And God gave Solomon wisdom and understanding beyond measure, and breadth of mind like the sand on the seashore...*  *1Kings 4:29 ESV*

> *And the whole earth sought the presence of Solomon to hear his wisdom, which God had put into his mind.*  *1Kings 10:24 ESV*

> *And all the kings of the earth sought the presence of Solomon to hear his wisdom, which God had put into his mind.*  *2Chronicles 9:23 ESV*

> *Good and upright is the LORD; therefore he instructs sinners in his ways. He guides the humble in what is right and teaches them his way.*  *Psalm 25:8-9 NIV*

> *For the LORD gives wisdom; from his mouth come knowledge and understanding.*  *Proverbs 2:6 NIV*

> *As for these four youths, God gave them learning and skill in all literature and wisdom, and Daniel had understanding in all visions and dreams.*  *Daniel 1:17 ESV*

> *Consider what I say, and may the Lord give you understanding in all things.*  *2Timothy 2:7 WEB*

> *And we know that the Son of God has come and has given us understanding, so that we may know him who is true; and we are in him who is true, in his Son Jesus Christ. He is the true God and eternal life.*  *1John 5:20 ESV*

# Ask God for Understanding

Since God is clearly a factor in gaining understanding, it seems obvious that we should ask God for help in this area. Here are some verses that support this:

*Only, may the LORD grant you discretion and understanding, that when he gives you charge over Israel you may keep the law of the LORD your God.*

*1Chronicles 22:12 ESV*

*"Give your servant therefore an understanding mind to govern your people, that I may discern between good and evil, for who is able to govern this your great people?" It pleased the Lord that Solomon had asked this.*

*1Kings 3:9-10 ESV*

*Show me your ways, LORD, teach me your paths. Guide me in your truth and teach me, for you are God my Savior, and my hope is in you all day long.*

*Psalm 25:4-5 NIV*

*Make me understand the way of your precepts, and I will meditate on your wondrous works.*

*Psalm 119:27 ESV*

*Give me understanding, that I may keep your law and observe it with my whole heart.*

*Psalm 119:34 ESV*

*Your hands have made and fashioned me; give me understanding that I may learn your commandments.*

*Psalm 119:73 ESV*

*I am your servant; give me understanding, that I may know your testimonies!*

*Psalm 119:125 ESV*

*Your testimonies are righteous forever; give me understanding that I may live.*

*Psalm 119:144 ESV*

*"Ask, and it will be given to you; seek, and you will find; knock, and it will be opened to you. For everyone who asks receives, and the one who seeks finds, and to the one who knocks it will be opened."*

*Matthew 7:7-8 ESV*

*And so, from the day we heard, we have not ceased to pray for you, asking that you may be filled with the knowledge of his will in all spiritual wisdom and understanding...*                    *Colossians 1:9 ESV*

*If any of you lacks wisdom, let him ask God, who gives generously to all without reproach, and it will be given him.  But let him ask in faith, with no doubting, for the one who doubts is like a wave of the sea that is driven and tossed by the wind.  For that person must not suppose that he will receive anything from the Lord; he is a double-minded man, unstable in all his ways.*
                    *James 1:5-8 ESV*

## The Holy Spirit

While understanding often appears in scripture to come directly from God, it is also associated with God giving us his Holy Spirit.  Those who truly trust in Jesus have received the Holy Spirit, who dwells in all true believers (Romans 8:9).  The Holy Spirit teaches us, reminds us, helps our understanding, brings us freedom and gives us power (John 14:26, 1 Corinthians 2:12, 2 Corinthians 3:17, Ephesians 3:16).

Jesus said to his disciples:

*"When the Spirit of truth comes, he will guide you into all the truth..."*                    *John 16:13 ESV*

I believe that same help is available to us today. As we individually abide in Christ and learn to walk by the Spirit, the Holy Spirit will guide us into truth.

The apostle John gives some additional perspective in his first letter:

*You have an anointing from the Holy One, and you all have knowledge.  I have not written to you because you don't know the truth, but because you know it, and because no lie is of the truth.*                    *1John 2:20-21 WEB*

*These things I have written to you concerning those who would lead you astray. As for you, the anointing which you received from him remains in you, and you don't need for anyone to teach you. But as his anointing teaches you concerning all things, and is true, and is no lie, and even as it taught you, you will remain in him.*

*1John 2:26-27 WEB*

John reminds us that there are many false teachers in the world *"who would lead you astray"* (see also Acts 20:29-31, 2 Peter 2:1-22, Jude 3-19). To avoid being deceived, we should each learn to be led by the Holy Spirit, rather than just depend on other people to lead and teach us.

Here are some additional verses about the Holy Spirit giving understanding:

*Then Moses said to the people of Israel, "See, the LORD has called by name Bezalel the son of Uri, son of Hur, of the tribe of Judah; and he has filled him with the Spirit of God, with skill, with intelligence, with knowledge, and with all craftsmanship..."*

*Exodus 35:30-31 ESV*

*Now we have received not the spirit of the world, but the Spirit who is from God, that we might understand the things freely given us by God.*

*1Corinthians 2:12 ESV*

*I do not cease to give thanks for you, remembering you in my prayers, that the God of our Lord Jesus Christ, the Father of glory, may give you the Spirit of wisdom and of revelation in the knowledge of him, having the eyes of your hearts enlightened, that you may know what is the hope to which he has called you, what are the riches of his glorious inheritance in the saints...*

*Ephesians 1:16-18 ESV*

So, we see that understanding is often given by God, and is often associated with the Holy Spirit living within us. Now, let's look at some ways God calls us to cooperate with him in growing in *knowledge, understanding,* and *wisdom.*

# Look to Scripture

Scripture is clearly an important source of spiritual truth. By looking to scripture we can grow in both knowledge and understanding. Consider these verses:

*Through your precepts I get understanding; therefore I hate every false way.*            *Psalm 119:104 ESV*

*The unfolding of your words gives light; it imparts understanding to the simple.*            *Psalm 119:130 ESV*

*Let my cry come before you, O LORD; give me understanding according to your word!*  *Psalm 119:169 ESV*

*Now these Jews were more noble than those in Thessalonica; they received the word with all eagerness, examining the Scriptures daily to see if these things were so.*            *Acts 17:11 ESV*

*Now these things happened to them as an example, but they were written down for our instruction, on whom the end of the ages has come.*            *1Corinthians 10:11 ESV*

*All Scripture is breathed out by God and profitable for teaching, for reproof, for correction, and for training in righteousness, that the man of God may be complete, equipped for every good work.*            *2Timothy 3:16-17 ESV*

*Jesus said to them, "Is this not the reason you are wrong, because you know neither the Scriptures nor the power of God?"*            *Mark 12:24 ESV*

While simply reading scripture is likely beneficial, it is often more beneficial to reflect on scripture, meditate on scripture, and memorize scripture. Consider these verses:

*I have hidden your word in my heart, that I might not sin against you.*            *Psalm 119:11 WEB*

*I will meditate on your precepts, and consider your ways.*            *Psalm 119:15 WEB*

*Your commandment makes me wiser than my enemies, for it is ever with me.* Psalm 119:98 ESV

*I have more understanding than all my teachers, for your testimonies are my meditation.* Psalm 119:99 ESV

*My son, pay attention to what I say; turn your ear to my words. Do not let them out of your sight, keep them within your heart; for they are life to those who find them and health to one's whole body.* Proverbs 4:20-22 NIV

*Turn your ear, and listen to the words of the wise. Apply your heart to my teaching. For it is a pleasant thing if you keep them within you, if all of them are ready on your lips.* Proverbs 22:17-18 WEB

## Do It, and Know

Jesus said to the Jews who had believed him:

*"If you abide in my word, you are truly my disciples, and you will know the truth, and the truth will set you free."*
John 8:31-32 ESV

*"If you abide in my word"* may be translated as *"If you hold to my teaching"* (NIV). I understand those verses to support this: Doing what Jesus says to do will lead to increasing knowledge and understanding, and that will lead to great freedom. James encourages us with similar words:

*But be doers of the word, and not hearers only, deceiving yourselves.* James 1:22 ESV

Just listening to truth can lead to deception. To avoid deception, it is important to be a *doer* and not a *hearer only*. We must put what we know to be true into practice, if we expect to continue to grow in knowledge and understanding.

## Delight in Understanding & Wisdom

Do you delight in knowledge, understanding, and wisdom? Or, do you prefer ignorance in some situations? If something in your life is displeasing to God, do you truly desire to know the truth about it and deal with it, or do you avoid that issue?

Consider these verses that focus on delighting in God's ways:

> *Praise the LORD! Blessed is the man who fears the LORD, who greatly delights in his commandments!*
> *Psalm 112:1 ESV*

> *I will delight myself in your statutes. I will not forget your word.*
> *Psalm 119:16 WEB*

> *Indeed your statutes are my delight, and my counselors.*
> *Psalm 119:24 WEB*

> *The law of your mouth is better to me than thousands of pieces of gold and silver.*
> *Psalm 119:72 WEB*

> *How I love your law! It is my meditation all day.*
> *Psalm 119:97 WEB*

> *How sweet are your words to my taste, sweeter than honey to my mouth!*
> *Psalm 119:103 ESV*

> *I opened my mouth wide and panted, for I longed for your commandments.*
> *Psalm 119:131 WEB*

> *Your promises have been thoroughly tested, and your servant loves them.*
> *Psalm 119:140 WEB*

> *I rejoice at your word, as one who finds great plunder.*
> *Psalm 119:162 WEB*

> *I hate and abhor falsehood, but I love your law.*
> *Psalm 119:163 ESV*

If you find yourself to be weak in this area, ask God to help you to delight in his words and his ways. Make a conscious choice to seek after truth even though you may not have a strong desire to do so.

As we grow in *understanding* and *wisdom* we should increasingly delight to *do* things God's way. Consider these verses that focus on delighting to *do* things God's way:

> ***Blessed is the man who walks not in the counsel of the wicked, nor stands in the way of sinners, nor sits in the seat of scoffers; but his delight is in the law of the LORD, and on his law he meditates day and night.***
>
> Psalm 1:1-2 ESV

> ***"I delight to do your will, O my God; your law is within my heart."***
> Psalm 40:8 ESV

> ***I rejoice in following your statutes as one rejoices in great riches.***
> Psalm 119:14 NIV

> ***Direct me in the path of your commands, for there I find delight.***
> Psalm 119:35 NIV

> ***A fool finds pleasure in wicked schemes, but a person of understanding delights in wisdom.***
> Proverbs 10:23 NIV

Note in that last verse that *"A fool finds pleasure in wicked schemes."* Many people delight in doing wrong rather than delighting in doing what is right. Solomon also wrote this about such people:

> ***Wisdom will save you from the ways of wicked men, from men whose words are perverse, who have left the straight paths to walk in dark ways, who delight in doing wrong and rejoice in the perverseness of evil, whose paths are crooked and who are devious in their ways.***
> Proverbs 2:12-15 NIV

Desiring to do things God's way not only involves wisdom, but also involves love for God. Recall what Jesus said:

> ***"If you love me, you will keep my commandments."***
> John 14:15 ESV

Love for Jesus naturally results in a desire to please Jesus, which naturally leads us to do things his way rather than our own way. This, of course, relates to the greatest commandment:

*One of them, an expert in the law, tested him with this question: "Teacher, which is the greatest commandment in the Law?"*

*Jesus replied: "'Love the Lord your God with all your heart and with all your soul and with all your mind.' This is the first and greatest commandment."*

Matthew 22:35-38 NIV

John said it this way:

*For this is the love of God, that we keep his commandments. And his commandments are not burdensome.*

1John 5:3 ESV

## Gifted Teachers

Some people have been gifted by God to have special ability to communicate spiritual truth and understanding to others. We would do well to learn from such people, while being careful to not be deceived by false teachers, or by true believers who may be deceived in some areas. Consider a few verses:

*"And I will give you shepherds after my own heart, who will feed you with knowledge and understanding."*

Jeremiah 3:15 ESV

*And he gave the apostles, the prophets, the evangelists, the shepherds and teachers, to equip the saints for the work of ministry, for building up the body of Christ...*

Ephesians 4:11-12 ESV

*You then, my child, be strengthened by the grace that is in Christ Jesus, and what you have heard from me in the presence of many witnesses entrust to faithful men who will be able to teach others also.*     *2Timothy 2:1-2 ESV*

*Having gifts that differ according to the grace given to us, let us use them: if prophecy, in proportion to our faith; if service, in our serving; the one who teaches, in his teaching...*     *Romans 12:6-7 ESV*

*This is how one should regard us, as servants of Christ and stewards of the mysteries of God.* 1Corinthians 4:1 ESV

So, we should take advantage of opportunities to learn from others.

## Good Relationships

One of the reasons God has directed his people to meet together is to encourage one another and help each other grow in *knowledge, understanding,* and *wisdom.* Consider these verses:

*Whoever walks with the wise becomes wise, but the companion of fools will suffer harm.* Proverbs 13:20 ESV

*Brothers, join in imitating me, and keep your eyes on those who walk according to the example you have in us.* Philippians 3:17 ESV

*But exhort one another every day, as long as it is called "today," that none of you may be hardened by the deceitfulness of sin.* Hebrews 3:13 ESV

*And let us consider how to stir up one another to love and good works, not neglecting to meet together, as is the habit of some, but encouraging one another, and all the more as you see the Day drawing near.*
Hebrews 10:24-25 ESV

*Do not be deceived: "Bad company ruins good morals."*
1Corinthians 15:33 ESV

## Listen to Advice

One of the characteristics of people who are wise is that they listen to advice. Consider these verses:

*The way of a fool is right in his own eyes, but he who is wise listens to counsel.* Proverbs 12:15 WEB

*A wise son listens to his father's instruction, but a*

*scoffer doesn't listen to rebuke.*    *Proverbs 13:1 WEB*

*Listen to counsel and receive instruction, that you may be wise in your latter end.*    *Proverbs 19:20 WEB*

*Listen, my son, and be wise, and keep your heart on the right path!*    *Proverbs 23:19 WEB*

## Different Viewpoints

One common problem many people have is a tendency to listen to only one viewpoint about various subjects. Often that viewpoint is simply their own viewpoint. It's common for people to tune-out other perspectives, and only listen to what they already agree with. One way to gain under-standing is to listen to differing perspectives with the intent to understand why people view things differently. Consider what Solomon wrote:

*The one who states his case first seems right, until the other comes and examines him.*    *Proverbs 18:17 ESV*

Scripture doesn't appear to repeat this truth much. However, I think we can all affirm its truth based on personal experience. Most of us have had reason to change our understanding about something when we hear a different viewpoint that is explained clearly.

Consider an example from scripture, which is often referred to as "the Gibeonite deception" (recorded in Joshua 9). Some Gibeonites pretended to come from a distant land to make a treaty with Israel. Joshua and his people only heard the one viewpoint, and *"did not ask counsel from the LORD"* (Joshua 9:14 ESV). They didn't properly understand the situation, and made a decision they later regretted. They didn't look for an alternate viewpoint. What is the obvious lesson here? We should always seek to know God's perspective, and embrace it! As Solomon wrote:

*Trust in the LORD with all your heart, and do not lean*

*on your own understanding. In all your ways acknowledge him, and he will make straight your paths.*

*Proverbs 3:5-6 ESV*

## Observation and Reason

Consider the tremendous amount of scientific knowledge and understanding that is now available. This has been developed by many people over many years, largely through *experiments*, *observation*, and *reason*. These are valuable tools in acquiring knowledge and understanding in general, and these tools are not limited to scientific topics. *Observation* and *reason* are tools we can use to learn spiritual truth as well as truth about the natural world. Consider these verses:

*The heavens declare the glory of God; the skies proclaim the work of his hands. Day after day they pour forth speech; night after night they reveal knowledge.*

*Psalm 19:1-2 NIV*

*For what can be known about God is plain to them, because God has shown it to them. For his invisible attributes, namely, his eternal power and divine nature, have been clearly perceived, ever since the creation of the world, in the things that have been made. So they are without excuse.*

*Romans 1:19-20 ESV*

*Go to the ant, you sluggard; consider its ways and be wise! It has no commander, no overseer or ruler, yet it stores its provisions in summer and gathers its food at harvest.*

*Proverbs 6:6-8 NIV*

*The prudent sees danger and hides himself, but the simple go on and suffer for it.*

*Proverbs 22:3 ESV*

*I passed by the field of a sluggard, by the vineyard of a man lacking sense, and behold, it was all overgrown with thorns; the ground was covered with nettles, and its stone wall was broken down. Then I saw and considered it; I looked and received instruction. A little sleep, a little slumber, a little folding of the hands to rest, and poverty will come upon you like a robber, and want like an armed man.* Proverbs 24:30-34 ESV

In those last verses, please note that Solomon **saw and considered it**, and **received instruction.** Even Solomon, who was clearly given understanding by God, used observation and reason to grow in understanding.

In the English language, the word "reason" has multiple shades of meaning. Something can be said to be right or wrong for some "reason." We can use "reason" to logically arrive at a new truth based on what we observe, or based on other truths we already know. We can also "reason" with other people to try to convince them of things we believe to be true, and other people can "reason" with us to try to persuade us also. Here are some more verses related to using reason:

> **The one who states his case first seems right, until the other comes and examines him.** Proverbs 18:17 ESV

> **It is the glory of God to conceal things, but the glory of kings is to search things out.** Proverbs 25:2 ESV

> **And Paul went in, as was his custom, and on three Sabbath days he reasoned with them from the Scriptures, explaining and proving that it was necessary for the Christ to suffer and to rise from the dead, and saying, "This Jesus, whom I proclaim to you, is the Christ."** Acts 17:2-3 ESV

> **And he reasoned in the synagogue every Sabbath, and tried to persuade Jews and Greeks.** Acts 18:4 ESV

How important is it that we use our reasoning ability to understand spiritual things? Consider Jesus' words to the Pharisees, who failed to understand *"the signs of the times"*:

> **And the Pharisees and Sadducees came, and to test him**

*they asked him to show them a sign from heaven. He answered them, "When it is evening, you say, 'It will be fair weather, for the sky is red.' And in the morning, 'It will be stormy today, for the sky is red and threatening.' You know how to interpret the appearance of the sky, but you cannot interpret the signs of the times. An evil and adulterous generation seeks for a sign, but no sign will be given to it except the sign of Jonah." So he left them and departed.*      Matthew 16:1-4 ESV

Jesus said similar things to the crowds that followed him:

*He also said to the crowds, "When you see a cloud rising in the west, you say at once, 'A shower is coming.' And so it happens. And when you see the south wind blowing, you say, 'There will be scorching heat,' and it happens. You hypocrites! You know how to interpret the appearance of earth and sky, but why do you not know how to interpret the present time? And why do you not judge for yourselves what is right?"*

Luke 12:54-57 ESV

The people Jesus was speaking to had knowledge about the *"present time"* and *"signs of the times"* through simple observation, but they didn't try to *"interpret"* that knowledge to gain understanding. They apparently preferred ignorance over understanding. Jesus was not pleased with that. He appears to rebuke the crowds for not judging for themselves *what is right* (Luke 12:57).

## Not by Worldly Learning and Philosophy

While observation and reason are valuable tools, we should be aware of how reasoning can be distorted and misused. Reasoning based on worldly perspectives or human traditions may result in deception rather than true understanding. Consider these verses:

*See to it that no one takes you captive through hollow and deceptive philosophy, which depends on human*

*tradition and the elemental spiritual forces of this world rather than on Christ.*     *Colossians 2:8 NIV*

*For the word of the cross is folly to those who are perishing, but to us who are being saved it is the power of God. For it is written, "I will destroy the wisdom of the wise, and the discernment of the discerning I will thwart." Where is the one who is wise? Where is the scribe? Where is the debater of this age? Has not God made foolish the wisdom of the world? For since, in the wisdom of God, the world did not know God through wisdom, it pleased God through the folly of what we preach to save those who believe. For Jews demand signs and Greeks seek wisdom, but we preach Christ crucified, a stumbling block to Jews and folly to Gentiles, but to those who are called, both Jews and Greeks, Christ the power of God and the wisdom of God. For the foolishness of God is wiser than men, and the weakness of God is stronger than men.*

*1Corinthians 1:18-25 ESV*

*Avoid the irreverent babble and contradictions of what is falsely called "knowledge," for by professing it some have swerved from the faith. Grace be with you.*

*1Timothy 6:20-21 ESV*

So, avoid worldly reasoning, and ask God for understanding about how to avoid such deceptions.

## Don't Reject Truth

So far, we have mostly focused on things we should do to acquire understanding. It is important also to consider what we should NOT do.

Similar to how God gives understanding to those who diligently seek him, God appears to actively hinder the understanding of those who reject truth. Consider this passage of scripture, speaking about unbelievers:

*The coming of the lawless one is by the activity of Satan with all power and false signs and wonders, and with all wicked deception for those who are perishing, because they refused to love the truth and so be saved. Therefore God sends them a strong delusion, so that they may believe what is false, in order that all may be condemned who did not believe the truth but had pleasure in unrighteousness.*     *2Thessalonians 2:9-12 ESV*

Those who **refused to love the truth** are **sent a strong delusion, so that they may believe what is false.** It appears here that God purposely hinders the understanding of people who reject truth.

Consider Jesus' words to his disciples after speaking the parable of the sower and the seed:

*Then the disciples came and said to him, "Why do you speak to them in parables?"*

*And he answered them, "To you it has been given to know the secrets of the kingdom of heaven, but to them it has not been given. For to the one who has, more will be given, and he will have an abundance, but from the one who has not, even what he has will be taken away. This is why I speak to them in parables, because seeing they do not see, and hearing they do not hear, nor do they understand. Indeed, in their case the prophecy of Isaiah is fulfilled that says: 'You will indeed hear but never understand, and you will indeed see but never perceive. For this people's heart has grown dull, and with their ears they can barely hear, and their eyes they have closed, lest they should see with their eyes and hear with their ears and understand with their heart and turn, and I would heal them.'"*     *Matthew 13:10-15 ESV*

Again we have the sense that understanding is withheld from some people. In this case it is people whose **"heart has grown dull, and with their ears they can barely hear, and** *their eyes they have closed..."* These people have apparently previously rejected truth, and are unable to receive new truth.

For an additional perspective on this subject, see Proverbs 1:20-33.

So, do you truly want understanding? Be careful to not reject truth.

## Don't Be Proud

Pride, meaning a haughty attitude, is another thing that can hinder understanding.

> *At that time Jesus, full of joy through the Holy Spirit, said, "I praise you, Father, Lord of heaven and earth, because you have hidden these things from the wise and learned, and revealed them to little children. Yes, Father, for this is what you were pleased to do."*
> *Luke 10:21 NIV*

Here Jesus indicates that God reveals some things to *"little children"* while hiding them from those he calls *"wise and learned."* Apparently, the *"wise and learned"* are proud in their own knowledge, and do not humble themselves before God to obtain true understanding. This is consistent with other verses dealing with pride and humility:

> *Surely he mocks the mockers, but he gives grace to the humble.*
> *Proverbs 3:34 WEB*

> *Clothe yourselves, all of you, with humility toward one another, for 'God opposes the proud but gives grace to the humble."*
> *1Peter 5:5 ESV*

So, do you truly want understanding? Be careful not to be proud. Aim to be humble.

## Affliction and Suffering

Consider some of the most valuable things you have learned. Were some of them learned because of affliction or suffering?   We may not like it, but hardship is often an effective teacher.   Sometimes God uses difficulties to teach people truth.  Consider these verses:

*Whenever God slew them, they would seek him; they eagerly turned to him again.   They remembered that God was their Rock, that God Most High was their Redeemer.   But then they would flatter him with their mouths, lying to him with their tongues; their hearts were not loyal to him, they were not faithful to his covenant.*                                          *Psalm 78:34-37 NIV*

*It is good for me that I was afflicted, that I might learn your statutes.*                                          *Psalm 119:71 ESV*

*"Then they will know that I am the LORD, when I have made the land a desolation and a waste because of all their abominations that they have committed."*
                                                     *Ezekiel 33:29 ESV*

*When your judgments come upon the earth, the people of the world learn righteousness.*                  *Isaiah 26:9 NIV*

*And have you forgotten the exhortation that addresses you as sons?   "My son, do not regard lightly the discipline of the Lord, nor be weary when reproved by him.   For the Lord disciplines the one he loves, and chastises every son whom he receives."   It is for discipline that you have to endure.   God is treating you as sons.   For what son is there whom his father does not discipline?   If you are left without discipline, in which all have participated, then you are illegitimate children and not sons.   Besides this, we have had earthly fathers who disciplined us and we respected them.   Shall we not much more be subject to the Father of spirits and live?   For they disciplined us for a short time as it seemed best to them, but he disciplines us for our good, that we may share his holiness.   For the moment all discipline seems painful rather than pleasant, but later it yields the peaceful fruit of righteousness to those who have been trained by it.* *Hebrews 12:5-11 ESV*

*Count it all joy, my brothers, when you meet trials of various kinds, for you know that the testing of your faith produces steadfastness. And let steadfastness have its full effect, that you may be perfect and complete, lacking in nothing.* *James 1:2-4 ESV*

## Wisdom Makes Right Choices

Again, please recall how I have defined wisdom:

**Wisdom:** Having knowledge and understanding, and putting them into practice for right living.

Living by knowledge and understanding involves right actions. We have already discussed that some in chapter 4, when we introduced *wisdom*. It's not enough to just know truth and understand how it can be used effectively; we must *choose* to apply our knowledge and understanding to make *right choices* that result in *right living*. This involves *choosing* to do the things we understand we should do, and *choosing* to NOT do the things we understand we shouldn't do. Consider these verses that encourage us to make *right choices*:

*"And if it is evil in your eyes to serve the LORD, choose this day whom you will serve, whether the gods your fathers served in the region beyond the River, or the gods of the Amorites in whose land you dwell. But as for me and my house, we will serve the LORD."*
*Joshua 24:15 ESV*

*Who is the man who fears the LORD? Him will he instruct in the way that he should choose.* *Psalm 25:12 ESV*

*Because they hated knowledge and did not choose the fear of the LORD, would have none of my counsel and despised all my reproof, therefore they shall eat the fruit of their way, and have their fill of their own devices.*
*Proverbs 1:29-31 ESV*

*Do not envy a man of violence and do not choose any of his ways...*
                                                    *Proverbs 3:31 ESV*

*How much better to get wisdom than gold! To get understanding is to be chosen rather than silver.*
                                                    *Proverbs 16:16 ESV*

Some people seem to be waiting for God to make *right choices* for them, waiting for God to somehow override their free will. However, the scriptures are full of verses instructing us how we should live because the *choice* whether to do so or not is ours. When scripture tells us to do something, it is a good indication that God will not do it for us, but rather expects us to make a *choice* to do it ourselves. Generally, God will not make those *choices* for us.

Yes, there are many things we don't have a *choice* about. Some things may be determined by God, while other things may be determined by other people, or by circumstances beyond our control. But there are many things about which we do have the ability to *choose*. Here are just a few of the many verses in scripture instructing us about things we should be making *right choices* about:

*Do not present your members to sin as instruments for unrighteousness, but present yourselves to God as those who have been brought from death to life, and your members to God as instruments for righteousness.*
                                                    *Romans 6:13 ESV*

*I therefore, a prisoner for the Lord, urge you to walk in a manner worthy of the calling to which you have been called, with all humility and gentleness, with patience, bearing with one another in love, eager to maintain the unity of the Spirit in the bond of peace.*
                                                    *Ephesians 4:1-3 ESV*

*Beloved, I urge you as sojourners and exiles to abstain from the passions of the flesh, which wage war against your soul.*
                                                    *1Peter 2:11 ESV*

*Rejoice always, pray without ceasing, give thanks in all circumstances; for this is the will of God in Christ Jesus for you.*                                        *1Thessalonians 5:16-18 ESV*

Doing these kinds of things involves *choosing* to exercise our will to make *right choices.* If we are truly Christ followers, we have the Holy Spirit to empower us to be able to make *right choices.* However, the *choice* is still ours. Where scripture urges us to do something, the *choice* is ours whether or not to do it. Wisdom makes the *right choice,* and looks to the Holy Spirit for strength to do it.

## Wisdom Chooses God's Way

Part of making right choices is affirming that God's way is always the right way, whether God's way makes sense to us or not. Recall what Solomon wrote:

*There is a way that seems right to a man, but its end is the way to death.*                                     *Proverbs 14:12, 16:25 ESV*

Wisdom involves knowing God's ways and choosing to do things his way, even though another way may *"seem right"* to us. Wisdom relies on God's understanding ahead of our own understanding. Consider this verse again:

*Trust in the LORD with all your heart, and do not lean on your own understanding. In all your ways acknowledge him, and he will make straight your paths.*
*Proverbs 3:5-6 ESV*

Consider also what a psalmist wrote about knowing God's ways and living accordingly:

*Teach me, O LORD, the way of your statutes; and I will keep it to the end.*                                        *Psalm 119:33 ESV*

*I will always obey your law, for ever and ever.*
*Psalm 119:44 NIV*

*I hasten and do not delay to keep your commandments.*
*Psalm 119:60 ESV*

*I understand more than the aged, for I keep your precepts.*
*Psalm 119:100 ESV*

*I hold back my feet from every evil way, in order to keep your word.*
*Psalm 119:101 ESV*

*I do not turn aside from your rules, for you have taught me.*
*Psalm 119:102 ESV*

*I incline my heart to perform your statutes forever, to the end.*
*Psalm 119:112 ESV*

Note especially that last verse. The psalmist is not requesting for God to incline his heart to keep God's statutes, rather he is making a *choice* to incline his heart himself, and is declaring that *choice.*

Finally, consider Jesus' words:

*"Everyone then who hears these words of mine and does them will be like a wise man who built his house on the rock. And the rain fell, and the floods came, and the winds blew and beat on that house, but it did not fall, because it had been founded on the rock."*
*Matthew 7:24-25 ESV*

## Jesus

There is a sense in which Jesus coming in the flesh and dying on a cross for us reveals, or is, *"wisdom from God."* Consider these verses:

*Where is the one who is wise? Where is the scribe? Where is the debater of this age? Has not God made foolish the wisdom of the world? For since, in the wisdom of God, the world did not know God through wisdom, it pleased God through the folly of what we preach to save those who believe. For Jews demand signs and Greeks seek wisdom, but we preach Christ crucified, a stumbling block to Jews and folly to Gentiles, but to those who are called, both Jews and*

**Greeks, Christ the power of God and the wisdom of God.**
*1 Corinthians 1:20-24 ESV*

**And because of him you are in Christ Jesus, who became to us wisdom from God, righteousness and sanctification and redemption, so that, as it is written, "Let the one who boasts, boast in the Lord."**
*1 Corinthians 1:30-31 ESV*

In this section of scripture (1 Corinthians 1:18-31), Paul contrasts the *"wisdom of this world"* (vs. 20) with the *"wisdom of God"* (vs. 21). *The wisdom of this world* considers the message of Christ and the cross to be *foolishness.* True wisdom knows that Christ is *the power of God and the wisdom of God.*

In closing this chapter, consider again the value of wisdom:

**Blessed is the one who finds wisdom, and the one who gets understanding, for the gain from her is better than gain from silver and her profit better than gold. She is more precious than jewels, and nothing you desire can compare with her.** *Proverbs 3:13-15 ESV*

## For Further Reflection

- Ask God to show you if you have rejected truth or understanding in the past.

- Ask God to show you if pride hinders your understanding.

- Ask God for understanding. Are there important areas of your life that you don't have much understanding about? If so, consider asking God for understanding specifically in those areas.

- Are you walking in wisdom? If not, what new choices should you make to start walking in wisdom?

\*\*\*\*\*\*\*\*\*\*\*\*

# PART 2
# Understanding Deception

*But evil men and impostors will grow worse and worse,*
*deceiving and being deceived.*
2Timothy 3:13 WEB

---

*Deception* involves believing something to be *true* which is actually *false,* or believing something to be *false* which is actually *true.* We are all subject to being *deceived* at times, and some people intentionally *deceive* other people. People who are *deceived* naturally tend to pass on *deception* to others. We can be deceived even when no one is intentionally trying to deceive us. In this section we will explore the nature of deception and some things we can do to avoid being deceived.

As mentioned in the Preface, we should keep in mind that salvation is primarily about coming to Jesus, trusting in Jesus, and following Jesus. He is the Christ, the Son of God, Lord of all. As we consider various issues relating to deception, we should keep in mind the simplicity of the gospel, and look *"to Jesus, the founder and perfecter of our faith"* (Hebrews 12:2 ESV). He sees all these things clearly, and he is the Good Shepherd of all us sheep (John 10).

\*\*\*\*\*\*\*\*\*\*\*\*

*Building on Foundations for Eternal Life*

# Chapter 6
# "Deceived"

*Let no one deceive you with empty words.*
*Ephesians 5:6 WEB*

---

In *"Beneath Foundations for Eternal Life"* (a previous book by the same author), these are some of the topics discussed:

- The existence of absolute truth.

- Some things are true and some things are false.

- Some truths are "grey," rather than black and white.

- Good or bad?  Right or wrong?  Righteous or unrighteous?

- We are all members of various groups.

- Different people and groups follow different paths, resulting in different destinies.

It may be helpful to review that book, if you haven't read it recently (free ebook versions should be available online).

*Deception* was also discussed some in *"Beneath Foundations for Eternal Life."* This is how *deception* was introduced in chapter 21:

> We looked at the concept of "true or false."  We saw that some things are true and some things are false.
>
> It follows that it is possible for each of us to believe something to be true which is actually false, or to believe something to be false which is actually true.  It is common to say that a person who has such wrong beliefs is "deceived" regarding those beliefs.  Based on this, I propose a simple definition for the word "deceived":
>
> **Deceived:**  A state of believing something to be true which is actually false, or believing something to be false which is actually true.

It should be clear that all of us have been deceived, at times, about some things. Perhaps we preferred to say we were "mistaken," but it probably fits the above definition of being "deceived." For most of us, the older we get, the more things we are aware of that we have been deceived about. Those who think they have never been deceived about anything are perhaps the most deceived of all!

We should note that being deceived is different than being neutral or ignorant about something. If I don't have a settled opinion or belief about something I cannot be deceived about it. I am either just neutral regarding it, or perhaps I am just ignorant about it (or some of both). I can only be deceived about things I claim to know truth about. If I don't claim to know the truth about something (either openly or secretly), then I cannot be deceived about it. I think the same is true of you.

Now it seems obvious that being deceived about something is generally NOT good. With few exceptions (I can't think of any) it is generally BAD to be deceived about anything. Being deceived generally leads to doing things that are harmful rather than helpful. So, I hope you already make it your goal to NOT be deceived. Assuming that is the case, it raises an important issue:

How can we avoid being deceived?

A primary theme of this present book is that very question: "How can we avoid being deceived?" If you want a short answer, see chapter 21 of the previous book. Otherwise, please stay with me and explore *deception* in more detail.

## For Further Reflection

- Consider some ways you have seen deception play out in other people's lives. What were some of the consequences of being deceived?

\*\*\*\*\*\*\*\*\*\*\*\*

# Chapter 7
# You Can Be Deceived

*The woman said, "The serpent deceived me, and I ate."*
*Genesis 3:13 WEB*

*But I am afraid that somehow, as the serpent deceived Eve*
*in his craftiness, so your minds might be corrupted from*
*the simplicity that is in Christ.*
*2Corinthians 11:3 WEB*

---

A first step in avoiding deception is to realize that *you can be deceived.* Let's look at some scriptures relating to deception. The problem is first seen in Genesis 3:

> *But the serpent said to the woman, "You will not surely die. For God knows that when you eat of it your eyes will be opened, and you will be like God, knowing good and evil."* Genesis 3:4-5 ESV

By believing the serpent's lies, Eve became deceived. Sin entered the world, and paradise was lost. Paul clarifies that we can also be deceived in a similar way if we aren't careful:

> *But I am afraid that somehow, as the serpent deceived Eve in his craftiness, so your minds might be corrupted from the simplicity that is in Christ.* 2Corinthians 11:3 WEB

Moses also warned the people about the possibility and consequences of being deceived:

> *Take care lest your heart be deceived, and you turn aside and serve other gods and worship them; then the anger of the LORD will be kindled against you, and he will shut up the heavens, so that there will be no rain, and the land will yield no fruit, and you will perish quickly off the good land that the LORD is giving you.*
> Deuteronomy 11:16-17 ESV

Paul found, in his own experience, that we can even be

deceived as we try to follow God's laws:

> *I found that the very commandment that was intended to bring life actually brought death.  For sin, seizing the opportunity afforded by the commandment, deceived me, and through the commandment put me to death.*
>
> *Romans 7:10-11 NIV*

Scripture warns us repeatedly of the possibility of being deceived by false teachers:

> *For I know that after my departure, vicious wolves will enter in among you, not sparing the flock.  Men will arise from among your own selves, speaking perverse things, to draw away the disciples after them.  Therefore watch, remembering that for a period of three years I didn't cease to admonish everyone night and day with tears.*
>
> *Acts 20:29-31 WEB*

> *Now I beg you, brothers, look out for those who are causing the divisions and occasions of stumbling, contrary to the doctrine which you learned, and turn away from them.  For those who are such don't serve our Lord, Jesus Christ, but their own belly; and by their smooth and flattering speech, they deceive the hearts of the innocent.*
>
> *Romans 16:17-18 WEB*

> *But false prophets also arose among the people, just as there will be false teachers among you, who will secretly bring in destructive heresies, even denying the Master who bought them, bringing upon themselves swift destruction.  And many will follow their sensuality, and because of them the way of truth will be blasphemed.  And in their greed they will exploit you with false words.*
>
> *2Peter 2:1-3 ESV*

> *I write these things to you about those who are trying to deceive you.*
>
> *1John 2:26 ESV*

> *For certain individuals whose condemnation was written about long ago have secretly slipped in among you. They*

*are ungodly people, who pervert the grace of our God into a license for immorality and deny Jesus Christ our only Sovereign and Lord.*                     *Jude 4 NIV*

Scripture also indicates that we can deceive ourselves. This kind of deception often involves pride:

*"The pride of your heart has deceived you, you who dwell in the clefts of the rock, whose habitation is high, who says in his heart, 'Who will bring me down to the ground?'"*                     *Obadiah 1:3 WEB*

*Let no one deceive himself. If anyone thinks that he is wise among you in this world, let him become a fool, that he may become wise.*                     *1Corinthians 3:18 WEB*

*For if anyone thinks he is something, when he is nothing, he deceives himself.*                     *Galatians 6:3 ESV*

*If we say that we have no sin, we deceive ourselves, and the truth is not in us.*                     *1John 1:8 WEB*

In summary, all these verses affirm that we can be deceived. Acknowledging that we can be deceived is an important part of avoiding deception, as well as an important step in being set free from deception.

Furthermore, please note that none of these verses indicate that good intentions will protect anyone from deception. It is a widespread deception itself that good intentions will protect people from deception. You can be deceived. Good intentions won't protect you. However, knowledge, understanding, and wisdom can protect you from deception.

## For Further Reflection

- What are some things you have been deceived about?

- Might you presently be deceived about something?

***********

# Chapter 8
# "Don't Be Deceived..."

*Don't be deceived. God is not mocked,*
*for whatever a man sows, that he will also reap.*
Galatians 6:7 WEB

We have just discussed that we can all be deceived. No one is immune from the possibility of being deceived

Being deceived about something is almost always a bad thing. Exceptions may include things like surprise parties, thrown for someone who may be temporarily "deceived" about the event in order to make it a surprise. However, for most kinds of deceptions, if we find out that we have been deceived, then we regret the consequences of that deception and wish we had not been deceived. Spiritual deception can have especially severe consequences. Consider Jesus' words regarding some people who apparently think they are his followers, but who are apparently deceived about that:

> *"Not everyone who says to me, 'Lord, Lord,' will enter into the Kingdom of Heaven; but he who does the will of my Father who is in heaven. Many will tell me in that day, 'Lord, Lord, didn't we prophesy in your name, in your name cast out demons, and in your name do many mighty works?' Then I will tell them, 'I never knew you. Depart from me, you who work iniquity.'"*
> Matthew 7:21-23 WEB

Scripture repeatedly encourages us to NOT be deceived. Scripture appears to be written from a perspective that presumes that we each have some level of control regarding whether or not we are deceived. Scripture often communicates how to NOT be deceived. Scripture does this by pointing out some important areas of truth and knowledge that people are commonly deceived about. Let's look at some verses that directly warn us to NOT be deceived about something. As you read them, consider whether or not you have been deceived, or may presently be deceived, regarding the subject of each verse.

*Or don't you know that the unrighteous will not inherit the Kingdom of God? Don't be deceived.*    *1 Cor. 6:9 WEB*

*Do not be deceived: "Bad company ruins good morals."*
*1Corinthians 15:33 ESV*

*Don't be deceived. God is not mocked, for whatever a man sows, that he will also reap.*    *Galatians 6:7 WEB*

*Know this for sure, that no sexually immoral person, nor unclean person, nor covetous man, who is an idolater, has any inheritance in the Kingdom of Christ and God. Let no one deceive you with empty words. For because of these things, the wrath of God comes on the children of disobedience.*    *Ephesians 5:5-6 WEB*

*Do not be deceived, my beloved brothers. Every good gift and every perfect gift is from above, coming down from the Father of lights with whom there is no variation or shadow due to change.*    *James 1:16-17 ESV*

*Little children, let no one deceive you. Whoever practices righteousness is righteous, as he is righteous. Whoever makes a practice of sinning is of the devil, for the devil has been sinning from the beginning. The reason the Son of God appeared was to destroy the works of the devil.*    *1John 3:7-8 ESV*

Note that all of these verses have to do with right versus wrong or good versus evil. That seems to be at the heart of scripture when it comes to deception. Know what is good; choose it; do it. Know what is bad; reject it; don't do it. *"Don't be deceived."*

## For Further Reflection

- Have you been deceived about something that is evil?

\*\*\*\*\*\*\*\*\*\*\*

# Chapter 9
# Darkness or Light?

*He who walks in darkness, and has no light, let him trust in*
*the Yahweh's name, and rely on his God.*
*Isaiah 50:10 WEB*

*"I am the light of the world.  He who follows me will not*
*walk in the darkness, but will have the light of life."*
*John 8:12 WEB*

*He has delivered us from the domain of darkness*
*and transferred us to the kingdom of his beloved Son,*
*in whom we have redemption, the forgiveness of sins.*
*Colossians 1:13-14 ESV*

---

We saw in the last chapter how avoiding deception involves
discerning right versus wrong, righteous versus unrighteous,
and good versus evil.  Scripture often refers to these differences as "light" versus "darkness."  Consider these verses:

*When I looked for good, then evil came; When I waited*
*for light, there came darkness.*          *Job 30:26 WEB*

*Woe to those who call evil good, and good evil; who put*
*darkness for light, and light for darkness; who put bitter*
*for sweet, and sweet for bitter!*          *Isaiah 5:20 WEB*

*Therefore is justice far from us, and righteousness*
*doesn't overtake us.  We look for light, but see darkness;*
*for brightness, but we walk in obscurity.*
*Isaiah 59:9 WEB*

Let's consider what else scripture has to say about *darkness*
and *light*.

## Those in Darkness Can't See

Scripture also associates light and darkness with seeing or
not seeing, knowing or not knowing, being saved or not
being saved.  Just as people in physical darkness can't see or

easily understand physical things, likewise people in spiritual darkness can't see or understand spiritual things. Consider these verses:

> *Jesus therefore said to them, "Yet a little while the light is with you. Walk while you have the light, that darkness doesn't overtake you. He who walks in the darkness doesn't know where he is going."*John 12:35 WEB

> *"The eye is the lamp of the body. If your eyes are healthy, your whole body will be full of light. But if your eyes are unhealthy, your whole body will be full of darkness. If then the light within you is darkness, how great is that darkness!"*          Matthew 6:22-23 NIV

> *"Your eye is the lamp of your body. When your eye is healthy, your whole body is full of light, but when it is bad, your body is full of darkness. Therefore be careful lest the light in you be darkness. If then your whole body is full of light, having no part dark, it will be wholly bright, as when a lamp with its rays gives you light."*          Luke 11:34-36 ESV

> *He who says he is in the light and hates his brother, is in the darkness even until now. He who loves his brother remains in the light, and there is no occasion for stumbling in him. But he who hates his brother is in the darkness, and walks in the darkness, and doesn't know where he is going, because the darkness has blinded his eyes.*          1John 2:9-11 WEB

## Light Comes from God

Spiritual light comes from God through Jesus. We enter into that light through faith in Jesus. We all start out in spiritual darkness. Consider these verses:

> *"...the people who sat in darkness saw a great light, to those who sat in the region and shadow of death, to them light has dawned."*          Matthew 4:16 WEB

*In the beginning was the Word, and the Word was with God, and the Word was God. The same was in the beginning with God. All things were made through him. Without him was not anything made that has been made. In him was life, and the life was the light of men. The light shines in the darkness, and the darkness hasn't overcome it.* John 1:1-5 WEB

*The true light that enlightens everyone was coming into the world.* John 1:9 WEB

*Again, therefore, Jesus spoke to them, saying, "I am the light of the world. He who follows me will not walk in the darkness, but will have the light of life."* John 8:12 WEB

*"I have come as a light into the world, that whoever believes in me may not remain in the darkness."* John 12:46 WEB

*...seeing it is God who said, "Light will shine out of darkness," who has shone in our hearts, to give the light of the knowledge of the glory of God in the face of Jesus Christ.* 2Corinthians 4:6 WEB

*This is the message which we have heard from him and announce to you, that God is light, and in him is no darkness at all.* 1John 1:5 WEB

Though spiritual light comes from God, and the devil is associated with spiritual darkness, the devil and those who follow him try to deceive people into thinking that their ways are spiritual light. Paul warns us:

*For such people are false apostles, deceitful workers, masquerading as apostles of Christ. And no wonder, for Satan himself masquerades as an angel of light. It is not surprising, then, if his servants also masquerade as servants of righteousness. Their end will be what their actions deserve.* 2Corinthians 11:13-15 ESV

# Jesus' Followers Are in Light

Jesus gives spiritual light to those who follow him. Those who don't follow Jesus remain in spiritual darkness. Consider these verses:

*"... I have appeared to you for this purpose: ... to open their eyes, that they may turn from darkness to light and from the power of Satan to God, that they may receive remission of sins and an inheritance among those who are sanctified by faith in me."* Acts 26:16,18 WEB

*For you were once darkness, but are now light in the Lord. Walk as children of light...* Ephesians 5:8 WEB

*He has delivered us from the domain of darkness and transferred us to the kingdom of his beloved Son, in whom we have redemption, the forgiveness of sins.* Colossians 1:13-14 ESV

*For you are all children of light, children of the day. We are not of the night or of the darkness.* 1Thessalonians 5:5 ESV

*But you are a chosen race, a royal priesthood, a holy nation, a people for his own possession, that you may proclaim the excellencies of him who called you out of darkness into his marvelous light.* 1Peter 2:9 ESV

# People Who Do Evil Hate the Light

Many unsaved people don't want spiritual light. Consider these verses:

*This is the judgment, that the light has come into the world, and men loved the darkness rather than the light; for their works were evil. For everyone who does evil hates the light, and doesn't come to the light, lest his works would be exposed.* John 3:19-20 WEB

*"The world can't hate you, but it hates me, because I testify about it, that its works are evil."* John 7:7 WEB

# Light and Darkness Don't Mix Well

Just as physical light and darkness are incompatible with each other, likewise spiritual light and darkness are incompatible.  Consider these verses:

*Don't be unequally yoked with unbelievers, for what fellowship have righteousness and iniquity?  Or what fellowship has light with darkness?*  2Corinthians 6:14 WEB

*If we say that we have fellowship with him and walk in the darkness, we lie, and don't tell the truth.*
1John 1:6 WEB

*He who says he is in the light and hates his brother, is in the darkness even until now.*  1John 2:9 WEB

## Expose Works of Darkness

We should not participate in works of darkness, but rather expose them.  Consider these verses:

*The night is far gone, and the day is near.  Let's therefore throw off the works of darkness, and let's put on the armor of light.*  Romans 13:12 WEB

*Take no part in the unfruitful works of darkness, but instead expose them.  For it is shameful even to speak of the things that they do in secret.  But when anything is exposed by the light, it becomes visible, for anything that becomes visible is light.  Therefore it says, "Awake, O sleeper, and arise from the dead, and Christ will shine on you."*  Ephesians 5:11-14 ESV

## For Further Reflection

- Have you been deceived, thinking something is spiritual light that is actually spiritual darkness?

\*\*\*\*\*\*\*\*\*\*\*\*

# Chapter 10
# Spirits of Deception

*And you were dead in the trespasses and sins in which you once walked, following the course of this world, following the prince of the power of the air, the spirit that is now at work in the sons of disobedience—among whom we all once lived in the passions of our flesh, carrying out the desires of the body and the mind, and were by nature children of wrath, like the rest of mankind.*
Ephesians 2:1-3 ESV

*Be sober and self-controlled. Be watchful.*
*Your adversary the devil, walks around like a roaring lion, seeking whom he may devour.*
1Peter 5:8 WEB

---

The existence of the devil and evil spirits is discussed in *"Foundations for Eternal Life"* (in chapter 12 *"Your Adversary the Devil"*). We will now focus on how deception is used by the devil and evil spirits to accomplish their purposes.

## A United Kingdom

The devil and evil spirits basically operate in similar ways. They are part of a united spiritual realm that opposes the kingdom of God. The devil is widely understood to be the leader of evil spirits. This understanding is supported by these verses:

> *Then one possessed by a demon, blind and mute, was brought to him and he healed him, so that the blind and mute man both spoke and saw. All the multitudes were amazed, and said, "Can this be the son of David?" But when the Pharisees heard it, they said, "This man does not cast out demons, except by Beelzebul, the prince of the demons."*

*Knowing their thoughts, Jesus said to them, "Every kingdom divided against itself is brought to desolation, and every city or house divided against itself will not stand. If Satan casts out Satan, he is divided against himself. How then will his kingdom stand? If I by Beelzebul cast out demons, by whom do your children cast them out? Therefore they will be your judges. But if I by the Spirit of God cast out demons, then the Kingdom of God has come upon you."*

*Matthew 12:22-28 WEB*

The devil and other evil spirits are not divided. They function with a clear united purpose: to oppose Christ and all who are his. This may be why scripture often seems to attribute demonic activity to the devil himself, since all evil spirits are basically his agents of evil in this world.

## The Devil Deceives

Scripture doesn't often reveal how the devil and evil spirits are involved in people's lives. However, there are several references that clearly associate the devil with deception and lies. Deception appears to be a primary tool that the devil uses to oppose God's people and promote his own purposes. Consider these verses:

*Yahweh God said to the woman, "What have you done?" The woman said, "The serpent deceived me, and I ate."*

*Genesis 3:13 WEB*

*But I am afraid that somehow, as the serpent deceived Eve in his craftiness, so your minds might be corrupted from the simplicity that is in Christ.* *2Corinthians 11:3 WEB*

*"Why do you not understand what I say? It is because you cannot bear to hear my word. You are of your father the devil, and your will is to do your father's desires. He was a murderer from the beginning, and does not stand in the truth, because there is no truth in him. When he lies, he speaks out of his own character,*

*for he is a liar and the father of lies. But because I tell the truth, you do not believe me."* John 8:43-45 ESV

*The great dragon was thrown down, the old serpent, he who is called the devil and Satan, the deceiver of the whole world. He was thrown down to the earth, and his angels were thrown down with him.* Revelation 12:9 WEB

*And he seized the dragon, that ancient serpent, who is the devil and Satan, and bound him for a thousand years, and threw him into the pit, and shut it and sealed it over him, so that he might not deceive the nations any longer, until the thousand years were ended. After that he must be released for a little while.* Revelation 20:2-3 ESV

*The devil who deceived them was thrown into the lake of fire and sulfur, where the beast and the false prophet are also.* Revelation 20:10 WEB

## The Devil's Purpose in Deception

The devil uses deception

- to cause people to believe various lies,
- to lead people away from God,
- to lead people into sin and increasing bondage to sin.

We see several examples of this in scripture:

- **Adam and Eve, in the garden** (Genesis 3): *"The serpent"* is widely understood to be the devil. His deception leads them to not trust what God said, which led to the first human sin. This resulted in spiritual death, expulsion from the garden, separation from God, and eventual physical death.

- **David counting Israel** (1 Chronicles 21): *"Satan stood up against Israel, and moved David to number Israel"* (1 Chronicles 21:1 WEB). We aren't told any details of how the devil accomplished this deception. However, its effect was that David believed the lie, that it was good to count the people, even with Joab's strong advice against doing so (1 Chronicles 21:3). David was led away from trusting God and into sin. Seventy thousand people died from the plague that resulted (1 Chronicles 21:14).

- **Job** (Job 1 & 2): Job was *"blameless and upright, a man who fears God and shuns evil"* (Job 1:8 NIV). God normally did not allow the devil to harass Job (Job 1:10). This all bothered the devil. He wanted to destroy Job's prosperity, lead him into sin, and ruin his relationship with God. So, the devil said to God: *"But now stretch out your hand and strike everything he has, and he will surely curse you to your face"* (Job 1:11 NIV). By afflicting Job, the devil intended to get Job to believe a lie (that God is not good, or that God does not care about him); lead him away from God, and lead him into sin.

- **Jesus' temptation** (Matthew 4:1-11, Luke 4:1-13): The devil tried three different deceptions to try to get Jesus to turn away from God and toward sin. The three deceptions the devil tried fall into these basic categories:
  - Choose present comfort rather than godly trials.
  - Choose immediate power and glory rather than following God and future power and glory.
  - Show how great you are.

  We each face similar temptations. Jesus used scripture to successfully resist these temptations and stay true to his calling.

- **Judas' betrayal:** Judas was led by the devil to betray Jesus. Apparently, Judas had a problem with greed, since *"he was a thief, and having the money box, used to steal what was put into it."* (John 12:6 WEB). The devil apparently used Judas' greed to deceive him into betraying Jesus in exchange for money. Luke indicates Satan had entered into him ahead of the plan to betray Jesus (Luke 22:1-6). John also indicates the devil's involvement prompting the betrayal (John 13:2). On the night Jesus was betrayed, the devil entered into Judas again (John 13:27). It was only after the betrayal that the reality of the deception set in, and Judas tried to undo the betrayal, but it was too late. He ended up hanging himself (Matthew 27:3-5).

God's purpose in our lives is opposite to the devil's purpose:

- to help people know truth,
- to lead people to himself,
- to free people from bondage to sin.

Jesus summarized the differences this way:

*"The thief only comes to steal, kill, and destroy. I came that they may have life, and may have it abundantly."*

*John 10:10 WEB*

## Evil Spirits

Before reading this section, please stop for a moment and ask God for the ability to read it and understand it well. Ask him to show you whether or not you have been deceived regarding the influence of evil spirits in your own life. Affirm to God that you want to be free from their influence and deception, and affirm again that you choose to follow him in all areas of your life.

Evil spirits, also called *demons* or *unclean spirits*, are spirits who are in rebellion against God, who look to the devil as their leader. While scripture is clear on the existence of evil spirits, it does not say much about their origins or how they operate. Much of the knowledge we have about them is based on believers' experience with them. However, there is a problem with that. It is easy to underestimate their power of deception.

Consider the great advantage they have. Apparently, they can readily see into our world, but we cannot readily see into their world, and we cannot normally see them. They have thousands of years of experience deceiving people; we have but a few years of experience in spiritual matters. Many believers are hardly even aware of their existence, presuming that if they don't manifest themselves the same way they did in Jesus' day, then they must not be a problem for us.

Let's consider briefly how people may be deceived and influenced by evil spirits. It is not my intent here to give a thorough review of this subject, but rather just to raise some issues to be aware of.

In response to those who think that believers cannot be influenced by evil spirits at all, consider with me what a first level of deception may involve. If you accept that evil spirits exist, and that they may dwell in people (at least in some unbelievers), and that evil spirits can influence at least some people to do evil and promote evil, and if you accept that we are all influenced to varying degrees by other people, then it follows that we can all be influenced indirectly by evil spirits as they influence other people.

Here are some ways I believe evil spirits indirectly influence believers today:

- Sexually immoral people (who may be influenced by evil spirits) may seduce believers into sexual immorality.

- Screenwriters and authors (who may be influenced by evil spirits) may promote sexual immorality in their works. Believers, who see or hear their work, may be tempted toward sexual immorality.

- Advertisers (who may be influenced by evil spirits) may promote materialism and greed to believers to sell more of their product.

- Teachers and college professors (who may be influenced by evil spirits) may treat faith in God as stupid and archaic, thereby weakening the faith of believers.

- Journalists, reporters, and editors (who may be influenced by evil spirits) may report news in such a way as to distort the truth, causing believers to be deceived about various matters. Or, they may choose to **not** report on various stories, or aspects of stories, that don't support their own bias. Again, the result is that believers may be deceived (or remain ignorant) about various matters.

- Operators of social media (who may be influenced by evil spirits) may censor various viewpoints, thereby promoting unrighteous viewpoints to believers, and hindering believers from freely communicating about alternative viewpoints.

- Friends and acquaintances (who may be influenced by evil spirits) may encourage believers to do worldly things with them.

- Unbelievers (who may be influenced by evil spirits) may physically persecute believers, even to the point of torture and death, as has been widely documented throughout history (including Revelation 2:10).

- False teachers (who may be influenced by evil spirits) may deceive believers into believing false doctrines, and believers then teach false doctrines to other believers.

Let's be clear here. While each of the types of people listed above *may be influenced by evil spirits* to do evil or promote evil, those types of people may do similar evil or promote similar evil just based on their own fallen sinful natures, apart from direct influence by evil spirits. I think most believers aren't usually able to discern to what degree an unsaved person is influenced by evil spirits.

Scripture is clear that many evil spirits prefer to dwell within people (or animals; see Matthew 8:28-32) rather than simply existing outside of people (consider Matthew 12:43-45 and Luke 11:24-26). The degree to which evil spirits may directly influence people while existing external to a person is not clear in scripture. Most of the accounts of evil spirits in the New Testament involve evil spirits living within people and usually being forced to leave by Jesus or his followers.

Scripture and experience show that people afflicted by evil spirits may have a wide range of symptoms. Many believers make a distinction between a person being "demonized" or being "demon possessed." Being "possessed" by a demon is understood to be more serious than being "demonized" (though scripture does not clearly discuss this difference).

Being "demonized" is often said to involve such things as hearing voices in one's mind, and various forms of emotional agitation. Nightmares also may be associated with the influence of evil spirits (I have experienced nightmares myself, which I believe were the result of influence by evil spirits).

On the other hand, "demon possession" is often understood to involve a demon directly controlling a person's speech and actions. After an episode of being "possessed," the person who was "demon possessed" may be totally unaware of what happened while he or she was in the "possessed" state. It has been said that some demons are able to imitate a person's own voice and manners well enough that other people may not be aware of the transition to being in a "possessed" state. The confusion and damage resulting from this level of demonic influence can be great indeed.

Experience also shows that evil spirits are masters at making things appear to be different than they really are. For example, a believer may confront a demon within a person, with apparent success in casting it out. However, the departure may have only been a deception, leading to confusion and discouragement when the demon then re-manifests itself at a later date, claiming to have returned, when, in fact, it may have never left. (Note the difficulty the disciples had in driving out demons in Matthew 17:14-20, and Mark 9:14-29.) There is no end to the deceptive games they can play this way, when root spiritual issues are not dealt with.

Here are some other examples of how evil spirits are effective in making things appear different than they really are:

- They deceive people into thinking they don't exist or don't have any influence over them. Western secular viewpoints (and many western religious viewpoints) have largely dismissed evil spirits as mere folklore. This leads many people to not even consider that some of their problems may be related to the influence of evil spirits.

- They deceive people into thinking that they are "gods" that should be served and worshiped. Many animist and eastern religions appear to be following evil spirits rather than the one true God. As Paul wrote: ***"But I say that the things which the Gentiles sacrifice, they sacrifice to demons, and not to God, and I don't desire that you would have fellowship with demons"*** (1 Corinthians 10:20, WEB).

- They deceive people into thinking that some evil spirits are good and some are bad. For protection from "bad" evil spirits, many people trust and follow so-called "good" evil spirits. Evil spirits pretending to be good is just a hoax used to keep naive people in bondage to them. Remember, ***"even Satan masquerades as an angel of light"*** (2 Corinthians 11:14 WEB).

- They deceive people into thinking they have more power than they actually have. Most of the power they have over people has to do with controlling people through deception and fear. People are naturally afraid of spiritual forces they can't see and don't understand. Evil spirits thrive on fear and ignorance. Followers of Jesus should not be afraid of them.

Resolving the spiritual issues that allowed a demon to have influence in the first place is often key to a person gaining freedom from demonic influence. Often, unforgiveness and anger are contributing factors to demonic influence (Matthew 18:21-35, Ephesians 4:26-27). Helping people resolve those kinds of issues can bring freedom without an overt deliverance being necessary. Vocally renouncing any prior participation in occult-type activities or sexual sin may also be helpful (whether as a willing or unwilling participant).

James indicates that submitting ourselves to God and resisting the devil is an effective strategy against the devil:

> *Submit yourselves therefore to God. Resist the devil, and he will flee from you. Draw near to God, and he will draw near to you. Cleanse your hands, you sinners, and purify your hearts, you double-minded.*
>
> *James 4:7-8 ESV*

Likewise, lesser evil spirits may be overcome the same way. Vocally declaring things like "I submit myself to God; I resist the devil" and "I choose the will of God; I refuse the will of Satan" may be helpful, but only if those statements reflect the true intent of the person seeking freedom. Repenting of specific sins and submitting ourselves to God in those specific areas is usually more effective than general statements. However, sometimes a person may not know the specific sins associated with demonic influence, and general statements may be a helpful way to begin in those cases. Ask God for discernment regarding what the root issues are, and deal with those root issues as they become apparent.

In getting rid of demonic influence, some people think it is only necessary to resist the devil, without fully submitting themselves to God. That is, I believe, one of the devil's most effective deceptions.

How do we submit ourselves to God and resist the devil? Knowing, understanding, and living by truth is an important aspect of doing that. That's what this book is about.

In chapter 14 *"Deception goes Both Ways,"* we'll look at the importance of finding the correct middle ground regarding many difficult issues. Discerning to what degree, if any, a person's emotional, psychological, or physical problems may be related to demonic influence is an especially difficult area. However, most of the above recommendations regarding how to be set free from demonic influence are good things to do whether or not a person is influenced by evil spirits. Submitting ourselves to God, resisting the devil, repenting of sin, choosing God's will, and turning from anger and unforgiveness are all important things for all of us to do to grow spiritually. **Don't let uncertainty about the source of your problems keep you from doing those things.**

I'm not claiming to know precisely where the middle-ground truth lies on this subject of evil spirits. However, I am certain it does not lie at either extreme viewpoint ("demons don't exist," or "demons are everywhere"). Evil spirits are real, as indicated in many places in scripture. They can impact us in ways we may be unaware of. However, there is not a demon behind every aspect of life. As we abide in Christ, we can rest in the truth of Paul's words:

*For I am convinced that neither death nor life, neither angels nor demons, neither the present nor the future, nor any powers, neither height nor depth, nor anything else in all creation, will be able to separate us from the love of God that is in Christ Jesus our Lord.*

*Romans 8:38-39 NIV*

## For Further Reflection

- How have you experienced opposition from the devil or evil spirits in your own life?

\*\*\*\*\*\*\*\*\*\*\*

# Chapter 11
# Deceivers Among Us

*"For I know that after my departure, vicious wolves will enter in among you, not sparing the flock. Men will arise from among your own selves, speaking perverse things, to draw away the disciples after them. Therefore watch, remembering that for a period of three years I didn't cease to admonish everyone night and day with tears."*

*Acts 20:29-31 WEB*

---

It seems to be common among believers to watch out for false teachers and false teaching from groups other than their own. It seems seldom that believers consider the possibility of false teachers in their own midst. But that is a recurring theme in scripture. In the verses above, Paul warns the Ephesian elders that *Men will arise from among your own selves, speaking perverse things, to draw away the disciples after them.* Peter and Jude give similar strong warnings:

*But false prophets also arose among the people, just as there will be false teachers among you, who will secretly bring in destructive heresies, even denying the Master who bought them, bringing upon themselves swift destruction. And many will follow their sensuality, and because of them the way of truth will be blasphemed. And in their greed they will exploit you with false words.*

*2Peter 2:1-3 ESV*

*Dear friends, although I was very eager to write to you about the salvation we share, I felt compelled to write and urge you to contend for the faith that was once for all entrusted to God's holy people. For certain individuals whose condemnation was written about long ago have secretly slipped in among you. They are ungodly people, who pervert the grace of our God into a license for immorality and deny Jesus Christ our only*

To understand this issue better, consider the many different people who may be among those who gather with us:

- Saved believers, who are mature in faith.

- Saved believers, who are partly mature in faith.

- Saved believers, who are still fleshly (to be discussed in chapter 18 *"The Flesh"*).

- Unsaved people, who come to learn about salvation.

- Unsaved people who think they are saved, who are deceived by poor understanding.

- Unsaved people who pretend to be saved in order to fit in socially.

- Unsaved people, who pretend to be saved, who intend to do harm to believers.

- Unsaved people, who don't pretend to be saved, who intend to do harm to believers.

Note that, especially among unsaved people, various levels of demonic influence may be at work. Some people influenced by evil spirits may be very good at pretending to be mature believers (or may really think they are mature believers), and may even be in positions of leadership, and may lead many people astray. How does your local assembly of believers discern the difference between true believers and false believers? Do they have understanding and wisdom in this area? A first step is to be aware of the possibility, and, as Paul wrote, *"Therefore, watch"* (Acts 20:31 WEB).

Note also that even those who are mature believers are likely to be deceived in some areas (I include myself here). Given the various conflicting beliefs of different groups of believers in the world today, this is a logical conclusion that is hard to escape. It may not be a reassuring thought, but it is likely that the people you most look up to are not completely free of deception.

Further, keep in mind that spiritual communication and spiritual manifestations can have various sources:

- God / good angels
- Evil spirits
- A person's own self (spirit/soul/body)

Those who accept all spiritual communication and spiritual manifestations, without questioning their source, open themselves up to being deceived.

Jesus gave us these instructions, which seem to correlate well with Paul's warning to the Ephesian elders (Acts 20:29-31):

> *"Beware of false prophets, who come to you in sheep's clothing, but inwardly are ravening wolves. By their fruits you will know them. Do you gather grapes from thorns, or figs from thistles? Even so, every good tree produces good fruit; but the corrupt tree produces evil fruit. A good tree can't produce evil fruit, neither can a corrupt tree produce good fruit. Every tree that doesn't grow good fruit is cut down, and thrown into the fire. Therefore, by their fruits you will know them."*
>
> *Matthew 7:15-20 WEB*

We understand that the *"fruits"* Jesus speaks of are not religious words or outward works of ministry, for Jesus then says:

> *"Not everyone who says to me, 'Lord, Lord,' will enter into the Kingdom of Heaven; but he who does the will of my Father who is in heaven. Many will tell me in that day, 'Lord, Lord, didn't we prophesy in your name, in your name cast out demons, and in your name do many mighty works?' Then I will tell them, 'I never knew*

*you. Depart from me, you who work iniquity.'"*

*Matthew 7:21-23 WEB*

Rather we understand *"fruits"* to refer to things like the works of the flesh and fruit of the Spirit spoken of by Paul:

*Now the works of the flesh are evident: sexual immorality, impurity, sensuality, idolatry, sorcery, enmity, strife, jealousy, fits of anger, rivalries, dissensions, divisions, envy, drunkenness, orgies, and things like these. I warn you, as I warned you before, that those who do such things will not inherit the kingdom of God. But the fruit of the Spirit is love, joy, peace, patience, kindness, goodness, faithfulness, gentleness, self-control; against such things there is no law.* Galatians 5:19-23 ESV

Note that, in Matthew 7:21-23 (above), people who didn't truly know Jesus will say *"Lord, Lord, didn't we prophesy in your name, in your name cast out demons, and in your name do many mighty works?"* Jesus doesn't deny they did such works, but rather indicates he *never knew* them.

Later, Jesus warns us again to not be deceived by people who perform miracles, but who are false christs or false prophets:

*"Then if anyone says to you, 'Look, here is the Christ!' or 'There he is!' do not believe it. For false christs and false prophets will arise and perform great signs and wonders, so as to lead astray, if possible, even the elect. See, I have told you beforehand."* Matthew 24:23-25 ESV

Of course, a primary characteristic of false teachers is that they distort the truth of the gospel. Having a clear understanding of the truths of scripture is a primary way we can identify false teachers. Consider these verses:

*I am astonished that you are so quickly deserting him who called you in the grace of Christ and are turning to a different gospel—not that there is another one, but*

*there are some who trouble you and want to distort the gospel of Christ. But even if we or an angel from heaven should preach to you a gospel contrary to the one we preached to you, let him be accursed. As we have said before, so now I say again: If anyone is preaching to you a gospel contrary to the one you received, let him be accursed.* Galatians 1:6-9 ESV

*But I am afraid that as the serpent deceived Eve by his cunning, your thoughts will be led astray from a sincere and pure devotion to Christ. For if someone comes and proclaims another Jesus than the one we proclaimed, or if you receive a different spirit from the one you received, or if you accept a different gospel from the one you accepted, you put up with it readily enough.*
2Corinthians 11:3-4 ESV

*For such people are false apostles, deceitful workers, masquerading as apostles of Christ. And no wonder, for Satan himself masquerades as an angel of light. It is not surprising, then, if his servants also masquerade as servants of righteousness. Their end will be what their actions deserve.* 2Corinthians 11:13-15 ESV

## For Further Reflection

- Have you been watching out for false teachers among us?

- What are some false teachings that are being promoted today?

\*\*\*\*\*\*\*\*\*\*\*\*

# Chapter 12
# Passivity

*Every athlete exercises self-control in all things. They do it to receive a perishable wreath, but we an imperishable. So I do not run aimlessly; I do not box as one beating the air. But I discipline my body and keep it under control, lest after preaching to others I myself should be disqualified.*
1Corinthians 9:25-27 ESV

*A simple man believes everything, but the prudent man carefully considers his ways.*
Proverbs 14:15 WEB

---

How does God want us to relate to him? Does God want active cooperation from us, or does God want us to be mere robots controlled by him? Should we exercise our wills and intellects to make wise choices and do right things, or should we just be passive so that God can somehow directly control us to do his will?

From beginning to end, scripture is filled with information that we are instructed to know and to act on. Scripture repeatedly finds fault with people for failing to actively follow God and do what he says to do. Nowhere in scripture do I see anyone rebuked for not being passive enough for God to use them.

Consider these verses:

> *I will give thanks to Yahweh with my whole heart. I will tell of all your marvelous works. I will be glad and rejoice in you. I will sing praise to your name, O Most High.* Psalm 9:1-2 WEB

> *I hold back my feet from every evil way, in order to keep your word.* Psalm 119:101 ESV

> *I incline my heart to perform your statutes forever, to*

*the end.* *Psalm 119:112 ESV*

*But the fruit of the Spirit is ... self-control.*
*Galatians 5:22-23 WEB*

*Like a city whose walls are broken through is a person who lacks self-control.* *Proverbs 25:28 NIV*

*We demolish arguments and every pretension that sets itself up against the knowledge of God, and we take captive every thought to make it obedient to Christ.*
*2Corinthians 10:5 NIV*

*Set your mind on the things that are above, not on the things that are on the earth.* *Colossians 3:2 WEB*

*Therefore, preparing your minds for action, and being sober-minded, set your hope fully on the grace that will be brought to you at the revelation of Jesus Christ.*
*1Peter 1:13 ESV*

*Therefore don't let sin reign in your mortal body, that you should obey it in its lusts. Neither present your members to sin as instruments of unrighteousness, but present yourselves to God, as alive from the dead, and your members as instruments of righteousness to God.*
*Romans 6:12-13 WEB*

*To him therefore who knows to do good, and doesn't do it, to him it is sin.* *James 4:17 WEB*

*Finally, be strong in the Lord, and in the strength of his might. Put on the whole armor of God, that you may be able to stand against the wiles of the devil. For our wrestling is not against flesh and blood, but against the principalities, against the powers, against the world's rulers of the darkness of this age, and against the spiritual forces of wickedness in the heavenly places. Therefore, put on the whole armor of God, that you may be able to withstand in the evil day, and, having done all, to stand. Stand therefore...*
*Ephesians 6:10-14 WEB*

These verses are calling us to use our wills and minds to actively follow God. They do not call us to a passive approach to spiritual things.

## Other Religious Perspectives

It may be helpful to consider the opposite teaching and practices found in many religions. Many religions promote the need to *empty* one's mind and to become *passive* to better connect with the spiritual realm. By doing so, many people hope to be influenced or indwelt by spirits associated with those religions. Scripture frequently refers to spirits that indwell people (other than the Holy Spirit of God) as "evil spirits" or "unclean spirits." Evil spirits have already been discussed some in Chapter 10 *"Spirits of Deception."*

In contrast, I am not aware of any scriptures in the Bible that call us to empty our minds or to not use our willpower in following God. The Holy Spirit indwells all who are truly saved (Romans 8:9). Salvation happens by turning to God in repentance and having faith in our Lord Jesus (Acts 20:21), not by becoming passive. Often, a genuine "born again" salvation experience occurs when a person makes an active choice to turn from sin and worldly things and to follow Jesus in all things (not by emptying oneself and being passive).

However, some followers of Jesus promote the idea that an empty mind and passive attitude are necessary for the Holy Spirit to work in us, or to fill us, or to give us a spiritual gift. It is the experience of many people that doing so may open the door to influence by evil spirits, leading to deception and bondage. Consider these verses about evil spirits pretending to be good:

> **For such people are false apostles, deceitful workers, masquerading as apostles of Christ. And no wonder, for Satan himself masquerades as an angel of light.**
> *2Corinthians 11:13-14 ESV*

*Beloved, don't believe every spirit, but test the spirits, whether they are of God, because many false prophets have gone out into the world.*                    *1John 4:1 WEB*

Regarding having a passive mind, consider Solomon's words:

*In everything the prudent acts with knowledge, but a fool flaunts his folly.*                    *Proverbs 13:16 ESV*

Prudent people's actions are based on having knowledge about what they are doing, not having an empty mind. On the other hand, fools act without appropriate knowledge, and that results in "folly." Let's now consider a few ways believers are sometimes led astray regarding having a passive attitude.

## "Let Go and Let God"?

Someone has said "Let go and let God." That has been a somewhat common saying for a long time (though it is not in scripture). In a positive light, we can understand it to be encouraging us to stop trusting in our own effort and ability and to place our trust in God to help us through a difficult situation. That's good. However, in a negative light, some may understand it to mean to stop using their wills and minds to actively follow God; to simply be passive and simply accept whatever happens. That's not so good.

## "No Longer I That Live"?

Here is a verse in scripture that leads some toward a passive perspective:

*I have been crucified with Christ, and it is no longer I that live, but Christ lives in me. That life which I now live in the flesh, I live by faith in the Son of God, who loved me, and gave himself up for me.*

*Galatians 2:20 WEB*

Some people interpret *"it is no longer I that live, but Christ lives in me"* as indicating that they should suppress their own consciousness and will, and instead somehow be controlled by *"Christ lives in me."* However, this viewpoint is inconsistent with other scripture, as already discussed. It is also inconsistent with the same verse, since Paul also said *"That life which I now live in the flesh, I live by faith in the Son of God..."* This suggests that Paul is speaking figuratively about a change in the focus of his life, not a cessation of his own consciousness and will.

Later, in his same letter to the Galatians, Paul writes:

> *Those who belong to Christ have crucified the flesh with its passions and lusts.* Galatians 5:24 WEB

This suggests that Paul's previous reference to being *crucified with Christ* (Galatians 2:20) has to do with no longer living according sinful desires. Paul no longer lives to satisfy his own fleshly desires, but rather to please God. That is a common theme in scripture, and involves an active attitude against sin. Paul writes more about being *crucified with Christ* in Romans 6:

> *We know that our old self was crucified with him in order that the body of sin might be brought to nothing, so that we would no longer be enslaved to sin. For one who has died has been set free from sin.*
> Romans 6:6-7 ESV

Reading further in Romans 6 we see that this involves our active participation:

> *Let not sin therefore reign in your mortal body, to make you obey its passions.* Romans 6:12 ESV

So, we see that in Galatians 2:20 Paul is showing us the importance of being united with Christ in his death, in order to die to sin and receive new life through Christ's resurrection (see Romans 6:3-14 for more on this theme). Paul is not calling us to a passive life.

# "It Is God Who Works in You"

Let's look at another verse that some interpret to promote a passive attitude:

> *So then, my beloved, even as you have always obeyed, not only in my presence, but now much more in my absence, work out your own salvation with fear and trembling. For it is God who works in you both to will and to work, for his good pleasure.* Philippians 2:12-13 WEB

These verses can be confusing. The first part (verse 12) instructs us to *obey*, and to *"work out your own salvation with fear and trembling."* That seems consistent with the emphasis of this chapter.

But then the later part (verse 13) says *"For it is God who works in you both to will and to work, for his good pleasure."* Who is willing and working here? God or us? I think there are two ways to understand this.

First, it is widely taught in scripture that the Holy Spirit living in us gives us understanding and power to follow God and to obey God (otherwise we generally fail). This verse (Philippians 2:13) may simply be referring to the Holy Spirit working in us, giving us power both to will and to work in a way that pleases God (using our own strengthened understanding and willpower to live in a way that pleases God).

Alternatively, it could be understood that God actively helps us to will and work in a way that pleases him (God contributing to our understanding and willpower to make right decisions, yet without controlling us like robots).

An interpretation that is NOT consistent with scripture is this: God alone controls our wills and actions; we do not need to exercise our will because God does that for us.

# "Walk in a Manner Worthy"

Finally, let's consider how knowledge, understanding, and wisdom relate to NOT being passive. Paul wrote to the believers at Colossae:

> *And so, from the day we heard, we have not ceased to pray for you, asking that you may be filled with the knowledge of his will in all spiritual wisdom and understanding, so as to walk in a manner worthy of the Lord, fully pleasing to him, bearing fruit in every good work and increasing in the knowledge of God.*
>
> *Colossians 1:9-10 ESV*

Here we see the purpose of having knowledge, understanding, and wisdom is *to walk in a manner worthy of the Lord, fully pleasing to him, bearing fruit in every good work.* We need knowledge, understanding, and wisdom because we are to actively follow God, not as passive robots with God controlling us, but as intelligent beings freely following God using our own wills and intellects to do so.

# For Further Reflection

• Have you been too passive in how you follow Jesus?

************

# Chapter 13
# A Neutral Attitude

*Therefore judge nothing before the appointed time;*
*wait until the Lord comes. He will bring to light what is*
*hidden in darkness and will expose the motives of the heart.*
*At that time each will receive their praise from God.*
1Corinthians 4:5 NIV

*The one who states his case first seems right,*
*until the other comes and examines him.*
Proverbs 18:17 ESV

*Beloved, don't believe every spirit,*
*but test the spirits, whether they are of God,*
*because many false prophets have gone out into the world.*
1John 4:1 WEB

———————

We have discussed how acquiring "knowledge" involves learning various "truths." We have also discussed how we may be deceived regarding truth, resulting in false knowledge and false understanding.

Regarding any particular subject, there are four possible positions we can each have regarding whether something is true or not:

1. **Ignorance:** Having little or no knowledge about the subject.

2. **A Neutral Attitude:** Having partial knowledge about the subject, but **not** having a settled opinion regarding its truth or how it should be understood.

3. **Assumed Understanding:** Having partial knowledge about the subject, and having a settled opinion regarding its truth and how to understand it.

4. **True Understanding:** Having fairly complete knowledge of the subject, and accurately under-

standing the truth about it.

Note that the lines between these four positions are not always clear. There may often be some overlap of these positions as our knowledge and understanding of a subject changes over time.

Many of us would like to have *"true understanding"* about everything, but that is not a realistic possibility in this life. As Paul wrote:

> **For now we see in a mirror, dimly, but then face to face. Now I know in part, but then I will know fully, even as I was also fully known.**        *1 Corinthians 13:12 WEB*

Anyone who takes a realistic view of the tremendous amount of information available today will quickly realize how ignorant all of us are about a great many subjects.

As we grow in our knowledge and understanding of a subject, there tends to be a natural progression through the first three possible positions.

1. Regarding any particular subject, we start in a state of **ignorance**.

2. As we first become aware of the subject, we tend to first have a **neutral attitude** toward it.

3. As we learn more about the subject, and are influenced by various people and opinions, we tend to come to a settled opinion about its truth and how it should be understood. This often happens before we have adequate knowledge and understanding to form an accurate conclusion. So, we often arrive at **assumed understanding** (rather than *true understanding*).

This third position, *"assumed understanding,"* is where deception often occurs. By leaving behind a *neutral attitude* too soon, we can easily end up being *deceived*, and not arrive at *true understanding*. Recall the definition of *deceived* we are using from chapter 6:

**Deceived:** A state of believing something to be true which is actually false, or believing something to be false which is actually true.

Ideally, we would skip the third stage of *assumed understanding*, and transition from a *neutral attitude* directly to *true understanding*. In practice, however, it seems that most people's *pride* leads them to assume they understand things much better and sooner than they actually do. It is *sinful pride* that often leads to *assumed understanding*, and contributes to being easily *deceived*.

Unfortunately, progress often stops with assumed understanding and some level of deception. Once we think we understand something, it is often difficult for us to consider a different viewpoint, acknowledge we may have been wrong, and embrace a different viewpoint.

So, do you want to avoid deception? Then be slower to leave a position of neutrality. Aim to understand things more deeply before arriving at settled conclusions. Look at all sides of an issue to better understand it. Keep in mind:

*The one who states his case first seems right, until the other comes and examines him.*          *Proverbs 18:17 ESV*

*Beloved, don't believe every spirit, but test the spirits, whether they are of God, because many false prophets have gone out into the world.*          *1John 4:1 WEB*

There are some subjects about which it is important that we arrive at *true understanding*, and not settle for long-term *ignorance* or *neutrality*. For example, consider spiritual and religious things. If Jesus is truly the only Son of God, who came in the flesh to redeem lost sinners; and if trusting in Jesus is necessary to obtain eternal life; then remaining an "agnostic" forever (one who is either ignorant regarding Jesus, or who maintains a neutral attitude about Jesus) is not a good path to follow.

Ultimately, our goal should be *true understanding* that

enables us to serve God with clarity. We cannot stand firmly with God and against evil if we do not have at least some *true understanding* about what is of God and what isn't. However, holding to a wrong *assumed understanding* of things can have serious consequences. Let's look at an example of this in scripture.

## The Man Born Blind

Consider the man who was born blind, whose story we read about in John 9. Jesus healed him! However, this happened on a Sabbath day, and some of the Pharisees had an *assumed understanding* that the command to keep the Sabbath day holy (the 3$^{rd}$ command of the Ten Commandments given through Moses; Exodus 20:8-11) meant that it was wrong for Jesus to heal people on the Sabbath. This was a primary reason that they opposed Jesus:

> *Some of the Pharisees said, "This man is not from God, for he does not keep the Sabbath." But others said, "How can a man who is a sinner do such signs?" And there was a division among them.*           John 9:16 ESV

This wrong *assumed understanding* about Jesus being a Sabbath breaker caused them to reject Jesus. However, some were questioning that *assumed understanding* and rightly held a more *neutral attitude*: *"How can a man who is a sinner do such signs?"* Notice how strongly some of the Pharisees hold to their wrong understanding:

> *So they called the man who was blind a second time, and said to him, "Give glory to God. We know that this man is a sinner."*
>
> *He therefore answered, "I don't know if he is a sinner. One thing I do know: that though I was blind, now I see."*           John 9:24-25 WEB

We see here that the man born blind saw through their wrong *assumed understanding* and rejected it. The man born blind was right to have a *neutral attitude* on the subject of whether or not Jesus was a sinner, saying ***"I don't know if he is a sinner."*** And, he had *true understanding* that Jesus had healed him, saying ***"One thing I do know: that though I was blind, now I see."*** This proper perspective, having a *neutral attitude* about some things that aren't so clear, combined with *true understanding* of things that are clear, helped the man born blind to avoid deception and embrace the truth about Jesus.

On the other hand, some of the Pharisees appear to be prideful about their knowledge about Moses, and they couldn't accept any challenges to their *assumed understanding*:

> ***They insulted him and said, "You are his disciple, but we are disciples of Moses. We know that God has spoken to Moses. But as for this man, we don't know where he comes from."***
>
> ***The man answered them, "How amazing! You don't know where he comes from, yet he opened my eyes. We know that God doesn't listen to sinners, but if anyone is a worshipper of God, and does his will, he listens to him. Since the world began it has never been heard of that anyone opened the eyes of someone born blind. If this man were not from God, he could do nothing."***
>
> ***They answered him, "You were altogether born in sins, and do you teach us?" They threw him out.***
>
> *John 9:28-34 WEB*

The man born blind arrives at *true understanding* that Jesus must be ***"from God"*** based on the clear evidence of his own healing, and communicates this clearly to the Pharisees. He also points out to them their lack of *true understanding* about Jesus, saying ***"How amazing! You don't know where he comes from, yet he opened my eyes."***

It is a common problem that religious people with partial

knowledge tend to think they have all the right answers. This is another wrong *assumed understanding* implied in this account. The Pharisees tended to look at themselves as the final authority regarding truth and right religion. Since Jesus was not part of them, nor subject to them, they looked at Jesus as a threat to true religion. True followers of Jesus today tend to get the same kind of treatment by religious people as Jesus received from them (John 15:18-21).

Another point of wrong *assumed understanding* by the Pharisees is observed in verse 34: ***"You were altogether born in sins, and do you teach us?"*** They believed anyone born blind had a problem with sin, and this was a good reason for them to reject the clear truth about Jesus which the man born blind spoke to them. However, Jesus told his disciples that sin was not the source of this man's blindness:

> *His disciples asked him, "Rabbi, who sinned, this man or his parents, that he was born blind?"*
>
> *Jesus answered, "Neither did this man sin, nor his parents; but, that the works of God might be revealed in him."*
> John 9:2-3 WEB

This account of the man born blind gives us several examples of how wrong *assumed understanding* can have serious negative consequences. However, let's not assume that these kinds of problems are limited to the Pharisees of Jesus' day. I think it is safe to say that we are all adversely impacted by wrong *assumed understandings* in our own lives, much more than we realize. Let us ask God to expose our areas of wrong understanding, and to lead us either to *true understanding* in those areas, or to a more *neutral attitude* regarding things that aren't very clear.

## For Further Reflection

- Has your religious background given you some traditional *assumed understanding* that is hindering you from *true understanding*? Should you have a more *neutral attitude* about some of those traditional viewpoints?

**\*\*\*\*\*\*\*\*\*\*\*\***

# Chapter 14
# Deception Goes Both Ways

*Let your eyes look straight ahead. Fix your gaze directly before you. Make the path of your feet level. Let all of your ways be established. Don't turn to the right hand nor to the left. Remove your foot from evil.* Proverbs 4:25-27 WEB

Truth is often NOT found in extreme or simple viewpoints, but rather somewhere between extreme or simple viewpoints. The easiest way to clarify what I mean is by an example. Consider the issue of our sexuality. Two extreme and simple viewpoints are:

- Sex is always bad and should always be avoided.

- Sex is always good and should always be embraced.

Clearly, from a scriptural viewpoint, neither extreme is true. Rather, scripture shows that sexual relationships can be very good within the context of marriage, but are not good outside of marriage.

So we see that holding onto truth in this area involves finding a correct middle-ground perspective, and not straying *to the right hand nor to the left.* A viewpoint that overly restricts sex may be just as wrong as a viewpoint that overly promotes sex. Deception can go both ways. Further, it is often difficult to discern the correct middle ground.

Continuing with this example, what about sexual self-gratification? Many seem to think God condemns any form of it, but I am not aware of any scriptures that specifically deal with it. I tend to think that many people's beliefs in this area are oversimplified. It's easy for people with a gift of self-control to condemn those without such a gift, but I doubt that's a correct middle-ground viewpoint. I suspect that neither extreme viewpoint on this subject is correct (always wrong, or never wrong). The truth is likely in the middle somewhere. I think the truth on this subject likely depends on a person's particular circumstances, to some degree. However, a clarification is in order here. We should keep in mind Jesus' words:

> *"You have heard that it was said, 'You shall not commit adultery;' but I tell you that everyone who gazes at a woman to lust after her has committed adultery with her already in his heart."* Matthew 5:27-28 WEB

From this we can conclude that pornography, in its many forms, is **not** a good option. Many lives have been ruined by going down that path.

As another example of how deception goes both ways, consider what happened after the spies searched out the Promised Land. Upon hearing a bad report from ten of the spies, most of the people were deceived into thinking they couldn't go forward, and responded with a lack of faith in God:

> *All the congregation lifted up their voice, and cried; and the people wept that night. All the children of Israel murmured against Moses and against Aaron. The whole congregation said to them, "We wish that we had died in the land of Egypt, or that we had died in this wilderness! Why does Yahweh bring us to this land, to fall by the sword? Our wives and our little ones will be captured or killed! Wouldn't it be better for us to return into Egypt?" They said to one another, "Let's make a captain, and let's return into Egypt."* Numbers 14:1-4 WEB

Then, after Moses spoke to God about it all, and told the people they would have to stay in the desert for forty years, the people went to the other extreme of deception:

> *Moses told these words to all the children of Israel, and the people mourned greatly. They rose up early in the morning and went up to the top of the mountain, saying,*

*"Behold, we are here, and will go up to the place which Yahweh has promised; for we have sinned."*

*Numbers 14:39-40 WEB*

Moses told them not to go, that God was not with them, but they went anyway, and they were defeated by their enemies (Numbers 14:41-45). Clearly, trusting and obeying God through difficult circumstances was always the right thing to do. However, the people were easily deceived, first not trusting God and thinking they couldn't win the battle (when they could, with God's help), then seeing they were wrong and thinking they could win the battle (when they couldn't, since God would not then help them). Deception went both ways.

As this example shows, it's easy to go from one form of deception to another form of deception when we become aware of the first deception. Finding the correct middle ground is often hard to do.

It's not my purpose in this chapter to define the precisely-correct middle-ground perspective on any subject, but simply to show that extreme or simple viewpoints are often wrong viewpoints, and to show that truth is often found somewhere between extreme or simple viewpoints.

Note that there can be a continuum of viewpoints between two or more extreme or simple viewpoints. The correct viewpoint may not be a black-and-white kind of issue. However, it should be clear that error doesn't just lie at the most extreme viewpoints, but is also found in many viewpoints that are between the extremes. We should be slow to think that our own viewpoints are completely without error.

There is a common problem associated with middle-ground kind of truth. Middle-ground viewpoints are usually more complicated and harder to understand than extreme or simple viewpoints. Often it is easier for people to hold an extreme or simple viewpoint than a more-complicated middle-ground viewpoint. As a result of this, it is not uncommon for a group of people to correctly see that one extreme position is wrong, and then embrace an opposite extreme position, which is also wrong. Reacting against one error often leads people into the opposite error. Many people seem to be unable to embrace a more-complicated correct middle-ground viewpoint.

We see this dynamic sometimes playing out in church history, where a group of believers see a problem, then moves to the other extreme to protect themselves, thereby moving into an opposite error.

For example, the Reformation was at least partly a response to a corrupt church hierarchy that wrongly emphasized good works and neglected the importance of faith and God's grace in salvation. In their reaction against that problem, some Reformation leaders taught that salvation is by God's "grace alone" through "faith alone." I believe those phrases oversimplify the issue, and have contributed to misunderstanding and division among believers. Many people may rightly understand the intent of those phrases in accordance with scripture, but it appears to me that many have been misled by them.

Scripture does say:

> *For by grace you have been saved through faith. And this is not your own doing; it is the gift of God, not a result of works, so that no one may boast.*
> *Ephesians 2:8-9 ESV*

However, note that the phrases *"grace alone"* and *"faith alone"* are not used here. Again, I believe those phrases are an oversimplification of the issue. Note that the next verse reads:

> *For we are his workmanship, created in Christ Jesus for good works, which God prepared beforehand, that we should walk in them.*
> *Ephesians 2:10 ESV*

While good works play no part in our initial salvation, scripture is clear that good works are an important part of a life of faith. James clarified this when he wrote:

> *What good is it, my brothers, if someone says he has faith but does not have works? Can that faith save him? If a brother or sister is poorly clothed and lacking in daily food, and one of you says to them, "Go in peace, be warmed and filled," without giving them the things needed for the body, what good is that? So also faith by itself, if it does not have works, is dead.* James 2:14-17 ESV

> *You see that a person is justified by works and not by faith alone.* James 2:24 ESV

That last verse is the only verse I find in the Bible that mentions *"faith alone."* Some Reformation leaders are said to have disputed whether the book of James should be included in scripture, partly because James clearly does not support their "faith alone" viewpoint. Some believers with other perspectives point to this verse as strong evidence of Reformation Theology error, and they therefore dismiss any truth that is in that perspective. Some believers intentionally divide from reformed-leaning believers based on the "faith alone" viewpoint appearing to be obviously contrary to scripture, per James 2:24.

For clarity, let's consider this issue from a broader perspective. Scripture appears to speak of salvation in three different senses:

1. We have been saved.
2. We are being saved.
3. We will be saved.

Here are some verses that support the first category, "We have been saved":

> *For by grace you have been saved through faith. And this is not your own doing; it is the gift of God, not a*

*result of works, so that no one may boast.*

*Ephesians 2:8-9 ESV*

*But when the kindness of God our Savior and his love toward mankind appeared, not by works of righteousness which we did ourselves, but according to his mercy, he saved us through the washing of regeneration and renewing by the Holy Spirit, whom he poured out on us richly, through Jesus Christ our Savior, so that being justified by his grace we might be made heirs according to the hope of eternal life.*

*Titus 3:4-7 WEB*

Here are some verses that support the second category, "We are being saved":

*In all my prayers for all of you, I always pray with joy because of your partnership in the gospel from the first day until now, being confident of this, that he who began a good work in you will carry it on to completion until the day of Christ Jesus.*    *Philippians 1:4-6 NIV*

*So then, my beloved, even as you have always obeyed, not only in my presence, but now much more in my absence, work out your own salvation with fear and trembling.*    *Philippians 2:12 WEB*

*But if we walk in the light, as he is in the light, we have fellowship with one another, and the blood of Jesus Christ, his Son, cleanses us from all sin.*

*1John 1:7 WEB*

Here are some verses that support the third category "We will be saved":

*You will be hated by all men for my name's sake, but he who endures to the end will be saved.*    *Matthew 10:22 WEB*

*If any man's work is burned, he will suffer loss, but he himself will be saved, but as through fire.*

*1Corinthians 3:15 WEB*

*Since, therefore, we have now been justified by his blood, much more shall we be saved by him from the wrath of God.*
*Romans 5:9 ESV*

Here is one perspective of how this issue of faith and works can be understood. When Paul says things like *"by grace you have been saved through faith... not a result of works"* (Ephesians 2:8-9) he is primarily referring to how *we have been saved.* When James emphasizes the importance of our faith being put into action (James 2:14-26), he is primarily referring to how *we are being saved.* If someone claims to have saving faith, but that faith has not changed how they live, then James calls that faith *dead*, and that person is likely still unsaved. True saving faith always expresses itself in how we live. However, the new life we live, and any good we do, is only done by the power of the Holy Spirit within us, so there is no place for boasting.

Paul also teaches that believers don't need to follow the Law of Moses (or do *"works of the law"*) to continue *being saved* or to *be saved* in the future. Some relevant verses regarding this are: Acts 15:1-29, Romans 3:19-31, 9:30-33, Galatians 2:1-21, and 3:1-26.

Saving faith is so closely associated with a changed life that salvation is sometimes spoken of in scripture as resulting from good works. An example of this is in Jesus' teaching about final judgment in Matthew 25:31-46. Here Jesus says that people will go to *"eternal punishment"* or *"eternal life"* based on how they treated other people, without mentioning their faith directly. Faith, or lack of faith, is evident in that passage only by the things people did or didn't do.

Oversimplifying things like this can lead to serious error. An emphasis on "grace alone" through "faith alone" has led many people to disregard scripture's call to a righteous life. Jude writes this in warning us about false teachers:

*For certain individuals whose condemnation was written*

*about long ago have secretly slipped in among you.*
*They are ungodly people, who pervert the grace of our*
*God into a license for immorality and deny Jesus Christ*
*our only Sovereign and Lord.*                    Jude 4 NIV

I am not claiming the Reformation leaders fit this profile. However, by oversimplifying salvation through grace and faith, some of them may have opened the door for false teachers *who pervert the grace of our God into a license for immorality.*

Oversimplifying issues like this also promotes division between believers. Each side sees the error of the other side, and tends to hold onto their opposite error. It would be easier for each side to consider middle-ground truth and move away from division if the other side was not so clearly wrong.

Consider some other issues which I think involve middle-ground truth.

- **Disputable Matters** (Romans 14): Disputable matters, such as whether we should be vegetarian or not, or consider some days special or not, can be divisive issues. A middle-ground perspective avoids offending one another regarding disputable matters (as Paul discusses in Romans 14:1 to 15:7).

- **Evangelism vs. Loving One Another** (The Great Commission vs. The Great Commandment): Some people seem to emphasize evangelism so much that they seem to neglect the love of God and love of others. Other people seem to want to focus on loving one another with no concern for sharing eternal life with the lost. A middle-ground perspective values both, while encouraging people to focus on their particular gifting.

- **Spiritual Gifts** (1 Corinthians 12-14): Some seem to promote spiritual gifts without any boundaries or without discerning the source of spiritual manifestations. Others deny that spiritual gifts are for today. The correct middle ground on this issue seems to be hard for many believers to find. This has resulted in huge divisions between believers. This will be discussed some in chapter 19 *"The Spirit"* and chapter 32 *"The Holy Spirit."*

- **Miracles:** Some reject all miracles, believing only in what can be proven scientifically, or believing that miracles no longer happen. Others accept and embrace anything that appears to be miraculous, without considering its source. Scripture gives examples of some miracles being done by powers of darkness (for example, the magicians of Egypt in Exodus 7; false christs and false prophets mentioned in Matthew 24:24; and the beast in Revelation 13:13-14). A middle-ground perspective acknowledges that miracles still happen, while rightly discerning their source and not having an unbalanced focus on miracles.

- **Demons in the World Today:** Some seem to be obsessed with demons being everywhere and influencing everything, while others deny they have any impact on us. This is another issue that is hard to discern the correct middle ground. This topic has already been discussed some in chapter 10 *"Spirits of Deception."*

- **God Speaking Today:** Some people claim that we should continually hear God speaking to us today in various ways, while others claim God only speaks through scripture today. Again, what is the correct middle ground? This topic will be discussed some in chapter 33 *"God Told Me..."*

- **Prosperity Gospel:** To what degree is God concerned with our material wealth? Some say we should expect God to bless us financially. Others say intentional poverty is the only way to spirituality. Again, what is the correct middle ground? This topic will be discussed some in chapter 28 *"Prosperity."*

- **Judging Others:** Some verses say we should judge, while others say we shouldn't judge. Many people today seem to embrace the "do not judge" verses, and ignore the "do judge" verses. What is the correct middle ground? This will be discussed in chapter 31 *"Do Not Judge."*

- **Right Doctrine:** While knowing truth is important, some people seem to put doctrinal beliefs ahead of loving God and loving others. Throughout church history, many people appear to have turned right beliefs about relatively minor issues into major points of division. Many beliefs that scripture is not clear about have been promoted in ways that have wrongly divided believers. In response to this error, others have promoted unity with little regard for what scripture clearly teaches. Clearly, we need to aim for the proper middle ground on these kinds of issues. This will be discussed some in chapter 30 *"Division."*

So, when dealing with many difficult issues, consider that truth may involve a middle-ground perspective, and we may be deceived if we hold simpler or more extreme viewpoints.

## For Further Reflection

- Are some of your viewpoints oversimplified?

\*\*\*\*\*\*\*\*\*\*\*\*

# Chapter 15
# "Heresy"

*But false prophets also arose among the people, just as there will be false teachers among you, who will secretly bring in destructive heresies, even denying the Master who bought them, bringing upon themselves swift destruction.*
2Peter 2:1 ESV

---

We should be careful how we handle matters of truth and deception. Many people wrongly use their own view of "truth" to cause division between believers. While faith in Jesus, and truth about Jesus, naturally divides believers from unbelievers, believers ought not to divide over secondary issues.

One of the greatest deceptions today among believers appears to be making truth about secondary issues more important than unity among believers. Secondary issues, often regarding secondary beliefs, are often the source of much unnecessary division and strife. One contributing factor to this problem is how people understand what scripture says about "heresy."

"Heresy" is one of those words that has taken on a much different meaning than its originally-intended meaning. It appears to me that the way many people use the word "heresy" today actually promotes "heresy" rather than exposing it. By accusing someone of "heresy" (using its common current meaning), people doing so may actually be promoting "heresy" (per its original meaning).

Our English word *"heresy"* appears to be directly derived from the Greek word *"hairesis"* (Strong's Exhaustive Concordance reference number G139). I count nine times that *hairesis* occurs in the New Testament, and in more-recent translations it is usually translated "sect," "faction," "party" or "division" (the nine verses are Acts 5:17, 15:5,

24:5, 24:14, 26:5, 28:22, 1 Corinthians 11:19, Galatians 5:20, and 2 Peter 2:1). Those nine verses together give a good sense of its original meaning.

However, in common English usage today, "heresy" is typically used to refer to any belief or doctrine that is so seriously wrong that the salvation of those who believe it is called into question. By some definitions, any belief or doctrine that is not *"orthodox"* is *"heresy"* (*"orthodox"* meaning to be in agreement with official church teaching). But it looks to me like that is not the meaning of the New Testament Greek word from which it is derived (*hairesis*). By New Testament usage, *hairesis* has to do with religious divisions, sects, parties, and factions.

Interestingly, 2 Peter 2:1 (above) is the only verse in which many more-recent translations still translate *hairesis* as "heresy." See if you can spot which word correlates with *hairesis* in the following passage:

> ***Now the works of the flesh are evident: sexual immorality, impurity, sensuality, idolatry, sorcery, enmity, strife, jealousy, fits of anger, rivalries, dissensions, divisions, envy, drunkenness, orgies, and things like these. I warn you, as I warned you before, that those who do such things will not inherit the kingdom of God.***   Galatians 5:19-21 ESV

Yes, *hairesis* correlates with ***"divisions."***

Consider 2nd Peter 2:1 (written out at the beginning of this chapter). Consider replacing the word ***"heresies"*** with "divisions," "factions," "sects," or "parties." Does that change how you understand that verse? It does for me. It changes the focus from an emphasis on right doctrine to a focus on the unity of believers and the importance of not dividing over secondary issues.

Our English word *"heretic"* is also directly derived from a Greek word: *"hairetikos"* (Strong's G141). Here is the only place I find in the New Testament that uses that word:

*As for a person who stirs up division, after warning him once and then twice, have nothing more to do with him, knowing that such a person is warped and sinful; he is self-condemned.* Titus 3:10-11 ESV

This translation, like many other translations, indicates that the original meaning of *"heretic"* also had more to do with causing division among believers than with holding to wrong beliefs (though promoting wrong beliefs is one way to cause division).

The history of the church is filled with divisions, resulting in the many "sects," "denominations," or *"heresies"* (per its original meaning) which we have today. Some of those divisions were necessary to preserve or restore important primary truths. However, many of those divisions occurred over secondary issues, and those who promoted those divisions may be guilty of promoting "heresy." "Heresy" not for promoting wrong doctrine, but for promoting division of believers over secondary issues.

The next time you hear a belief labeled "heresy," or hear someone accused of being a "heretic," consider whether or not the accuser may actually be promoting "heresy" (wrongly promoting divisions, factions, sects or parties). Don't be deceived!

## For Further Reflection

• Have you observed truth about secondary issues being made more important than unity among believers?

\*\*\*\*\*\*\*\*\*\*\*\*

# Chapter 16
# Test All Things

*Test all things, and hold firmly that which is good.*
*Abstain from every form of evil.*
*1Thessalonians 5:21-22 WEB*

---

While love and unity among believers is of primary importance, scripture frequently warns us to watch out for false doctrine, false teachers, false prophets, and even false christs. Though people in positions of leadership may have primary responsibility in this area, scripture warns us all to watch out for false doctrine and false teachers. Consider these verses.

*"Beware of false prophets, who come to you in sheep's clothing but inwardly are ravenous wolves. You will recognize them by their fruits. Are grapes gathered from thornbushes, or figs from thistles? So, every healthy tree bears good fruit, but the diseased tree bears bad fruit. A healthy tree cannot bear bad fruit, nor can a diseased tree bear good fruit. Every tree that does not bear good fruit is cut down and thrown into the fire. Thus you will recognize them by their fruits."*
*Matthew 7:15-20 ESV*

*Jesus, answering, began to tell them, "Be careful that no one leads you astray. For many will come in my name, saying, 'I am he!' and will lead many astray."*
*Mark 13:5-6 WEB*

*"Then if anyone tells you, 'Look, here is the Christ!' or, 'Look, there!' don't believe it. For there will arise false christs and false prophets, and will show signs and wonders, that they may lead astray, if possible, even the chosen ones."* *Mark 13:21-22 WEB*

*"I know that after I leave, savage wolves will come in*

*among you and will not spare the flock. Even from your own number men will arise and distort the truth in order to draw away disciples after them. So be on your guard! Remember that for three years I never stopped warning each of you night and day with tears."* Acts 20:29-31 NIV

*I appeal to you, brothers, to watch out for those who cause divisions and create obstacles contrary to the doctrine that you have been taught; avoid them. For such persons do not serve our Lord Christ, but their own appetites, and by smooth talk and flattery they deceive the hearts of the naive.* Romans 16:17-18 ESV

*See to it that no one takes you captive by philosophy and empty deceit, according to human tradition, according to the elemental spirits of the world, and not according to Christ.* Colossians 2:8 ESV

*Beloved, don't believe every spirit, but test the spirits, whether they are of God, because many false prophets have gone out into the world.* 1John 4:1 WEB

*But false prophets also arose among the people, just as there will be false teachers among you, who will secretly bring in destructive heresies, even denying the Master who bought them, bringing upon themselves swift destruction. And many will follow their sensuality, and because of them the way of truth will be blasphemed. And in their greed they will exploit you with false words. Their condemnation from long ago is not idle, and their destruction is not asleep.* 2Peter 2:1-3 ESV

*Regard the patience of our Lord as salvation; even as our beloved brother Paul also, according to the wisdom given to him, wrote to you; as also in all of his letters, speaking in them of these things. In those, there are some things that are hard to understand, which the ignorant and unsettled twist, as they also do to the other Scriptures, to their own destruction. You therefore, beloved, knowing these things beforehand, beware, lest being carried away with the error of the wicked, you fall from your own steadfastness.* 2Peter 3:15-17 WEB

*Dear friends, although I was very eager to write to you about the salvation we share, I felt compelled to write and urge you to contend for the faith that was once for all entrusted to God's holy people. For certain individuals whose condemnation was written about long ago have secretly slipped in among you. They are ungodly people, who pervert the grace of our God into a license for immorality and deny Jesus Christ our only Sovereign and Lord.* Jude 3-4 NIV

*But, dear friends, remember what the apostles of our Lord Jesus Christ foretold. They said to you, "In the last times there will be scoffers who will follow their own ungodly desires." These are the people who divide you, who follow mere natural instincts and do not have the Spirit. But you, dear friends, by building yourselves up in your most holy faith and praying in the Holy Spirit, keep yourselves in God's love as you wait for the mercy of our Lord Jesus Christ to bring you to eternal life. Be merciful to those who doubt; save others by snatching them from the fire; to others show mercy, mixed with fear—hating even the clothing stained by corrupted flesh.* Jude 17-23 NIV

Scripture not only warns us about the problem of false doctrine and false teachers, but also encourages us to test and discern what is true. Consider these verses:

*The simple believe anything, but the prudent give thought to their steps.* Proverbs 14:15 NIV

*He said to the multitudes also, "When you see a cloud rising from the west, immediately you say, 'A shower is coming,' and so it happens. When a south wind blows, you say, 'There will be a scorching heat,' and it*

*happens. You hypocrites! You know how to interpret the appearance of the earth and the sky, but how is it that you don't interpret this time? Why don't you judge for yourselves what is right?"*  Luke 12:54-57 WEB

*Now the Berean Jews were of more noble character than those in Thessalonica, for they received the message with great eagerness and examined the Scriptures every day to see if what Paul said was true.*
Acts 17:11 NIV

*Do not be conformed to this world, but be transformed by the renewal of your mind, that by testing you may discern what is the will of God, what is good and acceptable and perfect.*  Romans 12:2 ESV

*For if we discerned ourselves, we wouldn't be judged.*
1Corinthians 11:31 WEB

*Examine yourselves to see whether you are in the faith; test yourselves. Do you not realize that Christ Jesus is in you—unless, of course, you fail the test?*
2Corinthians 13:5 NIV

*This I pray, that your love may abound yet more and more in knowledge and all discernment; so that you may approve the things that are excellent; that you may be sincere and without offense to the day of Christ; being filled with the fruits of righteousness, which are through Jesus Christ, to the glory and praise of God.*
Philippians 1:9-11 WEB

*Test all things, and hold firmly that which is good. Abstain from every form of evil.*
1Thessalonians 5:21-22 WEB

*About this we have much to say, and it is hard to explain, since you have become dull of hearing. For though by this time you ought to be teachers, you need someone to teach you again the basic principles of the oracles of God. You need milk, not solid food, for*

*everyone who lives on milk is unskilled in the word of righteousness, since he is a child. But solid food is for the mature, for those who have their powers of discernment trained by constant practice to distinguish good from evil.*  Hebrews 5:11-14 ESV

## For Further Reflection

- Have you been learning to distinguish good from evil?

\*\*\*\*\*\*\*\*\*\*\*\*

# PART 3
# Flesh or Spirit?

*For those who live according to the flesh set their minds on the things of the flesh, but those who live according to the Spirit, the things of the Spirit. For the mind of the flesh is death, but the mind of the Spirit is life and peace.*
Romans 8:5-6 WEB

*For the flesh lusts against the Spirit, and the Spirit against the flesh; and these are contrary to one another, that you may not do the things that you desire.*
Galatians 5:17 WEB

*"Watch and pray, that you may not enter into temptation. The spirit indeed is willing, but the flesh is weak."*
Mark 14:38 WEB

---

How do we discern the difference between living by the Spirit, and living by the flesh? Avoiding deception in this area is an important part of successfully following Jesus. This section aims to clarify that issue. However, before we discuss that, we first need to discuss some related information about how we are made (spirit, soul, and body) and clarify what is meant by "Spirit" (with a capital S), "spirit" (lower-case s), and "flesh."

As previously mentioned, we should continue to keep in mind that salvation is primarily about coming to Jesus, trusting in Jesus, and following Jesus. He is the Christ, the Son of God, Lord of all. As we consider the difference between *Spirit* and *flesh*, let's continue to look *"to Jesus, the founder and perfecter of our faith"* (Hebrews 12:2 ESV).

\*\*\*\*\*\*\*\*\*\*\*

*Building on Foundations for Eternal Life*

# Chapter 17
# Spirit, Soul, Body

*May the God of peace himself sanctify you completely.*
*May your whole spirit, soul, and body be preserved*
*blameless at the coming of our Lord Jesus Christ.*
*1Thessalonians 5:23 WEB*

Scripture shows that people are comprised of three parts: spirit, soul, and body (New-Testament Greek: *"pneuma,"* *"psuche,"* and *"soma"*). Some consider spirit and soul to be synonyms for the non-physical part of people. However, I find that a careful reading of scripture shows spirit and soul to be distinct from each other, as 1 Thessalonians 5:23 (above) indicates.

Another reference that shows spirit and soul to be distinct is in Hebrews:

> *For the word of God is living, and active, and sharper than any two-edged sword, and piercing even to the dividing of soul and spirit, of both joints and marrow, and is able to discern the thoughts and intentions of the heart.*
> *Hebrews 4:12 WEB*

Here we see clearly that soul and spirit can be divided, and that the *"word of God"* is able to divide them.

Scripture has many references to spirit and soul, but scripture does not say much directly about their differences or how they relate to each other and to salvation. To add to the difficulty of this subject, many English translations often translate the Greek word for soul (*"psuche"*) as "life." Also, scripture is not always clear whether the Greek word for spirit ("pneuma") refers to our own spirit (usually translated "spirit" with a lower-case "s") or the Holy Spirit (usually translated "Spirit" with an upper-case "S"). Different translations are often different in this regard.

As a result of these translation difficulties, the distinctions between spirit and soul tend to be obscured some. As a further result, many believers know little about this subject, and there are many diverse viewpoints about it. I present to you my understanding, for your prayerful consideration.

The three-part nature of man is evident at creation:

> **Yahweh God formed man from the dust of the ground, and breathed into his nostrils the breath of life; and man became a living soul.**   *Genesis 2:7 WEB*

Adam's body was made from *the dust of the ground*, his spirit correlates with *the breath of life*, and he *became a living soul*.

Scripture and experience appear to me to support this basic understanding: Our body gives us world consciousness; our soul gives us self-consciousness; and our spirit gives us God consciousness. Our soul interacts with the physical world through our physical body. Our soul interacts with the spiritual world through our spirit.

Generally speaking, our soul is positioned between our spirit and our body, and is the nonphysical part of us that we are clearly conscious of. Its functions are often understood to include our will, our intellect (mind), and our emotions.

Most people are less conscious of their spirit. Its functions are often understood to include conscience, intuition, and communion with God.

The functions of our physical body are readily apparent, and include such things as vision, taste, touch, smell, hearing, legs for walking, and hands for various tasks. Our soul relates directly with our body in a way that is readily apparent to us.

However, our soul's relationship with our spirit is not so clear. When Adam and Eve first sinned (Genesis 3), this impacted their spirits, which suffered a form of death, resulting in mankind becoming "dead" spiritually:

*Yahweh God commanded the man, saying, "You may freely eat of every tree of the garden; but you shall not eat of the tree of the knowledge of good and evil; for in the day that you eat of it, you will surely die."*

*Genesis 2:16-17 WEB*

Adam and Eve didn't immediately die a physical death when they ate the forbidden fruit, though physical death was an eventual consequence. Rather they appear to have immediately suffered a type of spiritual death. All of us inherited that spiritual death from them. As Paul writes:

*Therefore, as sin entered into the world through one man, and death through sin; so death passed to all men, because all sinned.* Romans 5:12 WEB

*And you were dead in the trespasses and sins in which you once walked, following the course of this world, following the prince of the power of the air, the spirit that is now at work in the sons of disobedience—among whom we all once lived in the passions of our flesh, carrying out the desires of the body and the mind, and were by nature children of wrath, like the rest of mankind.* Ephesians 2:1-3 ESV

Prior to being born again, we were spiritually *dead in trespasses and sins*, and we were dominated by *the passions of our flesh*.

New birth through faith in Christ brings new life to our spirits, restoring to us the spiritual life that Adam and Eve had before they sinned. As Paul continued:

*But God, being rich in mercy, because of the great love with which he loved us, even when we were dead in our trespasses, made us alive together with Christ—by grace you have been saved...* Ephesians 2:4-5 ESV

The understanding that we each have a spirit that is distinct from our soul plays an important part in understanding salvation and the new life we have in Christ. The new *born-again* life that God gives us at the point of salvation primarily has to do with God's Holy Spirit coming and dwelling within us, with our spirit, and giving new life to our own spirit. Our soul and body may initially be only indirectly affected by this new life in our spirit. The new life that our spirit receives needs to be embraced by our soul to allow the new life in our spirit to work its way out into our soul, and then our soul is able to pass benefits of this new life on to our body.

After receiving new life in Christ, there is still a process of growing in Christ to become spiritually mature. This growth does not happen automatically. It is a process that requires our cooperation with the Holy Spirit. It is possible to resist the new life within us and continue to live largely unchanged. This is apparently what happened in Corinth. The new believers there failed to mature:

> **Brothers, I couldn't speak to you as to spiritual, but as to fleshly, as to babies in Christ. I fed you with milk, not with meat; for you weren't yet ready. Indeed, not even now are you ready, for you are still fleshly.**
>
> *1Corinthians 3:1-3 WEB*

Next, we'll explore this failure to mature and what it means to still be *"fleshly."*

## For Further Reflection

- Do you agree that spirit and soul are distinctly different parts of us? Why or why not?

************

# Chapter 18
# The Flesh

*Brothers, I couldn't speak to you as to spiritual, but as to fleshly, as to babies in Christ. I fed you with milk, not with meat; for you weren't yet ready. Indeed, not even now are you ready, for you are still fleshly. For insofar as there is jealousy, strife, and factions among you, aren't you fleshly, and don't you walk in the ways of men?*

*1Corinthians 3:1-3 WEB*

The people in Corinth were blessed with many spiritual gifts (1 Corinthians 1:4-8), but that didn't make them spiritual. They were still *"fleshly"* (per 1 Corinthians 3:1-3 above). Note the characteristics listed as evidence of being *"fleshly"*: *jealousy, strife, and factions.* However, before we go further, we need to better clarify different ways the word "flesh" may be used.

The word "flesh" (New-Testament Greek: *"sarx"*) has somewhat different meanings in different contexts. Sometimes scripture uses "flesh" to refer to all of mankind. "Flesh" can also refer to our natural bodies, especially the soft tissues. In the New Testament, however, "flesh" is often used to refer to *all that we are apart from new life in Christ.* That is the meaning and usage we focus on in this chapter.

Jesus spoke of **flesh** in this sense when he spoke to Nicodemus about the need to be born again:

*"Most certainly I tell you, unless one is born of water and spirit, he can't enter into God's Kingdom. That which is born of the flesh is flesh. That which is born of the Spirit is spirit."*     *John 3:6 WEB*

All that we are prior to being **born of the Spirit** is **flesh.** While being born of the Spirit imparts new life to our spirit, many aspects of the flesh remain.

The desires and sins of the "flesh" are generally associated with our body and soul. These include physical desires as well as emotional desires and selfish tendencies, such as *jealousy, strife, and factions* (per 1 Corinthians 3:3 above). Paul gives us a partial list of the *works of the flesh*:

> *Now the works of the flesh are evident: sexual immorality, impurity, sensuality, idolatry, sorcery, enmity, strife, jealousy, fits of anger, rivalries, dissensions, divisions, envy, drunkenness, orgies, and things like these. I warn you, as I warned you before, that those who do such things will not inherit the kingdom of God.* Galatians 5:19-21 ESV

As Paul said, these kinds of sins are *evident*. Some translations use the word *"obvious"* here; the point being that these kinds of sins aren't usually difficult to discern. However, there are other problems associated with our flesh which are not so obvious, which I'll refer to as *"the righteousness of the flesh."* These problems generally involve spiritual pride and selfishness associated with religious activities and status. Paul wrote about the problem of having *confidence in the flesh* in his letter to the believers at Philippi:

> *Look out for the dogs, look out for the evildoers, look out for those who mutilate the flesh. For we are the circumcision, who worship by the Spirit of God and glory in Christ Jesus and put no confidence in the flesh—though I myself have reason for confidence in the flesh also. If anyone else thinks he has reason for confidence in the flesh, I have more: circumcised on the eighth day, of the people of Israel, of the tribe of Benjamin, a Hebrew of Hebrews; as to the law, a Pharisee; as to zeal, a persecutor of the church; as to righteousness under the law, blameless.* Philippians 3:2-6 ESV

Here we see that religious background and religious rituals

and activities can easily be in the realm of *the flesh*. Prior to following Jesus, Paul had a lot of religious success in life (from a religious point of view). He turned away from all that to follow Christ. He goes on to clarify that he has rejected trying to be righteous in his own strength (by following the law in his own strength) and instead values righteousness from God, which comes through faith in Christ:

> *But whatever gain I had, I counted as loss for the sake of Christ. Indeed, I count everything as loss because of the surpassing worth of knowing Christ Jesus my Lord. For his sake I have suffered the loss of all things and count them as rubbish, in order that I may gain Christ and be found in him, not having a righteousness of my own that comes from the law, but that which comes through faith in Christ, the righteousness from God that depends on faith...*
>
> Philippians 3:7-9 ESV

These verses hint at the problem of religious legalism, which will be discussed later, in the context of Paul's letter to the Galatians (a few paragraphs below).

Paul also speaks of religious people who have a *fleshly mind* associated with wrong spiritual perspectives:

> *Let no one rob you of your prize by a voluntary humility and worshipping of the angels, dwelling in the things which he has not seen, vainly puffed up by his fleshly mind, and not holding firmly to the Head, from whom all the body, being supplied and knit together through the joints and ligaments, grows with God's growth.*
>
> Colossians 2:18-19 WEB

Peter warns of false teachers among God's people, who entice people away from truth by *sensual passions of the flesh*:

> *These are waterless springs and mists driven by a storm. For them the gloom of utter darkness has been reserved.*

*For, speaking loud boasts of folly, they entice by sensual passions of the flesh those who are barely escaping from those who live in error.*          2Peter 2:17-18 ESV

Finally, *the righteousness of the flesh* frequently is associated with religious legalism.   Our *flesh* can prefer self-righteousness associated with following religious rules rather than righteousness from God through faith in Jesus.  We've already seen Paul mention this in his letter to the Philippians:

*...not having a righteousness of my own that comes from the law, but that which comes through faith in Christ, the righteousness from God that depends on faith...*
Philippians 3:9 ESV

In Paul's letter to the Galatians, he deals with the problem of believers turning from salvation through faith in Christ to religious legalism.  After being saved through faith in Jesus, they had started trusting in the Law of Moses and circumcision rather than simply continuing with faith in Jesus:

*Foolish Galatians, who has bewitched you not to obey the truth, before whose eyes Jesus Christ was openly portrayed among you as crucified?  I just want to learn this from you.  Did you receive the Spirit by the works of the law, or by hearing of faith?  Are you so foolish?  Having begun in the Spirit, are you now completed in the flesh?  Did you suffer so many things in vain, if it is indeed in vain?  He therefore who supplies the Spirit to you, and does miracles among you, does he do it by the works of the law, or by hearing of faith?*
Galatians 3:1-5 WEB

*As many as desire to make a good impression in the flesh compel you to be circumcised; just so they may not be persecuted for the cross of Christ.  For even they who receive circumcision don't keep the law themselves, but they desire to have you circumcised, that they may boast in your flesh.*          Galatians 6:12-13 WEB

So, we see that *the flesh* can be involved in more than just obviously sinful *works of the flesh*, it can also be active in *the righteousness of the flesh*: things like religious activities, religious pride, and religious legalism. We should understand and turn away from both the *unrighteousness* of the flesh, and the *self-righteousness* of the flesh.

## For Further Reflection

- Are there parts of your life that are still dominated by the old flesh rather than the new life of the Spirit?

************

# Chapter 19
# The Spirit

*Peter said to them, "Repent, and be baptized, every one of you, in the name of Jesus Christ for the forgiveness of sins, and you will receive the gift of the Holy Spirit."*
Acts 2:38 WEB

---

Before discussing living by the Spirit or living by the flesh, we need to review the importance of the Holy Spirit, and some of the ways the Holy Spirit helps us. As was previously mentioned, scripture is not always clear whether it is referring to our own spirit or the Holy Spirit living in us. However, when contrasting living by the spirit (or the Holy Spirit) and living by the flesh, the distinction is usually not critical, since any success our own spirit has is dependent on new life and power given by the Holy Spirit living in us.

The Holy Spirit is central to our salvation, and is central to our walk with Jesus. The pouring out of the Holy Spirit was prophesied in the Old Testament, hundreds of years before Jesus came:

*"It will happen afterward, that I will pour out my Spirit on all flesh; and your sons and your daughters will prophesy. Your old men will dream dreams. Your young men will see visions. And also on the servants and on the handmaids in those days, I will pour out my Spirit."*
Joel 2:28-29 WEB (quoted in Acts 2:17-18)

Before Jesus started his ministry, John the Baptist was preaching that the coming Christ would *"baptize you with the Holy Spirit"*:

*John answered them all, saying, "I baptize you with water, but he who is mightier than I is coming, the strap of whose sandals I am not worthy to untie. He will baptize you with the Holy Spirit and with fire."*
Luke 3:16 ESV

During Jesus' ministry, Jesus himself emphasized the importance of the coming Holy Spirit:

*"If anyone thirsts, let him come to me and drink. Whoever believes in me, as the Scripture has said, 'Out of his heart will flow rivers of living water.'"* Now this *he said about the Spirit, whom those who believed in him were to receive, for as yet the Spirit had not been given, because Jesus was not yet glorified.*

*John 7:37-39 ESV*

*"Nevertheless I tell you the truth: It is to your advantage that I go away, for if I don't go away, the Counselor won't come to you. But if I go, I will send him to you."*

*John 16:7 WEB*

After Jesus rose from the dead, he told his disciples to wait for **power from on high**, which is widely associated with the Holy Spirit:

*"Behold, I send out the promise of my Father on you. But wait in the city of Jerusalem until you are clothed with power from on high."*  *Luke 24:49 WEB*

The Holy Spirit was not **poured out** until the day of Pentecost, after Jesus was exalted:

*"Exalted to the right hand of God, he has received from the Father the promised Holy Spirit and has poured out what you now see and hear."*  *Acts 2:33 NIV*

Peter clarifies that the Holy Spirit is available to everyone, even those who are *"far off"*:

*And Peter said to them, "Repent and be baptized every one of you in the name of Jesus Christ for the forgiveness of your sins, and you will receive the gift of the Holy Spirit. For the promise is for you and for your children and for all who are far off, everyone whom the Lord our God calls to himself."*  *Acts 2:38-39 ESV*

The promise even extends to gentile believers, as Peter

learned:

> *"As I began to speak, the Holy Spirit fell on them, even as on us at the beginning. I remembered the word of the Lord, how he said, 'John indeed baptized in water, but you will be baptized in the Holy Spirit.' If then God gave to them the same gift as us, when we believed in the Lord Jesus Christ, who was I, that I could withstand God?"*
> *Acts 11:15-17 WEB*

Paul clarifies that every true believer has the Holy Spirit:

> *But if any man doesn't have the Spirit of Christ, he is not his.*
> *Romans 8:9 WEB*

Paul uses an analogy of a temple to explain that God's Spirit lives in us:

> *Don't you know that you are a temple of God, and that God's Spirit lives in you?*
> *1 Corinthians 3:16 WEB*

The Holy Spirit gives us an inner testimony that we belong to God:

> *The Spirit himself testifies with our spirit that we are children of God...*
> *Romans 8:16 WEB*

The Holy Spirit, living in us, empowers us to turn away from the *"works of the flesh"* (Galatians 5:19-21) and instead to have the *"fruit of the Spirit"*:

> *But the fruit of the Spirit is love, joy, peace, patience, kindness, goodness, faith, gentleness, and self-control. Against such things there is no law.* *Galatians 5:22-23 WEB*

This *"fruit of the Spirit"* should be the experience of all believers. However, the Holy Spirit also imparts particular gifts to people:

> *Now there are various kinds of gifts, but the same Spirit. There are various kinds of service, and the same Lord. There are various kinds of workings, but the same God, who works all things in all. But to each one is given the*

*manifestation of the Spirit for the profit of all. For to one is given through the Spirit the word of wisdom, and to another the word of knowledge, according to the same Spirit; to another faith, by the same Spirit; and to another gifts of healings, by the same Spirit; and to another workings of miracles; and to another prophecy; and to another discerning of spirits; to another different kinds of languages; and to another the interpretation of languages. But the one and the same Spirit produces all of these, distributing to each one separately as he desires.*                            *1Corinthians 12:4-11 WEB*

It is important to understand that these spiritual gifts are not given to everyone, but *"to each one separately as he desires."* Paul clarifies this further:

*God has set some in the assembly: first apostles, second prophets, third teachers, then miracle workers, then gifts of healings, helps, governments, and various kinds of languages. Are all apostles? Are all prophets? Are all teachers? Are all miracle workers? Do all have gifts of healings? Do all speak with various languages? Do all interpret? But earnestly desire the best gifts.*
                              *1Corinthians 12:28-31 WEB*

Being *"filled with the Spirit"* has to do with being influenced and empowered by the Holy Spirit; it's **not** about whether or not we have the Holy Spirit living in us (though the Holy Spirit must be living in us in order to be *"filled with the Spirit"*). That is why Paul wrote:

*Don't be drunken with wine, in which is dissipation, but be filled with the Spirit...*                            *Ephesians 5:18 WEB*

It is worth noting that just as the Holy Spirit can dwell in people along with their own spirit (as is the case with all true believers), so also evil spirits can live within people (as already discussed in chapter 10 *"Spirits of Deception"*). Evil spirits may have varying degrees of influence over people, depending on how much each person has yielded to their influence, due to either being deceived or deliberately yielding to them. Some people who are not truly saved may, perhaps through the influence of evil spirits, be deceived into thinking they are saved. Consider Jesus' words:

> *"Not everyone who says to me, 'Lord, Lord,' will enter into the Kingdom of Heaven; but he who does the will of my Father who is in heaven. Many will tell me in that day, 'Lord, Lord, didn't we prophesy in your name, in your name cast out demons, and in your name do many mighty works?' Then I will tell them, 'I never knew you. Depart from me, you who work iniquity.'"*
>
> *Matthew 7:21-23 WEB*

Finally, let's recall what a great blessing the Holy Spirit is! Just because some people have distorted beliefs about the Holy Spirit, that should not prevent us from fully embracing the marvelous gift of the Holy Spirit. Remember Paul's words to Titus:

> *But when the kindness of God our Savior and his love toward mankind appeared, not by works of righteousness which we did ourselves, but according to his mercy, he saved us through the washing of regeneration and renewing by the Holy Spirit, whom he poured out on us richly, through Jesus Christ our Savior, so that being justified by his grace we might be made heirs according to the hope of eternal life.*
>
> *Titus 3:4-7 WEB*

Some additional thoughts on the Holy Spirit will be discussed in chapter 32 *"The Holy Spirit."*

## For Further Reflection

- Have you experienced the testimony of the Holy Spirit, that you are a child of God (Romans 8:16)?

\*\*\*\*\*\*\*\*\*\*\*\*

# Chapter 20
# Spirit and Flesh in Conflict

*But I say, walk by the Spirit,*
*and you won't fulfill the lust of the flesh.*
*For the flesh lusts against the Spirit,*
*and the Spirit against the flesh;*
*and these are contrary to one another,*
*that you may not do the things that you desire.*
*Galatians 5:16-17 WEB*

---

Now that we've clarified Spirit and flesh some, let's look at some verses that emphasize the importance of living by the spirit/Holy Spirit rather than living by the flesh:

*"It is the spirit who gives life. The flesh profits nothing. The words that I speak to you are spirit, and are life."*
*John 6:63 WEB*

*Don't be deceived. God is not mocked, for whatever a man sows, that he will also reap. For he who sows to his own flesh will from the flesh reap corruption. But he who sows to the Spirit will from the Spirit reap eternal life.*
*Galatians 6:7-8 WEB*

*Let us walk properly, as in the day; not in reveling and drunkenness, not in sexual promiscuity and lustful acts, and not in strife and jealousy. But put on the Lord Jesus Christ, and make no provision for the flesh, for its lusts.*
*Romans 13:13-14 WEB*

*Beloved, I urge you as sojourners and exiles to abstain from the passions of the flesh, which wage war against your soul.*
*1Peter 2:11 ESV*

Paul goes into more detail about the conflict between S*pirit* and *flesh* in his letter to the believers in Rome, especially in chapters 7 and 8. However, before we focus on those chapters, let's briefly review previous parts of Paul's letter.

In Romans 1:1-18, Paul speaks briefly about who Jesus is, Paul's calling as an apostle, and his desire to visit those in Rome. When Paul wrote this letter, he had not yet been to Rome, and he writes that he is *"eager to preach the gospel to you also who are in Rome"* (Romans 1:15 ESV). So, of all Paul's letters in the New Testament, this letter is widely considered to be his most thorough presentation of the good news about Jesus.

In Romans 1:19 to 3:18 Paul talks about the problem of sin and God's righteous judgment, and how these relate to both gentiles and Jews.

In Romans 3:19 to 4:25 he clarifies that righteousness and salvation come through faith, not by trying to observe various rules and regulations.

In Romans 5:1-21 he speaks about the grace that is ours through Jesus' sacrifice for us. Sin and death came into the world through Adam. Righteousness and eternal life are now available to all people through faith in Jesus.

In Romans 6:1-23, Paul clarifies that God's grace should result in a righteous life. God's grace should not be used as an excuse to keep on sinning. In order for us to live a righteous life and be set free from the power of sin, Paul clarifies these important key points to make freedom from sin's dominion a practical reality:

- We must know that we have been united with Jesus in his death:

*Do you not know that all of us who have been baptized into Christ Jesus were baptized into his death? We were buried therefore with him by baptism into death, in order that, just as Christ was raised from the dead by the glory of the Father, we too might walk in newness of life.*

*For if we have been united with him in a death like his,*

*we shall certainly be united with him in a resurrection like his. We know that our old self was crucified with him in order that the body of sin might be brought to nothing, so that we would no longer be enslaved to sin. For one who has died has been set free from sin.*

Romans 6:3-7 ESV

- We must identify ourselves with Jesus' death and resurrection:

*So you also must consider yourselves dead to sin and alive to God in Christ Jesus.*       Romans 6:11 ESV

- We are to present ourselves to God:

*Do not present your members to sin as instruments for unrighteousness, but present yourselves to God as those who have been brought from death to life, and your members to God as instruments for righteousness.*

Romans 6:13 ESV

- We are to walk in newness of life:

*We were buried therefore with him by baptism into death, in order that, just as Christ was raised from the dead by the glory of the Father, we too might walk in newness of life.*       Romans 6:4 ESV

While these principles may appear to be rather straightforward, it is easy for us to continue in sinful habits and patterns. Paul goes on in Romans chapter 7 to share about some of his own struggles with overcoming sin.

In chapter 7 Paul focuses on the problem many people have had in trying to obey God's commands using their own strength and willpower. Paul starts out in chapter 7 explaining how the law no longer has authority over us, since we died with Christ. Counting Christ's death as our own should set us free from sin's power:

*For while we were living in the flesh, our sinful passions, aroused by the law, were at work in our*

*members to bear fruit for death. But now we are released from the law, having died to that which held us captive, so that we serve in the new way of the Spirit and not in the old way of the written code.* Romans 7:5-6 ESV

However, in his own life, Paul had at some point fallen into the problem of trying to follow God and be righteous by trying to obey *the law* in his own strength. Paul found that doing so actually strengthened sin's hold on him:

*But sin, seizing an opportunity through the commandment, produced in me all kinds of covetousness. For apart from the law, sin lies dead. I was once alive apart from the law, but when the commandment came, sin came alive and I died. The very commandment that promised life proved to be death to me. For sin, seizing an opportunity through the commandment, deceived me and through it killed me.*
Romans 7:8-11 ESV

Paul found that his flesh and sin were still active in his life after becoming a believer, and he had no ability in his own strength to stop sinning:

*For we know that the law is spiritual, but I am of the flesh, sold under sin. For I do not understand my own actions. For I do not do what I want, but I do the very thing I hate. Now if I do what I do not want, I agree with the law, that it is good. So now it is no longer I who do it, but sin that dwells within me. For I know that nothing good dwells in me, that is, in my flesh. For I have the desire to do what is right, but not the ability to carry it out. For I do not do the good I want, but the evil I do not want is what I keep on doing. Now if I do what I do not want, it is no longer I who do it, but sin that dwells within me. So I find it to be a law that when I want to do right, evil lies close at hand. For I delight in the law of God, in my inner being, but I see in my members another law waging war against the law of my mind and making me captive to the law of sin that dwells in my members.* *Romans 7:14-23 ESV*

Paul wanted to do the right thing, but he couldn't do the right thing. His desire to do good is evidence of new life in his spirit through the Holy Spirit. His inability to actually do the good that he wanted to do is evidence of how the flesh and sin are still active after salvation. Paul concludes with a summary of the struggle many believers experience:

> *Wretched man that I am! Who will deliver me from this body of death? Thanks be to God through Jesus Christ our Lord! So then, I myself serve the law of God with my mind, but with my flesh I serve the law of sin.*
> *Romans 7:24-25 ESV*

He saw Jesus as the solution, and acknowledges that in his own strength, by his own *flesh*, he cannot be free from sin.

Then, in Romans chapter 8, Paul clarifies how to have victory over sin: by living *according to the Spirit*:

> *There is therefore now no condemnation to those who are in Christ Jesus, who don't walk according to the flesh, but according to the Spirit. For the law of the Spirit of life in Christ Jesus made me free from the law of sin and of death. For what the law couldn't do, in that it was weak through the flesh, God did, sending his own Son in the likeness of sinful flesh and for sin, he condemned sin in the flesh; that the ordinance of the law might be fulfilled in us, who walk not after the flesh, but after the Spirit.*
> *Romans 8:1-4 WEB*

Walking *not after the flesh, but after the Spirit* implies a life that desires and chooses God's ways, a life that is led by the Holy Spirit. Such a life is not achieved by human effort to follow various religious rules, but is based on *"the law of the Spirit of life in Christ Jesus."*

Now, before moving on in Romans, let's backtrack briefly and consider Paul's focus on various *"laws."* The word *"law"* can be used in two different ways. First, in a moral or legal sense, *law* can refer to various rules that people are supposed to follow (whether or not people are naturally inclined to do so) such as the Law of Moses. Paul refers to *law* in this way when he says ***"I wouldn't have known sin, except through the law"*** (Romans 7:7 WEB). I'll refer to that kind of *law* as an *extrinsic law*.

Second, *law* can refer to a principle that is always true, such as the *law* of gravity. Paul refers to this kind of law when he says ***"So I find it to be a law that when I want to do right, evil lies close at hand"*** (Romans 7:21 ESV). I'll refer to this kind of law as an *intrinsic law*.

Extrinsic laws, like the Law of Moses and various religious rules, cannot make us righteous. Their main benefit is to expose our sin and make us aware of our need for salvation. As Paul wrote:

> *. . . the law has become our tutor to bring us to Christ, that we might be justified by faith. But now that faith has come, we are no longer under a tutor.*
>
> *Galatians 3:24-25 WEB*

Once we are saved, part of our new life in Christ is that God's law becomes an intrinsic law within us. Jeremiah foretold this when he wrote:

> *"But this is the covenant that I will make with the house of Israel after those days," says Yahweh: "I will put my law in their inward parts, and I will write it in their heart. I will be their God, and they shall be my people."*
>
> *Jeremiah 31:33 WEB (also Hebrews 8:10)*

Now let's look at some different laws Paul refers to.

> *For I delight in the law of God, in my inner being, but I see in my members another law waging war against the law of my mind and making me captive to the law of sin that dwells in my members.*   *Romans 7:22-23 ESV*

The *"law of God, in my inner being"* appears to be the same as *"the law of my mind."* Paul seems to be referring to the *law of God* as an intrinsic law within him, as foretold by Jeremiah 31:33 (above). However, Paul found, in regard to his actions, that the *law of sin* was always stronger than the *law of his mind*. So, in his own strength he could not do the good that he wanted to do. So, Paul declares:

> *What a wretched man I am! Who will deliver me out of the body of this death?* Romans 7:24 WEB

Then Paul gives us a solution to the problem of the *law of sin*. It is another intrinsic law, one that is more powerful than the *law of sin*. It is *the law of the Spirit of life in Christ Jesus:*

> *For the law of the Spirit of life in Christ Jesus made me free from the law of sin and of death.* Romans 8:2 WEB

Notice how Paul writes most of Romans 7 in present tense. I believe he does so to show that the *law of sin* is always present within us. Only as we walk *according to the Spirit* does *the law of the Spirit of life in Christ Jesus* overpower *the law of sin* and deliver us from the power of sin. If we don't walk *according to the Spirit,* then the *law of sin* has power over us.

Moving on now, Paul clarifies that living *according to the Spirit* involves setting our minds on *the things of the Spirit*:

> *For those who live according to the flesh set their minds on the things of the flesh, but those who live according to the Spirit, the things of the Spirit. For the mind of the flesh is death, but the mind of the Spirit is life and peace; because the mind of the flesh is hostile towards God; for it is not subject to God's law, neither indeed can it be. Those who are in the flesh can't please God.*
> Romans 8:5-8 WEB

Paul then clarifies that living *"according to the Spirit"* should be the case with all true believers, since we all have the Holy Spirit living in us:

> *But you are not in the flesh but in the Spirit, if it is so that the Spirit of God dwells in you. But if any man doesn't have the Spirit of Christ, he is not his. If Christ is in you, the body is dead because of sin, but the spirit is alive because of righteousness. But if the Spirit of him who raised up Jesus from the dead dwells in you, he who raised up Christ Jesus from the dead will also give life to your mortal bodies through his Spirit who dwells in you.*
>
> *Romans 8:9-11 WEB*

Here we see that, even after receiving new life through Christ, our body may still be referred to as *"dead because of sin."* However, *"the spirit is alive because of righteousness."* This verse shows how the new life we have in Christ starts in our spirit. Verse 11 shows how that life should be working its way out to our body.

Paul then deals with the reality that we can still choose to live after the flesh, even though as believers the Holy Spirit is living in us. Of course, he encourages us not to do that:

> *So then, brothers, we are debtors, not to the flesh, to live after the flesh. For if you live after the flesh, you must die; but if by the Spirit you put to death the deeds of the body, you will live. For as many as are led by the Spirit of God, these are children of God.*
>
> *Romans 8:12-14 WEB*

Paul indicates we have a choice whether or not we will live after the flesh or live after the Spirit. It is our responsibility to *by the Spirit put to death the deeds of the body.*

If instead we *live after the flesh*, Paul writes *"you must die."* Some translations say "you will die." This is one of those controversial verses which people may understand very differently. It may mean that Paul is calling those who still *live after the flesh* to enter into the death of Jesus in order to stop living after the flesh. Count the death of Jesus as your own death in order to start living after the Spirit. This is what the Spirit calls us to do, and those who *are led by the Spirit of God, these are children of God.* Alternatively, this verse is understood by some to be contrary to the doctrine of "once saved always saved." With this perspective, continuing to willfully live by the flesh will result in a return to spiritual death. Regardless of which perspective may be right, Paul is clearly calling us to a higher life that is *led by the Spirit*, not living *after the flesh*.

A change from living by the flesh to living by the Spirit does **not** involve new grace from God, but rather involves entering into a deeper experience of what God has already given us. All of us who are true believers have already been crucified with Christ; we have died with Christ; we have been raised with Christ; we have been born again; we have new life; we have been set free from sin. These are all spiritual blessings from God which he freely gives to all who trust in Jesus. However, our experience of the fullness of this new life is at least partly dependent on knowing and understanding all these blessings God has given us, acting on them in faith, and not trying to live a righteous life in our own fleshly strength. Rather, we should learn to walk by the Spirit, living by the power of the Holy Spirit who lives in us, and we will find that sin no longer has power over us.

Discerning the difference between living by the flesh and living by the Spirit is, for many, a difficult subject to understand. It is easy for us to be deceived in this area, to justify our own fleshly attitudes and actions, even thinking them to be spiritual. For example, there is such a thing as righteous anger, and I have sometimes believed my anger to be righteous anger. However, upon further review later, I usually have concluded my anger was fleshly, not righteous and not spiritual.

How do we discern the difference between the flesh and the spirit in our own lives? Humbly ask God to show you the difference, and don't reject his answer when he does show you. Rather, acknowledge and confess your sins (1 John 1:9). We all need God to shed his light on us to show us how we really are. This is an area where understanding comes from God, and we ought to ask God for such understanding. Along these lines, I often pray: *"Open my spiritual eyes to see myself as you see me."*

To summarize, learning the difference between walking by the Spirit and walking by the flesh is an important part of growing to spiritual maturity. Those who are spiritually mature understand the difference between *Spirit* and *flesh*, and consistently choose to, and delight to, *walk by the Spirit*.

After Paul lists the *works of the flesh* and the *fruit of the Spirit* in his letter to the believers in Galatia (Galatians 5:19-23), he concludes:

> *Those who belong to Christ have crucified the flesh with its passions and lusts. If we live by the Spirit, let's also walk by the Spirit.* Galatians 5:24-25 WEB

If we belong to Christ, our *flesh* has been crucified. By understanding that we have been united with Jesus in his death, we are set free from the power of sin (Romans 6:1-14). Through faith in Jesus, we have new life by the Spirit (*"we live by the Spirit"*). Since we have new life by the Spirit, *"let's also walk by the Spirit."* Let's depend on the Holy Spirit day by day to walk in victory over sin!

## For Further Reflection

- In what ways have you experienced the flesh and Spirit in conflict in your own life?

- **Book Reference:** *"The Normal Christian Life"* by Watchman Nee. A fuller discussion of how *the law of the Spirit of life in Christ Jesus* sets us free from *the law of sin and death* is found in chapters 9 and 10.

\*\*\*\*\*\*\*\*\*\*\*\*

# Chapter 21
# Other Perspectives

*Now the Berean Jews were of more noble character than those in Thessalonica, for they received the message with great eagerness and examined the Scriptures every day to see if what Paul said was true.*
*Act 17:11 NIV*

---

The Berean Jews wanted to be sure that what Paul told them was true, so they compared what he said with the scriptures they had at the time (scriptures now associated with the Old Testament). Up to this point, in discussing the differences between living by the Spirit or living by the flesh, we have largely been relying on New Testament letters written by the apostle Paul. If we understand Paul correctly, and if this topic is as important as I believe it is, we should be able to find similar teaching from other New Testament authors.

Other New Testament authors appear to discuss these concepts using somewhat different words, writing from a somewhat different perspective. Let's look at some of those scriptures, outside of Paul's letters, which deal with right and wrong ways to live, or a failure to mature spiritually.

Jesus appears to me to give a parallel way of understanding living by the Spirit. He referred to it as *abiding* in him:

*Abide in me, and I in you. As the branch cannot bear fruit by itself, unless it abides in the vine, neither can you, unless you abide in me. I am the vine; you are the branches. Whoever abides in me and I in him, he it is that bears much fruit, for apart from me you can do nothing. If anyone does not abide in me he is thrown away like a branch and withers; and the branches are gathered, thrown into the fire, and burned. If you abide in me, and my words abide in you, ask whatever you wish, and it will be done for you. By this my Father is glorified, that you bear much fruit and so prove to be my disciples. As the Father has loved me, so have I loved you. Abide in my love. If you keep my commandments, you will abide in my love, just as I have kept my Father's commandments and abide in his love.*

John 15:4-10 ESV

Jesus appears to teach about some people failing to mature in his parable about the sower and the seed (Matthew 13:3-23, Mark 4:3-20, Luke 8:5-14). Luke records it this way:

*"The farmer went out to sow his seed. As he sowed, some fell along the road, and it was trampled under foot, and the birds of the sky devoured it. Other seed fell on the rock, and as soon as it grew, it withered away, because it had no moisture. Other fell amid the thorns, and the thorns grew with it, and choked it. Other fell into the good ground, and grew, and produced one hundred times as much fruit." As he said these things, he called out, "He who has ears to hear, let him hear!"*

*Then his disciples asked him, "What does this parable mean?"*

*He said, "To you it is given to know the mysteries of God's Kingdom, but to the rest in parables; that 'seeing they may not see, and hearing they may not understand.' Now the parable is this: The seed is the word of God. Those along the road are those who hear, then the devil comes, and takes away the word from their heart, that they may not believe and be saved. Those on the rock are they who, when they hear, receive the word with joy; but these have no root, who believe for a while, then fall away in time of temptation. That which fell among the thorns, these are those who have heard, and as they go on their way they are choked with cares, riches, and pleasures of life, and bring no fruit to maturity. That in the good ground, these are those who with an honest and good heart, having heard the word, hold it tightly, and produce fruit with perseverance."* Luke 8:5-15 WEB

Those *among the thorns* are said to *bring no fruit to maturity*. They are choked by the *cares, riches, and pleasures of life*. Their focus appears to be on themselves rather than on loving, trusting, and following Jesus. Using Paul's words, they appear to be *walking according to the flesh*.

Jesus also gives us a picture here of what *walking according to the Spirit* looks like. This involves having an honest and good heart (from being born of the Spirit), hearing the word, holding the word tightly, and producing fruit with perseverance (Luke 8:15).

In Matthew chapter 23, Jesus condemns the religious leaders of his day, who were clearly influenced by what I have called the *righteousness of the flesh*. Here are just a few verses from that chapter:

> *Then Jesus spoke to the multitudes and to his disciples, saying, "The scribes and the Pharisees sat on Moses' seat. All things therefore whatever they tell you to observe, observe and do, but don't do their works; for they say, and don't do. For they bind heavy burdens that are grievous to be borne, and lay them on men's shoulders; but they themselves will not lift a finger to help them. But all their works they do to be seen by men. They make their phylacteries broad, enlarge the fringes of their garments, and love the place of honor at feasts, the best seats in the synagogues, the salutations in the marketplaces, and to be called 'Rabbi, Rabbi' by men."*
>
> Matthew 23:1-7 WEB

Similar words spoken by Jesus are found in Mark 12:38-40, Luke 11:37-54, and Luke 20:45-47.

Here is another example of the *righteousness of the flesh*:

> *He spoke also this parable to certain people who were convinced of their own righteousness, and who despised all others. "Two men went up into the temple to pray;*

*one was a Pharisee, and the other was a tax collector.*
*The Pharisee stood and prayed to himself like this:*
*'God, I thank you, that I am not like the rest of men,*
*extortionists, unrighteous, adulterers, or even like this*
*tax collector. I fast twice a week. I give tithes of all that*
*I get.'"*
*Luke 18:9-12 WEB*

James seems to refer to living by the Spirit or flesh as two different kinds of wisdom:

*Who is wise and understanding among you? Let him*
*show by his good conduct that his deeds are done in*
*gentleness of wisdom. But if you have bitter jealousy*
*and selfish ambition in your heart, don't boast and don't*
*lie against the truth. This wisdom is not that which*
*comes down from above, but is earthly, sensual, and*
*demonic. For where jealousy and selfish ambition are,*
*there is confusion and every evil deed. But the wisdom*
*that is from above is first pure, then peaceful, gentle,*
*reasonable, full of mercy and good fruits, without*
*partiality, and without hypocrisy.*
*James 3:13-17 WEB*

The author of Hebrews talks about a failure to grow to spiritual maturity in these verses:

*About this we have much to say, and it is hard to*
*explain, since you have become dull of hearing. For*
*though by this time you ought to be teachers, you need*
*someone to teach you again the basic principles of the*
*oracles of God. You need milk, not solid food, for*
*everyone who lives on milk is unskilled in the word of*
*righteousness, since he is a child. But solid food is for*
*the mature, for those who have their powers of*
*discernment trained by constant practice to distinguish*
*good from evil.*

*Therefore let us leave the elementary doctrine of Christ*
*and go on to maturity, not laying again a foundation of*
*repentance from dead works and of faith toward God,*

*and of instruction about washings, the laying on of hands, the resurrection of the dead, and eternal judgment. And this we will do if God permits.*

Hebrews 5:11 to 6:3 ESV

Peter, like the author of Hebrews, talks about spiritual milk and growing up:

*So put away all malice and all deceit and hypocrisy and envy and all slander. Like newborn infants, long for the pure spiritual milk, that by it you may grow up into salvation—if indeed you have tasted that the Lord is good.*

1Peter 2:1-3 ESV

Peter also talks about not following after fleshly passions:

*Beloved, I urge you as sojourners and exiles to abstain from the passions of the flesh, which wage war against your soul.*

1Peter 2:11 ESV

Peter encourages us to grow spiritually in specific areas, which appear to me to correlate with living by the Spirit:

*For this very reason, make every effort to supplement your faith with virtue, and virtue with knowledge, and knowledge with self-control, and self-control with steadfastness, and steadfastness with godliness, and godliness with brotherly affection, and brotherly affection with love. For if these qualities are yours and are increasing, they keep you from being ineffective or unfruitful in the knowledge of our Lord Jesus Christ. For whoever lacks these qualities is so nearsighted that he is blind, having forgotten that he was cleansed from his former sins. Therefore, brothers, be all the more diligent to confirm your calling and election, for if you practice these qualities you will never fall.*

2Peter 1:5-10 ESV

The apostle John refers to *walking in the light* or *walking in the darkness*, which appears to me to correlate with Paul referring to walking by the Spirit or walking by the flesh:

*This is the message which we have heard from him and announce to you, that God is light, and in him is no darkness at all. If we say that we have fellowship with him and walk in the darkness, we lie, and don't tell the truth. But if we walk in the light, as he is in the light, we have fellowship with one another, and the blood of Jesus Christ, his Son, cleanses us from all sin.*    *1John 1:5-7 WEB*

John also writes about the importance of not loving the world, and that *the lust of the flesh, the lust of the eyes, and the pride of life* are not from the Father, but from the world:

*Don't love the world, neither the things that are in the world. If anyone loves the world, the Father's love isn't in him. For all that is in the world, the lust of the flesh, the lust of the eyes, and the pride of life, isn't the Father's, but is the world's. The world is passing away with its lusts, but he who does God's will remains forever.*    *1John 2:15-17 WEB*

King David seems to have had at least a basic understanding of living by the Spirit when he wrote these words:

*Teach me to do your will, for you are my God! Let your good Spirit lead me on level ground!*    *Psalm 143:10 ESV*

## For Further Reflection

- Do you have a preferred way that you understand the difference between living by the flesh and living by the Spirit?

- **Book Reference:** *"The Law of Liberty in the Spiritual Life"* by Evan Henry Hopkins (1837-1918); originally published in 1884; available for free on the Internet. Scanned images of the original book may have better formatting and better notes than other ebook formats.

\*\*\*\*\*\*\*\*\*\*\*\*

# PART 4
# Common Deceptions

Up to this point, we have mostly looked at truth and deception in general terms. Now we venture into more difficult territory: specifics about right and wrong understanding regarding various topics.

Many of the topics we will look at have clear scriptural support, and I will try to support what I write with scripture wherever possible. However, some of these topics are **not** so clear in scripture. To the extent that what I write is **not** clear in scripture, please consider the beliefs I share to be my own. I do **not** claim that God has spoken to me *directly* about them. I have learned them through scripture, reason, other people, and experience. I believe the Holy Spirit has led me in this.

In accordance with chapter 16 *"Test All Things,"* you should prayerfully test and evaluate what I write, and decide for yourself whether or not my perspective is correct. May the Holy Spirit help you understand these things clearly. Please don't blindly accept my beliefs as your own!

> *See to it that no one takes you captive by philosophy and empty deceit, according to human tradition, according to the elemental spirits of the world, and not according to Christ.*
> *Colossians 2:8 ESV*

Some of these topics involve primary issues, while others involve secondary issues. Avoiding deception about both primary issues and secondary issues is important. However, as mentioned previously, believers ought not to be divisive about secondary issues. I'll try to write in a way that is not divisive; please try to receive what I write in the same way.

Some of the topics discussed are very basic, while others are more difficult and not so well known. While it may be beneficial to have some understanding on all of these topics, the needs of readers will vary. This part is organized so that it can be used somewhat as a topical reference. Most of the topics are not too dependent on other sections for understanding. While it would be good to read this part straight through, some may find it more beneficial to pick particular topics, especially if the time available to read this book is limited. May our Lord help you find truth that benefits you in these pages.

As previously mentioned, we should continue to keep in mind that salvation is primarily about coming to Jesus, trusting in Jesus, and following Jesus. He is the Christ, the Son of God, Lord of all. As we consider various areas of possible deception, let's continue to look *"to Jesus, the founder and perfecter of our faith"* (Hebrews 12:2 ESV). Again, he sees all these things clearly, and he is the Good Shepherd of all us sheep (John 10).

\*\*\*\*\*\*\*\*\*\*\*\*

# Chapter 22
# Truth and Scripture

*For the time is coming when people will not endure sound teaching, but having itching ears they will accumulate for themselves teachers to suit their own passions, and will turn away from listening to the truth and wander off into myths.*
*2Timothy 4:3-4 ESV*

*Every Scripture is God-breathed and profitable for teaching, for reproof, for correction, and for instruction in righteousness, that each person who belongs to God may be complete, thoroughly equipped for every good work.*
*2Timothy 3:16-17 WEB*

---

We began in chapter 1 with a simple definition of *truth*, and looked briefly at the importance of truth. Now let's look at some common deceptions regarding *truth*.

## Truth Does Not Exist

It was mentioned in the introduction to Part 1 that some people debate whether or not *truth* really exists, but that is not our concern in this book. This book is built upon the simple premise that *truth* does exist, and that it is to our advantage to embrace *truth* and reject *error*.

However, now that we are discussing common deceptions, it is fitting that we begin with this most basic deception: "Truth does not exist." Any discussion about deception is clearly based on the premise that truth does exist, and if truth exists, so does deception. If truth does not exist, then this book is clearly misguided and irrelevant. But, if "truth does not exist" is true, how could anyone even claim that "truth does not exist"? The claim itself is a claim to truth.

So, the claim that "Truth does not exist" is self-defeating. The claim itself is evidence that truth does exist, and that the claim itself is false.

Further, scripture is full of references to "truth" (per chapter 1), and, if one values scripture, this is clear evidence to the existence of truth.

The very fact that you are reading this book is an indication that you already acknowledge the existence of truth, and that you value knowing truth and don't want to be deceived. Since that is most likely the case with you, it seems unnecessary to spend more time justifying the existence of truth.

In summary, the existence of truth is self-evident. Be aware that claims to the contrary are a form of deception. Don't be deceived!

## Absolute Truth Does Not Exist

Not all truth is *absolute truth*. Many truths are grey in nature, not black and white. This has already been discussed in the book *"Beneath Foundations for Eternal Life,"* chapters 2 and 3. However, just because many truths are not clearly black-and-white absolute truths, that does not mean absolute truth does not exist. One important absolute truth is whether or not you yourself actually exist. Do you believe beyond doubt that you exist? If so, that should settle the matter; the existence of absolute truth is self-evident.

Claiming that absolute truth doesn't exist is a form of deception that seems to affect people who want to avoid dealing with truth in general. If absolute truth doesn't exist, then people can more easily justify anything they do. Sin is easily ignored in their own lives, because nothing can be clearly said to be wrong, because all truth is relative, nothing is absolute. This is clearly not the perspective that scripture is written from. Don't be deceived!

# Truth Changes with Time

Some truths obviously change with time. How old are you? Today you are one day older than yesterday. Are you still alive? As you read this, the answer apparently is "yes." Someday the answer will likely change to "no." Clearly, these kinds of truths change with time.

Other truths, however, clearly don't change. When were you born? Where were you born? Does God exist? Is Jesus the Christ? Did Jesus come in the flesh or not? Did he die on the cross for our sins? The answers to these kinds of questions are truths that clearly don't change with time.

Some people who don't want to deal with spiritual truth prefer to believe that all truth changes with time. This gives them a convenient excuse to disregard truths that may be contrary to how they prefer to think and live.

It is worth noting that modern science is largely based on the premise that scientific laws don't change with time (though our understanding of them may change with time). Without that basic understanding, most scientific progress would not be possible. It is reasonable to expect that spiritual principles also generally do not change with time. These verses lend some support to this:

> **Jesus Christ is the same yesterday, today, and forever.**
> *Hebrews 13:8 WEB*

> **"For I, Yahweh, don't change; therefore you, sons of Jacob, are not consumed."** *Malachi 3:6 WEB*

Now, let's be careful here. While spiritual principles don't generally change with time, the way God deals with us may change with time. For example, when someone genuinely turns to God, they are no longer under God's wrath, but are then under God's grace (while the principles of God's wrath and grace haven't changed). God may have different expectations of different people based on their different situations and different abilities (without changing any spiritual principles). And as we mature or backslide in our faith, different spiritual principles may come into play in our lives. Those wouldn't be new or changed spiritual principles, rather old spiritual principles that are new to our experience.

Finally, there has been a huge change in how God relates to his people. Due to people's persistence in sinning, God had implemented the "Law of Moses" in Old Testament times. With the coming of Jesus, the Law of Moses should no longer be the basis of our relationship with God:

> *For the law was given through Moses. Grace and truth came through Jesus Christ.*          John 1:17 ESV

> *For sin will not have dominion over you. For you are not under law, but under grace.*          Romans_6:14 WEB

> *So that the law has become our tutor to bring us to Christ, that we might be justified by faith. But now that faith has come, we are no longer under a tutor.*
> Galatians 3:24-25 WEB

## Old Scripture Is Irrelevant Today

This tends to be a popular corollary to the previous deception that "truth changes with time."

Modern technology has facilitated an increase in knowledge and access to huge amounts of information, both of which were not previously possible. Combining this with an evolutionary worldview leads many people to believe that old information and old ways of doing things are inferior to what we have today. As a result, many people simply disregard anything old, thinking the new is better. Likewise, many people are deceived into disregarding scripture.

However, the spiritual realm is not dependent on, or much influenced by, so-called "progress" in the physical realm. Worldly wealth, technology, and knowledge do not make us more spiritual, and they do not change spiritual truths. On the contrary, wealth, technology and worldly knowledge tend to be idols in many people's lives, leading them away from spiritual truth, causing them to neglect truth found in scripture.

Consider these verses:

> *For whatever was written in former days was written for our instruction, that through endurance and through the encouragement of the Scriptures we might have hope.*  Romans 15:4 ESV

> *Concerning this salvation, the prophets who prophesied about the grace that was to be yours searched and inquired carefully, inquiring what person or time the Spirit of Christ in them was indicating when he predicted the sufferings of Christ and the subsequent glories. It was revealed to them that they were serving not themselves but you, in the things that have now been announced to you through those who preached the good news to you by the Holy Spirit sent from heaven, things into which angels long to look.*  1Peter 1:10-12 ESV

> *We have the more sure word of prophecy; and you do well that you heed it, as to a lamp shining in a dark place, until the day dawns, and the morning star arises in your hearts: knowing this first, that no prophecy of Scripture is of private interpretation. For no prophecy ever came by the will of man: but holy men of God spoke, being moved by the Holy Spirit.*  2Peter 1:19-21 WEB

> *Every Scripture is God-breathed and profitable for teaching, for reproof, for correction, and for instruction in righteousness, that each person who belongs to God may be complete, thoroughly equipped for every good work.*  2Timothy 3:16-17 WEB

## New Revelation Supersedes the Old

Similar to claiming that old scriptures are no longer relevant, or claiming that truth changes with time, many people claim that new revelation supersedes older revelation. While not denying the inspiration and value of old revelation, they claim that newer revelation is better. When new revelation is in conflict with the old, they disregard the old in favor of the new.

Some believers try to avoid problems in this area by simply claiming that God no longer reveals anything new to anyone. Others seem to accept anything that is new and that appears to have a spiritual source; they are quick to disregard the old.

I believe this is one of those issues where *"Deception goes Both Ways"* (the title of chapter 14). I believe God still communicates with his people, as discussed later in chapter 33 *"God Told Me..."* However, I also believe that spiritual principles don't change with time, just as physical laws of science don't change with time. Spiritual truth communicated in scripture long ago is still true today. Any new "revelation" or communication thought to be from God, but which is not consistent with scripture, likely is not from God. Paul gives us this stern warning:

> ***I am astonished that you are so quickly deserting him who called you in the grace of Christ and are turning to a different gospel—not that there is another one, but there are some who trouble you and want to distort the gospel of Christ. But even if we or an angel from heaven should preach to you a gospel contrary to the one we preached to you, let him be accursed. As we have said before, so now I say again: If anyone is preaching to you a gospel contrary to the one you received, let him be accursed.*** *Galatians 1:6-9 ESV*

Here we are warned to not believe even *"an angel from heaven"* if the angel brings a message that is not consistent with Paul's message.

# Scripture Has Been Changed

Those who seek to deceive others often take a minor problem and greatly magnify it to suit their purposes. This correlates with the saying "making a mountain out of a molehill." Likewise, some people, who generally have little respect for scripture, discount the accuracy and validity of scripture by claiming "Scripture has been changed."

By "scripture" I am referring here to the Old and New Testament scriptures found in the Bible. The various "books" of the Bible were written over the course of more than a thousand years, and, generally speaking, the original documents are not in existence today. What we do have is very old copies of the original texts. Or, in most cases, copies of copies of copies... of the originals. So, some people simply claim that scripture is not a reliable source of truth because, they say, "Scripture has been changed." Their purpose is generally to discourage people from looking to scripture as a source of truth.

While it is true that there are some minor inconsistencies between old manuscripts of scripture, it is also true that the degree of consistency between the old manuscripts is remarkable. There is little significant dispute over the actual original texts (in the original Hebrew and Greek) of the vast majority of verses in the Bible, since there are so few differences between the old manuscripts. Most people who copied scripture long ago had such high regard for it that they took great care to copy the scriptures accurately. Relatively few verses appear to have "changed" significantly. As a result we can have a lot of confidence in the accuracy of the scriptures we have today.

This is one of those issues that rightly would take an entire book to do it justice. Such books have already been written. It is not my purpose here to duplicate that work, but merely to draw your attention to this issue, so that you will not be easily deceived. For those who want more information on this subject, I recommend the book *"Can I really trust the Bible"* by Barry Cooper.

Note that the issue of Bible *translation accuracy* is a separate issue. Translating the original scriptures from Hebrew and Greek into other languages introduces additional concerns about the accuracy of scripture. One way to reduce this problem is to compare different translations to better understand the original intent and get past translation biases. Learning to read the original Hebrew and/or Greek is also an option, but this is an option that most people don't have time or talent for.

Even though we should have a lot of confidence in scripture, our salvation is not dependent on having perfect scriptures, or having a perfect translation of scripture, or having a perfect understanding of scripture. Rather, salvation involves coming to Jesus, trusting in Jesus, and following Jesus. The scriptures point us to Jesus. Jesus said this to the religious people of his day:

> *"You search the Scriptures, because you think that in them you have eternal life; and these are they which testify about me. Yet you will not come to me, that you may have life."*    John 5:39-40 WEB

The scriptures are reliable sources of truth about God and spiritual things. However, keep in mind that salvation is about coming to Jesus, trusting in Jesus, and following Jesus; it's not about having perfect scriptures, or having perfect understanding of the scriptures.

## For Further Reflection

- Do you believe that there are truths that don't change with time?

- How do you view scripture?

***********

# Chapter 23
# God

*In the beginning, God created the heavens and the earth.*
*Genesis 1:1 WEB*

*The fool says in his heart, "There is no God."*
*Psalm 14:1, 53:1 ESV*

---

Having a correct understanding of God is important for developing correct understanding about many areas of life, including both natural things and supernatural things. In this chapter we'll look at some common misunderstandings about God that we should avoid.

## No God (Naturalism)

Clearly, this book is written with the understanding that God exists, and that scripture is a reliable source of information about God. Self-evident truths that support this viewpoint are discussed in the book *"Beneath Foundations for Eternal Life."* Please refer to that book for a non-scriptural justification for belief in God and why scripture is an important source of truth about God.

When a *fool says in his heart "There is no God,"* he is deceived.

## Many Gods (Polytheism)

The existence of many supernatural beings is a viewpoint common to most religions that acknowledge the existence of a spiritual realm (this has already been discussed in the book *"Beneath Foundations for Eternal Life,"* chapter 16, *"God or Gods"*). However, scripture makes clear that there is one God who created all other spiritual beings, and who is greater than all other spiritual beings. Scripture also makes clear that there are spiritual beings that are in rebellion against God, generally led by the devil (as previously discussed in chapter 10 *"Spirits of Deception"*). Some religions, however, do not acknowledge the one God who created everything, and some religions appear to be following created spiritual beings as though they are self-existent gods. Scripture clearly speaks against this. Consider these verses:

*Now at Lystra there was a man sitting who could not use his feet. He was crippled from birth and had never walked. He listened to Paul speaking. And Paul, looking intently at him and seeing that he had faith to be made well, said in a loud voice, "Stand upright on your feet." And he sprang up and began walking. And when the crowds saw what Paul had done, they lifted up their voices, saying in Lycaonian, "The gods have come down to us in the likeness of men!" Barnabas they called Zeus, and Paul, Hermes, because he was the chief speaker. And the priest of Zeus, whose temple was at the entrance to the city, brought oxen and garlands to the gates and wanted to offer sacrifice with the crowds. But when the apostles Barnabas and Paul heard of it, they tore their garments and rushed out into the crowd, crying out, "Men, why are you doing these things? We also are men, of like nature with you, and we bring you good news, that you should turn from these vain things to a living God, who made the heaven and the earth and the sea and all that is in them."* Acts 14:8-15 ESV

*For although there may be so-called gods in heaven or on earth—as indeed there are many "gods" and many "lords"—yet for us there is one God, the Father, from whom are all things and for whom we exist, and one Lord, Jesus Christ, through whom are all things and through whom we exist.* 1Corinthians 8:5-6 ESV

*There is one body, and one Spirit, even as you also were called in one hope of your calling; one Lord, one faith, one baptism, one God and Father of all, who is over all, and through all, and in us all.* Ephesians 4:4-6 WEB

*For there is one God and one mediator between God and mankind, the man Christ Jesus, who gave himself as a ransom for all people.* 1Timothy 2:5-6 NIV

We should take special note that the first two commands of the Ten Commandments deal with our relationship to other gods:

*"I am the LORD your God, who brought you out of the land of Egypt, out of the house of slavery.*

*"You shall have no other gods before me.*

*"You shall not make for yourself a carved image, or any likeness of anything that is in heaven above, or that is in the earth beneath, or that is in the water under the earth. You shall not bow down to them or serve them, for I the LORD your God am a jealous God, visiting the iniquity of the fathers on the children to the third and the fourth generation of those who hate me, but showing steadfast love to thousands of those who love me and keep my commandments."* Exodus 20:2-6 ESV

Polytheistic religions often encourage the making of idols, or various images, which represent other gods. Various forms of worship or service are promoted in relationship to these idols or images. However, God has prohibited the making of an idol, or any kind of image to represent him. Moses further clarified this:

*You saw no form of any kind the day the LORD spoke to you at Horeb out of the fire. Therefore watch yourselves very carefully, so that you do not become corrupt and make for yourselves an idol, an image of any shape, whether formed like a man or a woman, or like any animal on earth or any bird that flies in the air, or like any creature that moves along the ground or any fish in the waters below. And when you look up to the sky and see the sun, the moon and the stars—all the heavenly array—do not be enticed into bowing down to them and worshiping things the LORD your God has apportioned to all the nations under heaven.*     *Deuteronomy 4:15-19 NIV*

## All Is God (Pantheism)

At the other extreme from saying **"There is no God"** are people who believe that everything is God. However, scripture presents a much different viewpoint. The first verse in the Bible reads:

*In the beginning, God created the heavens and the earth.*     *Genesis 1:1 WEB*

Here we see God as the creator of the universe, being self-existing prior to the creation of *the heavens and the earth.* Scripture is consistent in its portrayal of God as creator and as distinctly separate from what he has created. Clearly, a belief that "all is God" is not consistent with scripture.

## God Not Personal

Some people claim that God is far off, not involved in people's lives, and, frankly, rather indifferent about everything. This perspective is clearly shown to be false by these kinds of truths:

- **For God so loved the world, that he gave his one and only Son, that whoever believes in him should not perish, but have eternal life** (John 3:16 WEB).

- Jesus, the "Son of God," left heaven and came to earth, became a person and lived among us.

- Jesus shed his blood and died for our sins, so that we might be forgiven and be delivered from the power of sin.

- Jesus rose from the dead, proving his authority over death and bringing new life to all who follow him.

- Jesus poured out the Holy Spirit on his followers after ascending to heaven.

- Jesus said: *"If anyone is thirsty, let him come to me and drink!"* (John 7:37 WEB).

- Jesus said: *"Are not two sparrows sold for a penny? And not one of them will fall to the ground apart from your Father. But even the hairs of your head are all numbered. Fear not, therefore; you are of more value than many sparrows"* (Matthew 10:29-31 ESV).

- Jesus said: *"Come to me, all you who labor and are heavily burdened, and I will give you rest. Take my yoke upon you, and learn from me, for I am gentle and lowly in heart; and you will find rest for your souls. For my yoke is easy, and my burden is light."* (Matthew 11:28-30 WEB)

## God Not Good

Some people claim that God is not good, that he doesn't want what is best for us. This deception played a role in the first sin in the Garden of Eden. The serpent deceived Eve into doubting God's goodness by implying God had lied to her to keep good things from her:

*"You won't surely die, for God knows that in the day you eat it, your eyes will be opened, and you will be like God, knowing good and evil."*     *Genesis 3:4-5 WEB*

Consider what is perhaps the most-repeated line in scripture:

*Give thanks to Yahweh, for he is good, for his loving kindness endures forever.*
*1Chronicles 16:34; Psalm 106:1, 107:1, 118:1, 118:29 136:1 WEB*

Note, however, that God's goodness causes him to oppose unrighteousness. Those who reject God's ways will eventually experience God's righteous judgment. Consider these verses:

*The way of the LORD is a refuge for the blameless, but it is the ruin of those who do evil.* Proverbs 10:29 NIV

*The righteous will never be uprooted, but the wicked will not remain in the land.* Proverbs 10:30 NIV

*Yahweh's eyes are toward the righteous. His ears listen to their cry. Yahweh's face is against those who do evil, to cut off the memory of them from the earth.*
Psalm 34:15-16 WEB

*"God opposes the proud but gives grace to the humble."*
James 4:6, 1Peter 5:5 ESV

## All Paths Lead to God

- It is self-evident that different paths here on earth (both physical and metaphorical) lead to different locations or destinies. This has been discussed previously in the book *"Beneath Foundations for Eternal Life,"* chapters 8 and 9. The same is true in the spiritual realm. All paths do NOT lead to God. Consider Jesus' words:

*"Enter in by the narrow gate; for wide is the gate and broad is the way that leads to destruction, and many are those who enter in by it. How narrow is the gate, and restricted is the way that leads to life! Few are those who find it."* Matthew 7:13-14 WEB

*"Not everyone who says to me, 'Lord, Lord,' will enter into the Kingdom of Heaven; but he who does the will of my Father who is in heaven. Many will tell me in that day, 'Lord, Lord, didn't we prophesy in your name, in your name cast out demons, and in your name do many mighty works?' Then I will tell them, 'I never knew you. Depart from me, you who work iniquity.'"*
Matthew 7:21-23 WEB

*"When the Son of Man comes in his glory, and all the angels with him, then he will sit on his glorious throne. Before him will be gathered all the nations, and he will*

*separate people one from another as a shepherd separates the sheep from the goats. And he will place the sheep on his right, but the goats on the left. Then the King will say to those on his right, 'Come, you who are blessed by my Father, inherit the kingdom prepared for you from the foundation of the world.'"*

*Matthew 25:31-34 ESV*

*"Then he will say to those on his left, 'Depart from me, you cursed, into the eternal fire prepared for the devil and his angels.'"*   *Matthew 25:41 ESV*

## For Further Reflection

- Are your beliefs about God consistent with scripture?

\*\*\*\*\*\*\*\*\*\*\*

# Chapter 24
# Jesus

*He has on his garment and on his thigh a name written,*
*"KING OF KINGS, AND LORD OF LORDS."*
Revelation 19:16 WEB

---

Since Jesus is central to our faith and salvation, those who oppose our faith often deny any or all of the important truths about who Jesus is, what Jesus has done, and what Jesus will do in the future. These deceptions should be apparent to anyone who understands and values scripture, but it is still necessary to briefly mention them here. Our faith in Jesus would likely be ruined if any of these deceptions are believed.

## Jesus Not the Christ

Clearly, the testimony of scripture is that Jesus is the Christ:

*Again the high priest asked him, "Are you the Christ, the Son of the Blessed?" And Jesus said, "I am, and you will see the Son of Man seated at the right hand of Power, and coming with the clouds of heaven."*
Mark 14:61-62 ESV

*Now Jesus did many other signs in the presence of the disciples, which are not written in this book; but these are written so that you may believe that Jesus is the Christ, the Son of God, and that by believing you may have life in his name.* John 20:30-31 ESV

## Didn't Come in the Flesh

Jesus, the Christ, has come, "in the flesh," to earth, and has lived among us. This is the testimony of the entire New Testament. In particular, John writes on this topic:

*By this you know the Spirit of God: every spirit who*

*confesses that Jesus Christ has come in the flesh is of God, and every spirit who doesn't confess that Jesus Christ has come in the flesh is not of God, and this is the spirit of the Antichrist, of whom you have heard that it comes. Now it is in the world already.* 1John 4:2-3 WEB

An important aspect of Jesus having *come in the flesh* is that Jesus existed prior to his life on earth, and that he came down from heaven to reveal God to us. Consider these verses:

*In the beginning was the Word, and the Word was with God, and the Word was God. He was in the beginning with God. All things were made through him, and without him was not any thing made that was made.*
John 1:1-3 ESV

*The Word became flesh, and lived among us.*
John 1:14 WEB

*"I am the living bread which came down out of heaven. If anyone eats of this bread, he will live forever. Yes, the bread which I will give for the life of the world is my flesh."*
John 6:51 WEB

*"I came from the Father and entered the world; now I am leaving the world and going back to the Father."*
John 16:28 NIV

*Have this in your mind, which was also in Christ Jesus, who, existing in the form of God, didn't consider equality with God a thing to be grasped, but emptied himself, taking the form of a servant, being made in the likeness of men.*
Philippians 2:5-7 WEB

## Didn't Exist

This is a variation of the previous deception, claiming that Jesus didn't even exist. Clearly, the entire New Testament is evidence against this view. Other historical sources also provide clear evidence that Jesus did actually live among us.

# Didn't Die

Some people claim that Jesus didn't really die on the cross, so he didn't really rise from the dead; he was just healed of his wounds. John seems to have anticipated this argument:

*Therefore the soldiers came, and broke the legs of the first, and of the other who was crucified with him; but when they came to Jesus, and saw that he was already dead, they didn't break his legs. However one of the soldiers pierced his side with a spear, and immediately blood and water came out. He who has seen has testified, and his testimony is true. He knows that he tells the truth, that you may believe.* John 19:32-35 WEB

It is widely understood that the *blood and water* that *came out* is a certain indication of death. John emphasizes that he personally witnessed the death of Jesus.

# Didn't Rise

As Paul wrote:

*If Christ has not been raised, then our preaching is in vain, and your faith also is in vain. Yes, we are found false witnesses of God, because we testified about God that he raised up Christ, whom he didn't raise up, if it is so that the dead are not raised. For if the dead aren't raised, neither has Christ been raised. If Christ has not been raised, your faith is vain; you are still in your sins. Then they also who are fallen asleep in Christ have perished. If we have only hoped in Christ in this life, we are of all men most pitiable. But now Christ has been raised from the dead.* 1Corinthians 15:14-20 WEB

Some of the strongest historical evidences that Jesus rose from the dead are the people who witnessed him alive after his crucifixion. The eleven Apostles devoted their lives to tell people about Jesus and his resurrection. Most of them were martyred for their faith. While many people may be willing to die for something they believe is true, few are willing to die for what they know to be a lie. Clearly, the original followers of Jesus were convinced that Jesus rose from the dead.

Paul also suffered greatly for following Jesus. He turned from persecuting followers of Jesus to being a follower of Jesus himself only after being confronted by Jesus on the road to Damascus. Paul wrote that Jesus

> *...appeared to more than five hundred brothers at one time, most of whom are still alive, though some have fallen asleep.*  1Corinthians 15:6 ESV

Clearly, scripture declares that Jesus has risen from the dead. Our entire salvation hinges on this truth. *If Christ has not been raised, your faith is vain; you are still in your sins.* (1 Corinthians 15:17 WEB).

If this issue is not settled for you, ask God for clarity on this subject. Your faith cannot mature without knowing that Jesus has risen from the dead.

**Christ is Risen!!** Can you respond **"He is risen indeed!!"**?

## Not Exalted

Here is a subject I think many believers do not understand well. We may have *knowledge* about this, but we may lack *understanding* and *wisdom* regarding it.

Most people who acknowledge that Jesus rose from the dead, and who accept the truth of scripture, will also acknowledge that Jesus ascended to heaven and is at the right hand of God. However, do we fully understand what it means that Jesus is *exalted?* Do we live according to the truth that Jesus is *exalted?*

Before exploring what it means that Jesus is exalted, let's first simply look at a few of the many verses which indicate that Jesus ascended to heaven and is at the right hand of

God:

*Again the high priest asked him, "Are you the Christ, the Son of the Blessed?" And Jesus said, "I am, and you will see the Son of Man seated at the right hand of Power, and coming with the clouds of heaven."*
*Mark 14:61-62 ESV*

*So then the Lord, after he had spoken to them, was received up into heaven, and sat down at the right hand of God.*
*Mark 16:19 WEB*

*And when he had said these things, as they were looking on, he was lifted up, and a cloud took him out of their sight. And while they were gazing into heaven as he went, behold, two men stood by them in white robes, and said, "Men of Galilee, why do you stand looking into heaven? This Jesus, who was taken up from you into heaven, will come in the same way as you saw him go into heaven."*
*Acts 1:9-11 ESV*

*God has raised this Jesus to life, and we are all witnesses of it. Exalted to the right hand of God, he has received from the Father the promised Holy Spirit and has poured out what you now see and hear.*
*Acts 2:32-33 NIV*

*When the members of the Sanhedrin heard this, they were furious and gnashed their teeth at him. But Stephen, full of the Holy Spirit, looked up to heaven and saw the glory of God, and Jesus standing at the right hand of God. "Look," he said, "I see heaven open and the Son of Man standing at the right hand of God."*
*Acts 7:54-56 NIV*

*If then you have been raised with Christ, seek the things that are above, where Christ is, seated at the right hand of God.*
*Colossians 3:1 ESV*

Now let's consider the significance of Jesus being *exalted*.

For me, part of my difficulty of understanding comes from

not living in an earthly kingdom with a powerful king who is shown great respect, so I don't naturally relate to Jesus being a great king who is highly exalted. I live in a country with a democratic form of government that emphasizes the equality of all people. Even the president of my country is often not shown much respect or honor, even though he holds the highest office in government. His power is limited by various laws and the country's Constitution. People in the country in which I live can speak openly against the president with little fear of retribution. So, I have a tendency to think of Jesus merely like a good president, rather than a powerful king.

However, Jesus is not limited like a president is limited. Jesus is *"**King of kings, and Lord of lords**"* (Revelation 17:14, 19:16). His power and authority are unlimited.

Let's look at how great Jesus is. Please consider these verses, along with my brief comments after each set of verses:

> *In the beginning was the Word, and the Word was with God, and the Word was God. He was in the beginning with God. All things were made through him, and without him was not any thing made that was made.*
>
> *John 1:1-3 ESV*

> *He is the image of the invisible God, the firstborn of all creation. For by him all things were created, in heaven and on earth, visible and invisible, whether thrones or dominions or rulers or authorities—all things were created through him and for him.* *Colossians 1:15-16 ESV*

All things were made through Jesus, and he is *the image of the invisible God.* The power and authority that Jesus has is hard to comprehend!

> *For the Father judges no one, but he has given all judgment to the Son, that all may honor the Son, even as they honor the Father. He who doesn't honor the Son*

***doesn't honor the Father who sent him.*** *John 5:22-23 WEB*

All judgment has been given to Jesus. We are to honor Jesus the same as we honor the Father. Whoever doesn't honor Jesus does not honor the Father.

> ***Have this in your mind, which was also in Christ Jesus, who, existing in the form of God, didn't consider equality with God a thing to be grasped, but emptied himself, taking the form of a servant, being made in the likeness of men. And being found in human form, he humbled himself, becoming obedient to death, yes, the death of the cross. Therefore God also highly exalted him, and gave to him the name which is above every name; that at the name of Jesus every knee should bow, of those in heaven, those on earth, and those under the earth, and that every tongue should confess that Jesus Christ is Lord, to the glory of God the Father.***
> *Philippians 2:5-11 WEB*

Every knee will bow before Jesus and acknowledge that Jesus Christ is Lord.

> ***The Son is the radiance of God's glory and the exact representation of his being, sustaining all things by his powerful word. After he had provided purification for sins, he sat down at the right hand of the Majesty in heaven. So he became as much superior to the angels as the name he has inherited is superior to theirs.***
> *Hebrews 1:3-4 NIV*

Jesus is superior to all angels.

> ***This is a symbol of baptism, which now saves you—not the putting away of the filth of the flesh, but the answer of a good conscience toward God, through the resurrection of Jesus Christ, who is at the right hand of God, having gone into heaven, angels and authorities and powers being made subject to him.*** *1Peter 3:21-22 WEB*

All angels, authorities, and powers are subject to Jesus.

*Now the point in what we are saying is this: we have such a high priest, one who is seated at the right hand of the throne of the Majesty in heaven, a minister in the holy places, in the true tent that the Lord set up, not man.*
*Hebrews 8:1-2 ESV*

Jesus is our perfect high priest.

*And after six days Jesus took with him Peter and James, and John his brother, and led them up a high mountain by themselves. And he was transfigured before them, and his face shone like the sun, and his clothes became white as light.*
*Matthew 17:1-2 ESV*

While Jesus lived among us, his appearance briefly changed from that of a normal person to an appearance closer to his normal glorified state.

*I turned to see the voice that spoke with me. Having turned, I saw seven golden lamp stands. And among the lamp stands was one like a son of man, clothed with a robe reaching down to his feet, and with a golden sash around his chest. His head and his hair were white as white wool, like snow. His eyes were like a flame of fire. His feet were like burnished brass, as if it had been refined in a furnace. His voice was like the voice of many waters. He had seven stars in his right hand. Out of his mouth proceeded a sharp two-edged sword. His face was like the sun shining at its brightest. When I saw him, I fell at his feet like a dead man.*
*Revelation 1:12-17 WEB*

Jesus' exalted appearance is striking, to say the least. John's natural reaction to seeing him was to fall at his feet.

*I saw, and I heard something like a voice of many angels around the throne, the living creatures, and the elders; and the number of them was ten thousands of ten thousands, and thousands of thousands; saying with a loud voice, "Worthy is the Lamb who has been killed to receive the power, wealth, wisdom, strength, honor, glory, and blessing!"*

*I heard every created thing which is in heaven, on the earth, under the earth, on the sea, and everything in them, saying, "To him who sits on the throne, and to the Lamb be the blessing, the honor, the glory, and the dominion, forever and ever! Amen!"*

*The four living creatures said, "Amen!" Then the elders fell down and worshiped.*     Revelation 5:11-14 WEB

Here we see all of heaven and earth worshiping Jesus (*the Lamb*) the same as they worship the Father (*him who sits on the throne*).

What about you? Jesus is highly exalted. Do you worship, honor, and respect Jesus as much as they do in Heaven? If not, why not?

## Won't Come Again

The understanding that Jesus will come again to Earth to reign is an important teaching throughout the New Testament. Jesus is the great king of the Kingdom of God, who will one day reign on Earth. While believers may disagree over many details associated with Jesus' return, scripture is clear that Jesus will return. Here are just a few of the many verses that speak of his return:

*"Then all the tribes of the earth will mourn, and they will see the Son of Man coming on the clouds of the sky with power and great glory."*     Matthew 24:30 WEB

*"But when the Son of Man comes in his glory, and all the holy angels with him, then he will sit on the throne of his glory."*     Matthew 25:31 WEB

*After he said this, he was taken up before their very eyes, and a cloud hid him from their sight. They were looking intently up into the sky as he was going, when*

*suddenly two men dressed in white stood beside them. "Men of Galilee," they said, "why do you stand here looking into the sky? This same Jesus, who has been taken from you into heaven, will come back in the same way you have seen him go into heaven."*   Acts 1:9-11 NIV

*Above all, you must understand that in the last days scoffers will come, scoffing and following their own evil desires. They will say, "Where is this 'coming' he promised? Ever since our ancestors died, everything goes on as it has since the beginning of creation." But they deliberately forget...*   2Peter 3:3-5 NIV

*The seventh angel sounded, and great voices in heaven followed, saying, "The kingdom of the world has become the Kingdom of our Lord, and of his Christ. He will reign forever and ever!"*   Revelation 11:15 WEB

This is, again, one of those truths that is easy to have knowledge about, but harder to understand and live by. Do you live with an awareness and hope that Jesus will return?

## Other Christs

Some people claim Jesus is just one of many "christs," and typically try to lead people to follow someone else as "Christ." Jesus himself addressed this issue:

*"Be careful that no one leads you astray. For many will come in my name, saying, 'I am the Christ,' and will lead many astray."*   Matthew 24:4-5 WEB

*"Then if any man tells you, 'Behold, here is the Christ,' or, 'There,' don't believe it. For there will arise false christs, and false prophets, and they will show great signs and wonders, so as to lead astray, if possible, even the chosen ones. Behold, I have told you beforehand. If therefore they tell you, 'Behold, he is in the wilderness,' don't go out; 'Behold, he is in the inner rooms,' don't believe it. For as the lightning flashes from the east,*

*and is seen even to the west, so will be the coming of the Son of Man."*   Matthew 24:23-27 WEB

What about you? Do you live with an awareness that Jesus is the Christ, the only true Messiah?

## For Further Reflection

- Which of these deceptions about Jesus have you heard promoted? In what context?

- Are there some changes you should make in your life to better honor, respect, and worship Jesus?

************

# Chapter 25
# Sin

*"From now on, sin no more."*
*John 8:11 WEB*

---

Sin, and salvation from sin, is a primary theme throughout scripture. A primary reason that Jesus came into the world was to deal with the problem of sin. As Paul said:

> **Here is a trustworthy saying that deserves full acceptance: Christ Jesus came into the world to save sinners—of whom I am the worst.** *1Timothy 1:15 NIV*

We first see the possibility of sin in Genesis chapter 2, with **"the tree of the knowledge of good and evil"** and God's command to not eat its fruit. In chapter 3 we see the serpent tempt Eve, and Adam and Eve then commit the first human sins by disobeying God and eating from that tree. Paul clarifies the impact that event has had on all of us:

> **Therefore as sin entered into the world through one man, and death through sin; so death passed to all men, because all sinned.** *Romans 5:12 WEB*

"Sin" can be simply defined as wrong thinking or wrong actions. As John said:

> **All wrongdoing is sin...** *1John 5:17 ESV*

In Genesis 3, Eve was tempted to think wrong before she and Adam acted wrong. As Eve said:

> **"The serpent deceived me, and I ate."** *Genesis 3:13 WEB*

Generally speaking, wrong thinking, some kind of deception or misunderstanding, usually precedes wrong actions.

What we believe about sin, what is morally *right* and *wrong,* should agree with God's perspective of sin. God is always right. If there is a conflict between you and God in some area, do not think for a moment that God is wrong.

However, our understanding of what is or isn't sinful may be wrong, and we may feel false condemnation if we are deceived in this area. Holding a neutral perspective about things that aren't clear may be helpful, as discussed in chapter 13 "A Neutral Attitude."

A primary purpose of God in creating us appears to be that he wants deep relationship with many people, because *"God is love"* (1 John 4:8). God desires that we also love him, and that is why the greatest commandment is that we should love God with our whole being (Matthew 22:35-40, Mark 12:28-34, Luke 10:25-28). Love for God results in us wanting to please him, and to do things his way. As Jesus said:

*"If you love me, you will keep my commandments."*
*John 14:15 ESV*

*"If anyone loves me, he will keep my word, and my Father will love him, and we will come to him and make our home with him. Whoever does not love me does not keep my words. And the word that you hear is not mine but the Father's who sent me."* *John 14:23-24 ESV*

If we are intentionally continuing to sin, this shows a lack of love for God, and this may bring our salvation into question. We have this warning in scripture:

*If we deliberately keep on sinning after we have received the knowledge of the truth, no sacrifice for sins is left, but only a fearful expectation of judgment and of raging fire that will consume the enemies of God. Anyone who rejected the law of Moses died without mercy on the testimony of two or three witnesses. How much more severely do you think someone deserves to be punished who has trampled the Son of God underfoot, who has treated as an unholy thing the blood of the covenant that sanctified them, and who has insulted the Spirit of grace?* *Hebrews 10:26-29 NIV*

Generally speaking, when we sin we are turning away from God, and our relationship with God is damaged. When we repent of sin, we are turning toward God, and our relationship with him is improved. By consistently *living by the Spirit* (chapter 20) we avoid sin, and our relationship with God grows stronger. When we are in right relationship with God, an underlying peace should characterize our lives, even in the midst of great trials. As Jesus said:

> **Peace I leave with you; my peace I give you. I do not give to you as the world gives. Do not let your hearts be troubled and do not be afraid.**
> John 14:27 NIV

Is there some conflict between you and God? Is there something in your life that you know is displeasing to him, but for some reason you are unwilling to do things his way? Dear friend, do not treat this lightly. God's ways are always right and good. Let us not delay turning away from sin and turning toward God for grace and forgiveness.

Now let's consider some common misunderstandings about "sin."

## No Sin

Some people claim "sin" does not exist, that it is just an invention of religion. However, those same people are usually quick to condemn people who believe or act differently than themselves regarding various issues. This shows that they actually do believe in right and wrong. What is sin, other than wrong thinking or wrong actions? It seems to me that a person has to deny right and wrong to deny the existence of sin. The rightness and wrongness of some things is self-evident (as discussed in chapters 5 and 6 of the book *"Beneath Foundations for Eternal Life"*). The existence of sin is likewise self-evident.

Also, scripture clearly shows that sin exists, and all of us are affected by sin:

*If we say we have no sin, we deceive ourselves, and the truth is not in us. If we confess our sins, he is faithful and just to forgive us our sins and to cleanse us from all unrighteousness. If we say we have not sinned, we make him a liar, and his word is not in us.* 1John 1:8-10 ESV

Indeed, a major theme in scripture is how sin entered the world (Genesis 3), and how God has been, and is, redeeming people from spiritual death caused by sin.

## Moral Relativism

Moral relativism proposes that what is morally right or wrong is only derived from culture and situations. Stated another way: There is no absolute truth regarding anything being morally right or morally wrong; it all depends on the particular situation and culture.

This is one of those subjects that is difficult because the truth regarding it is not black and white, but is instead rather grey (as discussed in chapter 3 *"Clean or Dirty"* in the book *"Beneath Foundations for Eternal Life"*). Let's look at some examples from scripture on both sides of this issue.

Paul seems to support a form of moral relativism in Romans 14, where he emphasizes the need for believers to respect each other regarding disputable matters (especially regarding what kind of food we eat). Here are a couple verses from that chapter:

*I know, and am persuaded in the Lord Jesus, that nothing is unclean of itself; except that to him who considers anything to be unclean, to him it is unclean.*
Romans 14:14 WEB

*But he who doubts is condemned if he eats, because it isn't of faith; and whatever is not of faith is sin.*
Romans 14:23 WEB

In Romans 14, Paul reasons that what is right and wrong for a particular person partly depends on what they themselves believe to be right or wrong. Further, in some situations at least, Paul instructs those who are stronger in faith to defer to those who are weaker in faith, so as to not unnecessarily offend someone (see Romans 14:1 through 15:7).

On the other hand, the believers in Corinth appear to have thought it to be okay for a man to have sexual relations with his father's wife. Perhaps they were looking at sexuality through the permissive perspective of their local culture. Paul clearly condemned their openness to such things:

> *It is actually reported that there is sexual immorality among you, and of a kind that is not tolerated even among pagans, for a man has his father's wife. And you are arrogant! Ought you not rather to mourn? Let him who has done this be removed from among you.*
> *1 Corinthians 5:1-2 ESV*

Later in that same letter, Paul provides a list of sins that are never morally right:

> *Or do you not know that the unrighteous will not inherit the kingdom of God? Do not be deceived: neither the sexually immoral, nor idolaters, nor adulterers, nor men who practice homosexuality, nor thieves, nor the greedy, nor drunkards, nor revilers, nor swindlers will inherit the kingdom of God. And such were some of you. But you were washed, you were sanctified, you were justified in the name of the Lord Jesus Christ and by the Spirit of our God.*
> *1 Corinthians 6:9-11 ESV*

So we see that some areas of morality are dependent on viewpoint or culture; while other areas are not.

## All Sins Are Equal

The idea that "all sins are equal" seems to be promoted among some believers based on reasoning that any sin is sufficient to condemn us before God, so "all sins are equal." Perhaps in that one sense they are equal, but scripture clearly refers to sins NOT being equal. Consider these verses:

*Yahweh said, "Because the cry of Sodom and Gomorrah is great, and because their sin is very grievous, I will go down now, and see whether their deeds are as bad as the reports which have come to me. If not, I will know."*
*Genesis 18:20-21 WEB*

*On the next day, Moses said to the people, "You have sinned a great sin. Now I will go up to Yahweh. Perhaps I shall make atonement for your sin." Moses returned to Yahweh, and said, "Oh, this people have sinned a great sin, and have made themselves gods of gold."*
*Exodus 32:30-31 WEB*

*The sin of the young men was very great before Yahweh; for the men despised the offering of Yahweh.*
*1Samuel 2:17 WEB*

*"Truly I tell you, people can be forgiven all their sins and every slander they utter, but whoever blasphemes against the Holy Spirit will never be forgiven; they are guilty of an eternal sin."*
*Mark 3:28-29 NIV*

*Pilate therefore said to him, "Aren't you speaking to me? Don't you know that I have power to release you, and have power to crucify you?"*
*Jesus answered, "You would have no power at all against me, unless it were given to you from above. Therefore he who delivered me to you has greater sin."*
*John 19:10-11 WEB*

*If anyone sees his brother sinning a sin not leading to death, he shall ask, and God will give him life for those who sin not leading to death. There is a sin leading to death. I don't say that he should make a request concerning this. All unrighteousness is sin, and there is a sin not leading to death.*
*1John 5:16-17 WEB*

The problem with wrongly believing "all sins are equal" is

that this belief encourages people to do greater evil, rather than avoid it. For example, if a man has a lustful look toward a woman, and that sin (Matthew 5:28) is equally as bad as physical adultery, why not do the latter sin once the former sin has happened? If there is no difference before God, then it is easy to rationalize the actual act of physical adultery. However, there ARE degrees of sin, and God deals with people accordingly.

## No Deliverance from Sin

Not only are our sins forgiven through faith in Jesus, but we are set free from the power of sin! This is not to say that believers have achieved perfection here on earth, but that we should no longer be controlled by the power of sin. However, many believers don't seem to understand this, and continue to live as though sin is still their master. Consider these verses

> *We know that our old self was crucified with him in order that the body of sin might be brought to nothing, so that we would no longer be enslaved to sin. For one who has died has been set free from sin.* Romans 6:6-7 ESV

> *For the death he died he died to sin, once for all, but the life he lives he lives to God. So you also must consider yourselves dead to sin and alive to God in Christ Jesus. Let not sin therefore reign in your mortal body, to make you obey its passions.* Romans 6:10-12 ESV

> *We know that everyone who has been born of God does not keep on sinning, but he who was born of God protects him, and the evil one does not touch him.*
> 1John 5:18 ESV

John goes so far as to say that having victory over sin, keeping God's word, is one of the ways we know that we are saved:

> *This is how we know that we know him: if we keep his*

*commandments. One who says, "I know him," and doesn't keep his commandments, is a liar, and the truth isn't in him. But whoever keeps his word, God's love has most certainly been perfected in him. This is how we know that we are in him: he who says he remains in him ought himself also to walk just like he walked.*

*1John 2:3-6 WEB*

For more on this subject, please refer back to chapter 20 "Spirit and Flesh in Conflict." This topic is also addressed in chapter 30, *"Set Free from Sin,"* in the book *"Foundations for Eternal Life."*

## No Consequences

God's abundant grace leads some people to think that there will be no consequences for sin in their life. God will forgive them, they think, and that will be the end of it.

Let us remember that when we sin we turn away from God, and when we repent we turn toward God. Intentional sin shows a lack of love for God, and hurts our relationship with God. If we intentionally turn away from God today, why would we expect to have a good relationship with God in the future? Why would we even expect to be able to genuinely repent in the future if we don't embrace a repentant attitude today?

Also, even if there is genuine repentance and forgiveness by God in the future, that does not mean that there won't be serious consequences for sin. Consider what Paul wrote:

*Don't be deceived. God is not mocked, for whatever a man sows, that he will also reap. For he who sows to his own flesh will from the flesh reap corruption. But he who sows to the Spirit will from the Spirit reap eternal life.*

*Galatians 6:7-8 WEB*

Consider the consequences that resulted from David's sins against Bathsheba and her husband Uriah (2 Samuel 11 and

12). Yes, David repented and God did forgive those sins, but consider the consequences that still followed:

- The sword would never depart from David's house (2 Samuel 12:10).

- God said: ***"I will take your wives and give them to one who is close to you, and he will sleep with your wives in broad daylight"*** (2 Samuel 12:11 NIV). This was fulfilled in 2 Samuel 16:20-22 when David's son Absalom led a rebellion against David.

- David's son born to Bathsheba died (2 Samuel 12:14-18).

- Uriah, a righteous man, was still dead.

Further, scripture gives us this sobering warning:

> *If we deliberately keep on sinning after we have received the knowledge of the truth, no sacrifice for sins is left, but only a fearful expectation of judgment and of raging fire that will consume the enemies of God. Anyone who rejected the law of Moses died without mercy on the testimony of two or three witnesses. How much more severely do you think someone deserves to be punished who has trampled the Son of God underfoot, who has treated as an unholy thing the blood of the covenant that sanctified them, and who has insulted the Spirit of grace?* Hebrews 10:26-29 NIV

However, for those who embrace repentance we have this promise:

> *If we confess our sins, he is faithful and just to forgive us our sins and to cleanse us from all unrighteousness.* 1John 1:9 ESV

## For Further Reflection

- Do your views about sin agree with God's views?

\*\*\*\*\*\*\*\*\*\*\*\*

# Chapter 26
# Salvation

*For by grace you have been saved through faith. And this is not your own doing; it is the gift of God, not a result of works, so that no one may boast. For we are his workmanship, created in Christ Jesus for good works, which God prepared beforehand, that we should walk in them.*     *Ephesians 2:8-10 ESV*

---

Salvation is a primary reason we follow Jesus, with benefits both in this life and in the life to come. Many aspects of salvation have already been discussed in the book *"Foundations for Eternal Life,"* with chapter 50 *"Salvation"* providing a brief summary of this topic. Now let's consider some common misunderstandings associated with salvation.

## Good Works

Believers should be doing good works; good works are simply part of following Jesus. As Paul wrote, we are **created in Christ Jesus for good works** (Ephesians 2:10 above).

However, we are saved **by grace**, **through faith**, **not by works** (Ephesians 2:8-9 above). As has often been said, *we do good works because we are saved, not to become saved.*

However, many people do not understand this, and view good works as necessary to becoming saved. Many try to earn salvation by doing good works rather than by trusting in Jesus. Consider these verses:

> *"Not everyone who says to me, 'Lord, Lord,' will enter into the Kingdom of Heaven; but he who does the will of my Father who is in heaven. Many will tell me in that day, 'Lord, Lord, didn't we prophesy in your name, in your name cast out demons, and in your name do many*

*mighty works?' Then I will tell them, 'I never knew you. Depart from me, you who work iniquity.'"*

Even prophesying, casting out demons, and doing *many mighty works*, all done in Jesus' name, will not gain entry into the Kingdom of Heaven. What is *"the will of my Father"* that Jesus spoke of, that will enable entry to the Kingdom of Heaven? Consider Jesus' answer elsewhere in scripture:

> *Then they asked him, "What must we do to do the works God requires?"*
>
> *Jesus answered, "The work of God is this: to believe in the one he has sent."*          John 6:28-29 NIV

John summarizes it this way:

> *This is his commandment, that we should believe in the name of his Son, Jesus Christ, and love one another, even as he commanded.*          1John 3:23 WEB

Keep in mind that the word usually translated *"believe"* in the New Testament (Greek: *pisteuo*) includes a sense of *having faith and trust* in something; not just mentally agreeing that something is true. It is by placing our faith and trust in Jesus that we are saved, not by doing good works to somehow earn God's approval, and not by simple mental agreement that Jesus existed and is the Son of God. Even the demons know that much (Mark 3:11, James 2:19), but that mental knowledge does not save them.

## Self-Denial

Self-denial is another way we can be deceived into a works salvation perspective.

First, let's acknowledge that self-denial is an important part of following Jesus. Jesus himself said:

> *"If anyone desires to come after me, let him deny*

*Building on Foundations for Eternal Life*          197

*himself, take up his cross, and follow me. For whoever desires to save his life will lose it, but whoever will lose his life for my sake, the same will save it."*

*Luke 9:23-24 WEB*

And Paul wrote:

*Do you not know that in a race all the runners run, but only one receives the prize? So run that you may obtain it. Every athlete exercises self-control in all things. They do it to receive a perishable wreath, but we an imperishable. So I do not run aimlessly; I do not box as one beating the air. But I discipline my body and keep it under control, lest after preaching to others I myself should be disqualified.*  1Corinthians 9:24-27 ESV

However, like so many spiritual things, this issue involves proper balance and perspective. In Isaiah's time God rebuked people for fasting while living unrighteously:

*"Is such the fast that I choose, a day for a person to humble himself? Is it to bow down his head like a reed, and to spread sackcloth and ashes under him? Will you call this a fast, and a day acceptable to the LORD? Is not this the fast that I choose: to loose the bonds of wickedness, to undo the straps of the yoke, to let the oppressed go free, and to break every yoke? Is it not to share your bread with the hungry and bring the homeless poor into your house; when you see the naked, to cover him, and not to hide yourself from your own flesh?"*  Isaiah 58:5-7 ESV

Paul takes it one step further, by saying anything not done in love profits nothing:

*If I give away all my goods to feed the poor, and if I give my body to be burned, but don't have love, it profits me nothing.*  1Corinthians 13:3 WEB

Paul also addresses how restrictive rules can merely be false religion:

*If you died with Christ from the elements of the world, why, as though living in the world, do you subject yourselves to ordinances, "Don't handle, nor taste, nor touch" (all of which perish with use), according to the precepts and doctrines of men? Which things indeed appear like wisdom in self-imposed worship, and humility, and severity to the body; but aren't of any value against the indulgence of the flesh.*

*Colossians 2:20-23 WEB*

*The Spirit clearly says that in later times some will abandon the faith and follow deceiving spirits and things taught by demons. Such teachings come through hypocritical liars, whose consciences have been seared as with a hot iron. They forbid people to marry and order them to abstain from certain foods, which God created to be received with thanksgiving by those who believe and who know the truth. For everything God created is good, and nothing is to be rejected if it is received with thanksgiving, because it is consecrated by the word of God and prayer.*

*1 Timothy 4:1-5 NIV*

So, it is important to keep self-denial in proper perspective. Jesus called people to deny themselves in order to truly follow him. We cannot truly follow Jesus without turning away from worldly and selfish activities. As John wrote:

*Do not love the world or the things in the world. If anyone loves the world, the love of the Father is not in him. For all that is in the world—the desires of the flesh and the desires of the eyes and pride of life—is not from the Father but is from the world. And the world is passing away along with its desires, but whoever does the will of God abides forever.*

*1 John 2:15-17 ESV*

And as Paul said:

*Whatever you do, in word or in deed, do all in the name of the Lord Jesus, giving thanks to God the Father, through him.*

*Colossians 3:17 WEB*

# Legalism

Many people today, and throughout history, appear to fall into the trap of legalism. They depend on following rules to be right with God, rather than truly loving God and loving others.

Consider Paul's own relationship with the law before his salvation:

> *If any other man thinks that he has confidence in the flesh, I yet more: circumcised the eighth day, of the stock of Israel, of the tribe of Benjamin, a Hebrew of Hebrews; concerning the law, a Pharisee; concerning zeal, persecuting the assembly; concerning the righteousness which is in the law, found blameless.*
>
> *Philippians 3:4-6 WEB*

Paul had been a *"Pharisee"* who was *"found blameless."* However, meeting Jesus changed all that. He no longer looked to legalism to make him righteous, but to Christ:

> *...not having a righteousness of my own, that which is of the law, but that which is through faith in Christ, the righteousness which is from God by faith; that I may know him, and the power of his resurrection, and the fellowship of his sufferings, becoming conformed to his death; if by any means I may attain to the resurrection from the dead.*
> *Philippians 3:9-11 WEB*

Further, Paul teaches us that those who try to be righteous by following laws may get dragged into sin by doing so:

> *What shall we say, then? Is the law sinful? Certainly not! Nevertheless, I would not have known what sin was had it not been for the law. For I would not have known what coveting really was if the law had not said, "You shall not covet." But sin, seizing the opportunity afforded by the commandment, produced in me every kind of coveting. For apart from the law, sin was dead. Once I was alive apart from the law; but when the*

*commandment came, sin sprang to life and I died. I found that the very commandment that was intended to bring life actually brought death. For sin, seizing the opportunity afforded by the commandment, deceived me, and through the commandment put me to death.*

*Romans 7:7-11 NIV*

Almost the entire letter that Paul wrote to the believers in Galatia deals with the need to trust in Jesus, to have faith in Jesus, rather than trying to become righteous through following various laws. Here are a few key verses:

*"For I, through the law, died to the law, that I might live to God. I have been crucified with Christ, and it is no longer I that live, but Christ lives in me. That life which I now live in the flesh, I live by faith in the Son of God, who loved me, and gave himself up for me. I don't reject the grace of God. For if righteousness is through the law, then Christ died for nothing!"*

*Galatians 2:19-21 WEB*

*Now before faith came, we were held captive under the law, imprisoned until the coming faith would be revealed. So then, the law was our guardian until Christ came, in order that we might be justified by faith. But now that faith has come, we are no longer under a guardian, for in Christ Jesus you are all sons of God, through faith.*

*Galatians 3:23-26 ESV*

*You are alienated from Christ, you who desire to be justified by the law. You have fallen away from grace.*

*Galatians 5:4 WEB*

The subject of legalism was also dealt with in what has become known as the *Jerusalem Council* (or *Council of Jerusalem*). In Acts 15, some people had come to Antioch and were teaching that the Gentiles had to be circumcised and obey the Law of Moses in order to be saved. This led to the apostles and elders gathering in Jerusalem to resolve the matter. Some Pharisees, who had become believers, said:

*"It is necessary to circumcise them, and to command them to keep the law of Moses."*                    Acts 15:5 WEB

Peter responded, in part:

*"Now therefore why do you tempt God, that you should put a yoke on the neck of the disciples which neither our fathers nor we were able to bear? But we believe that we are saved through the grace of the Lord Jesus, just as they are."*                    Acts 15:10-11 WEB

After additional discussion, the council concluded with a letter to be distributed to the Gentile believers:

*"The brothers, both the apostles and the elders, to the brothers who are of the Gentiles in Antioch and Syria and Cilicia, greetings. Since we have heard that some persons have gone out from us and troubled you with words, unsettling your minds, although we gave them no instructions, it has seemed good to us, having come to one accord, to choose men and send them to you with our beloved Barnabas and Paul, men who have risked their lives for the name of our Lord Jesus Christ. We have therefore sent Judas and Silas, who themselves will tell you the same things by word of mouth. For it has seemed good to the Holy Spirit and to us to lay on you no greater burden than these requirements: that you abstain from what has been sacrificed to idols, and from blood, and from what has been strangled, and from sexual immorality. If you keep yourselves from these, you will do well. Farewell."*                    Acts 15:23-29 ESV

The tendency to trust in rules and laws for salvation is an ongoing problem we all face. Let's keep in mind that salvation is about turning to God (repentance) and having faith in Jesus, not about keeping various laws. Stated somewhat differently, salvation involves coming to Jesus, trusting in Jesus, and following Jesus; not focusing on keeping various rules and regulations.

However, let us not go to the other extreme and pretend that morality doesn't matter. Part of coming to Jesus does involve turning from sin to God, and God's grace toward us includes deliverance from the power of sin. As Paul wrote:

*For sin will not have dominion over you. For you are not under law, but under grace.*

*What then? Shall we sin, because we are not under law, but under grace? May it never be!* Romans 6:14-15 WEB

## Church Membership

It is important to have good relationships with other believers. However, we should not confuse salvation with membership in an organized church, or with having good relationships with religious people, or with being born into a religious family. Many people seem to think that their salvation is assured by being a member of a church, or by being around religious people. Rather, salvation is assured through our own repentance toward God and faith in our Lord Jesus. This was Paul's message:

*I did not shrink from declaring to you anything that was profitable, and teaching you in public and from house to house, testifying both to Jews and to Greeks of repentance toward God and of faith in our Lord Jesus Christ.* Acts 20:20-21 ESV

Have you turned to God in repentance? Do you have faith in our Lord Jesus?

Let's look at faith and repentance in more detail.

## Faith and Repentance

The importance of faith and repentance has already been discussed in "Foundations for Eternal Life," in chapter 16 "What Must I Do to Be Saved." Repentance was said to speak of "a change in thinking; a change from unbelief to belief; a change in the direction of your life. Acknowledge that you have sinned, and turn to God for forgiveness of sins and for deliverance from the power of sin. Choose to follow God rather than continuing to follow after sinful desires." Repentance involves turning from my selfish way of living to God's way.

Now let's consider what *repentance* is **not**.

Repentance is not regret or sorrow. Paul mentioned two kinds of sorrow, Godly sorrow and worldly sorrow:

> ***Godly sorrow brings repentance that leads to salvation and leaves no regret, but worldly sorrow brings death.***
> *2Corinthians 7:10 NIV*

So, we see that sorrow can lead to repentance and salvation if it is Godly sorrow. However, worldly sorrow **brings death**.

What is the difference between worldly sorrow and Godly sorrow? Paul doesn't directly clarify that, but it seems to me that worldly sorrow typically focuses on one's own pain or loss, without seeking God, without a willingness to change and do things God's way. Godly sorrow takes us toward God, acknowledges that God's way is right, and, if we have sinned, results in a change of direction. Without a change in thinking and direction, there is no repentance.

Likewise, repentance is not merely feeling bad about your life or about what you have done. It is not merely feeling convicted about sin, though that should lead us to repent.

Repentance is not being afraid of the consequences of sin. It is not being afraid of God's judgment, though fear of God's judgment should also lead us to repent.

Repentance is not afflicting ourselves through fasting or harsh treatment of our bodies. It's not mentally beating ourselves up over our failures.

Repentance is not turning away from just one or two sins, while still holding onto other sins.

Repentance is not doing religious activities, while continuing to embrace sin. It is not reading the Bible, praying to God, or crying before God, though these are all generally good things to do.

Repentance involves acknowledging that God's ways are right, and turning toward God, and turning away from sin. When we sin, we turn away from God. When we repent, we turn toward God. Consider Paul's words:

> *"Therefore, O King Agrippa, I was not disobedient to the heavenly vision, but declared first to those in Damascus, then in Jerusalem and throughout all the region of Judea, and also to the Gentiles, that they should repent and turn to God, performing deeds in keeping with their repentance."* Acts 26:19-20 ESV

Now let's consider faith, and some misunderstandings about faith. Faith has already been discussed some in *"Foundations for Eternal Life"* in chapter 35 *"Faith,"* and in this book in chapter 4 *"Wisdom and Faith."*

Faith is belief and confidence in what is not seen, or in what we hope for in the future. As scripture says:

> *Now faith is confidence in what we hope for and assurance about what we do not see.* Hebrews 11:1 NIV

In chapter 4, we saw that faith involves *knowing*, *understanding*, and *acting* on spiritual truth, similar to how wisdom involves *knowing*, *understanding*, and *acting* on truth in general.

Saving faith also involves trust in God, which leads people to do things God's way. This is shown throughout Hebrews chapter 11, which lists various people of faith along with what they did *"by faith."* Here are just a couple examples:

> *By faith Noah, being warned by God concerning events as yet unseen, in reverent fear constructed an ark for the saving of his household. By this he condemned the*

*world and became an heir of the righteousness that comes by faith.*

*By faith Abraham obeyed when he was called to go out to a place that he was to receive as an inheritance. And he went out, not knowing where he was going.*

*Hebrews 11:7-8 ESV*

Saving faith is not merely mental agreement with religious doctrines. Nor is it merely good feelings associated with religious things. Saving faith involves coming to Jesus, trusting in Jesus, and following Jesus. Saving faith affects how we live. Consider what James wrote:

*What good is it, my brothers, if someone says he has faith but does not have works? Can that faith save him? If a brother or sister is poorly clothed and lacking in daily food, and one of you says to them, "Go in peace, be warmed and filled," without giving them the things needed for the body, what good is that? So also faith by itself, if it does not have works, is dead.*

*But someone will say, "You have faith and I have works." Show me your faith apart from your works, and I will show you my faith by my works. You believe that God is one; you do well. Even the demons believe—and shudder! Do you want to be shown, you foolish person, that faith apart from works is useless? Was not Abraham our father justified by works when he offered up his son Isaac on the altar? You see that faith was active along with his works, and faith was completed by his works; and the Scripture was fulfilled that says, "Abraham believed God, and it was counted to him as righteousness"—and he was called a friend of God. You see that a person is justified by works and not by faith alone. And in the same way was not also Rahab the prostitute justified by works when she received the messengers and sent them out by another way? For as the body apart from the spirit is dead, so also faith apart*

**from works is dead.**                         *James 2:14-26 ESV*

Faith and repentance go together. They can be considered to be what some call "two sides of the same coin." True repentance toward God only happens in the context of true faith, and true faith only exists when there is true repentance.

What about you? Have you turned to God in repentance? Do you have faith in our Lord Jesus? If not, why not? Do not delay any longer. If you don't see your need for repentance, ask God to make it clear to you, and be open to it when he does. Again, do not delay, for, as Paul wrote:

> *I tell you, now is the time of God's favor, now is the day of salvation.*                         *2Corinthians 6:2 NIV*

For those of us who have already turned to God in repentance and already have faith in Jesus, is there new or ongoing sin we need to confess and repent of today?

> *If we confess our sins, he is faithful and just to forgive us our sins and to cleanse us from all unrighteousness.*
> *1John 1:9 ESV*

Let us not delay to confess our sins and get right with God.

## Not for All

Some people promote the idea that salvation is only available to relatively few people to whom God gives special grace. Please consider these many verses which indicate that salvation is available to *all* people:

> *"Come to me, all you who labor and are heavily burdened, and I will give you rest. Take my yoke upon you, and learn from me, for I am gentle and humble in heart; and you will find rest for your souls. For my yoke is easy, and my burden is light."*                         *Matthew 11:28-30 WEB*

> *And an angel of the Lord appeared to them, and the glory of the Lord shone around them, and they were filled with great fear. And the angel said to them, "Fear*

*not, for behold, I bring you good news of great joy that will be for all the people."* Luke 2:9-10 ESV

*There was a man sent from God, whose name was John. He came as a witness, to bear witness about the light, that all might believe through him.* John 1:6-7 ESV

*The true light, which gives light to everyone, was coming into the world. He was in the world, and the world was made through him, yet the world did not know him. He came to his own, and his own people did not receive him. But to all who did receive him, who believed in his name, he gave the right to become children of God, who were born, not of blood nor of the will of the flesh nor of the will of man, but of God.* John 1:9-13 ESV

*From his fullness we all received grace upon grace.* John 1:16 WEB

*For God so loved the world, that he gave his one and only Son, that whoever believes in him should not perish, but have eternal life. For God didn't send his Son into the world to judge the world, but that the world should be saved through him.* John 3:16-17 WEB

*"And I, if I am lifted up from the earth, will draw all people to myself."* John 12:32 WEB

*"And everyone who calls on the name of the Lord will be saved."* Acts 2:21 NIV

*So Peter opened his mouth and said: "Truly I understand that God shows no partiality, but in every nation anyone who fears him and does what is right is acceptable to him."* Acts 10:34-35 ESV

*"In the past God overlooked such ignorance, but now he commands all people everywhere to repent. For he has set a day when he will judge the world with justice by the man he has appointed. He has given proof of this to*

*everyone by raising him from the dead."* Acts 17:30-31 NIV

*For I am not ashamed of the gospel, because it is the power of God that brings salvation to everyone who believes: first to the Jew, then to the Gentile.*
Romans 1:16 NIV

*There will be tribulation and distress for every human being who does evil, the Jew first and also the Greek, but glory and honor and peace for everyone who does good, the Jew first and also the Greek. For God shows no partiality.*
Romans 2:9-11 ESV

*But now the righteousness of God has been manifested apart from the law, although the Law and the Prophets bear witness to it—the righteousness of God through faith in Jesus Christ for all who believe. For there is no distinction: for all have sinned and fall short of the glory of God...*
Romans 3:21-23 ESV

*Consequently, just as one trespass resulted in condemnation for all people, so also one righteous act resulted in justification and life for all people.*
Romans 5:18 NIV

*For the Scripture says, "Everyone who believes in him will not be put to shame." For there is no distinction between Jew and Greek; for the same Lord is Lord of all, bestowing his riches on all who call on him. For "everyone who calls on the name of the Lord will be saved."*
Romans 10:11-13 ESV

*For God has bound everyone over to disobedience so that he may have mercy on them all.*
Romans 11:32 NIV

*For Christ's love compels us, because we are convinced that one died for all, and therefore all died. And he died for all, that those who live should no longer live for themselves but for him who died for them and was raised again.*
2Corinthians 5:14-15 NIV

*First of all, then, I urge that supplications, prayers, intercessions, and thanksgivings be made for all people, for kings and all who are in high positions, that we may lead a peaceful and quiet life, godly and dignified in every way. This is good, and it is pleasing in the sight of God our Savior, who desires all people to be saved and to come to the knowledge of the truth. For there is one God, and there is one mediator between God and men, the man Christ Jesus, who gave himself as a ransom for all, which is the testimony given at the proper time.*

*1Timothy 2:1-6 ESV*

*For to this end we both labor and suffer reproach, because we have set our trust in the living God, who is the Savior of all men, especially of those who believe.*

*1Timothy_4:10 WEB*

*For the grace of God has appeared that offers salvation to all people.* *Titus 2:11 NIV*

*The Lord is not slow concerning his promise, as some count slowness; but is patient with us, not wishing that any should perish, but that all should come to repentance.* *2Peter 3:9 WEB*

*And he is the atoning sacrifice for our sins, and not for ours only, but also for the whole world.* *1John 2:2 WEB*

## For Further Reflection

- Have you been trusting some in your own self-righteousness, rather than in Jesus?

- Is more self-denial needed in your life? If so, ask God for help in this area; don't try to do it in your own strength.

- Have you believed, in some way, that salvation through faith in Jesus is not intended for all people?

\*\*\*\*\*\*\*\*\*\*\*\*

# Chapter 27
# Self

*He said to all, "If anyone desires to come after me, let him deny himself, take up his cross, and follow me. For whoever desires to save his life will lose it, but whoever will lose his life for my sake, the same will save it. For what does it profit a man if he gains the whole world, and loses or forfeits his own self?"*

Luke 9:23-25 WEB

---

An unhealthy focus on self is natural for unbelievers, and is far-too-common among believers. In this chapter we will explore various aspects of that problem.

## Selfishness

It is natural for us to care more about ourselves than others. The command to *"Love your neighbor as yourself"* (Leviticus 19:18, Matthew 22:39, Mark 12:31, Luke 10:27) calls us to care as much for others as we care for ourselves. Paul wrote that love *"is not self-seeking"* (1 Corinthians 13:5 NIV).

What is the opposite of love? *"Hate"* might be a common answer. However, I think that *selfishness* is also the opposite of love. Genuine *agape love* results in us serving others. Selfishness results in us serving only ourselves, or serving others only when we ourselves get something for doing so.

Our old sinful nature generally wants everyone else to serve us. Jesus calls us to an opposite standard of us serving all:

*He came to Capernaum, and when he was in the house he asked them, "What were you arguing among yourselves on the way?"*

*But they were silent, for they had disputed one with another on the way about who was the greatest.*

*He sat down, and called the twelve; and he said to them, "If any man wants to be first, he shall be last of all, and servant of all."*                    *Mark 9:33-35 WEB*

*Jesus called them together and said, "You know that those who are regarded as rulers of the Gentiles lord it over them, and their high officials exercise authority over them. Not so with you. Instead, whoever wants to become great among you must be your servant, and whoever wants to be first must be slave of all. For even the Son of Man did not come to be served, but to serve, and to give his life as a ransom for many."*
*Mark 10:42-45 NIV*

Paul gives us this instruction:

*Do nothing from selfish ambition or conceit, but in humility count others more significant than yourselves. Let each of you look not only to his own interests, but also to the interests of others.*        *Philippians 2:3-4 ESV*

Paul also gives us this warning:

*But understand this, that in the last days there will come times of difficulty. For people will be lovers of self...*
*2Timothy 3:1-2 ESV*

## Pride or Humility?

Many problems and deceptions associated with "self" are related to the issue of *pride*. Pride is thought by many to be the root of all sins. *Humility* is often considered to be the opposite of pride. Pride and humility have already been discussed some in the book *"Foundations for Eternal Life"* in chapter 45 *"Pride."*

Paul shows us that Jesus himself is the ultimate example of humility, and he challenges us to have similar humility:

*If there is therefore any exhortation in Christ, if any consolation of love, if any fellowship of the Spirit, if any tender mercies and compassion, make my joy full, by being like-minded, having the same love, being of one accord, of one mind; doing nothing through rivalry or through conceit, but in humility, each counting others better than himself; each of you not just looking to his own things, but each of you also to the things of others. Have this in your mind, which was also in Christ Jesus, who, existing in the form of God, didn't consider equality with God a thing to be grasped, but emptied himself, taking the form of a servant, being made in the likeness of men. And being found in human form, he humbled himself, becoming obedient to death, yes, the death of the cross.*      *Philippians 2:1-8 WEB*

I am troubled by Paul using Jesus as our example of what our humility should be like: humbling ourselves to the point of willing to be crucified on a cross for the benefit of others. I clearly have room to grow in this area. What about you?

Consider again this passage of scripture:

*He came to Capernaum, and when he was in the house he asked them, "What were you arguing among yourselves on the way?"*

*But they were silent, for they had disputed one with another on the way about who was the greatest.*

*He sat down, and called the twelve; and he said to them, "If any man wants to be first, he shall be last of all, and servant of all."*      *Mark 9:33-35 WEB*

Again, I am troubled regarding humility. With that standard, I'm not so sure I want to be *great* in Jesus' eyes. Again, it looks like I have room to grow.

Consider another verse:

*Clothe yourselves, all of you, with humility toward one another, for "God opposes the proud but gives grace to the humble."*      *1Peter 5:5 ESV*

While scripture often condemns pride, I don't see scripture telling us to rid ourselves of pride. Rather, I see scripture instructing us to pursue humility. It appears that we cannot overcome pride by trying to not be proud. Rather, we must pursue humility, with God's help, and pride will then fall away as we become more humble. It is apparently not possible to overcome pride without becoming humble, and just focusing on overcoming pride doesn't work. Some may say this is just semantics, but I don't think so. Focusing our energies on doing something positive is usually more effective than focusing on stopping something that is negative.

Also, focusing on not being proud may simply put us in a similar situation as Paul's predicament with trying to not covet, as he discussed in Romans 7:7-24. As Paul writes in Romans 8, we can only truly overcome sin with the help of the Holy Spirit living in us.

There are lots of verses in scripture that deal with pride and humility. A thorough treatment of this subject would likely require a whole book, and such books have already been written. If you want to go deeper on this topic, and I encourage you to do so, I recommend the book *"Humility"* by Andrew Murray (ebook versions are available for free on the Internet).

## Individualism

Western culture tends to place a high value on the individual, and individual freedom. While there is some value in this, there can also be problems associated with it. Those who live in that culture should at least be aware that there are other viewpoints that should be considered. Of course, my main concern is to understand the viewpoint of scripture.

Solomon spoke of there being strength in more than one:

*Two are better than one, because they have a good*

*reward for their labor. For if they fall, the one will lift up his fellow; but woe to him who is alone when he falls, and doesn't have another to lift him up. Again, if two lie together, then they have warmth; but how can one keep warm alone? If a man prevails against one who is alone, two shall withstand him; and a threefold cord is not quickly broken.* Ecclesiastes 4:9-12 WEB

Jesus prayed for unity among his followers, not individualism:

*I am no more in the world, but these are in the world, and I am coming to you. Holy Father, keep them through your name which you have given me, that they may be one, even as we are.* John 17:11 WEB

*Not for these only do I pray, but for those also who will believe in me through their word, that they may all be one; even as you, Father, are in me, and I in you, that they also may be one in us; that the world may believe that you sent me. The glory which you have given me, I have given to them; that they may be one, even as we are one; I in them, and you in me, that they may be perfected into one; that the world may know that you sent me, and loved them, even as you loved me.* John 17:20-23 WEB

Throughout Paul's letters in the New Testament, he often returns to the theme of one body with many members. He emphasizes the need believers have for one another, and that all believers are members of Christ's one body:

*The cup of blessing which we bless, isn't it a sharing of the blood of Christ? The bread which we break, isn't it a sharing of the body of Christ? Because there is one loaf of bread, we, who are many, are one body; for we all partake of the one loaf of bread.* 1Corinthians 10:16-17 WEB

*For I say, through the grace that was given me, to every*

*man who is among you, not to think of himself more highly than he ought to think; but to think reasonably, as God has apportioned to each person a measure of faith. For even as we have many members in one body, and all the members don't have the same function, so we, who are many, are one body in Christ, and individually members of one another. Having gifts differing according to the grace that was given to us...*

*Romans 12:3-6 WEB*

*For as the body is one, and has many members, and all the members of the body, being many, are one body; so also is Christ. For in one Spirit we were all baptized into one body, whether Jews or Greeks, whether bond or free; and were all given to drink into one Spirit. For the body is not one member, but many. If the foot would say, "Because I'm not the hand, I'm not part of the body," it is not therefore not part of the body. If the ear would say, "Because I'm not the eye, I'm not part of the body," it's not therefore not part of the body. If the whole body were an eye, where would the hearing be? If the whole were hearing, where would the smelling be? But now God has set the members, each one of them, in the body, just as he desired. If they were all one member, where would the body be? But now they are many members, but one body. The eye can't tell the hand, "I have no need for you," or again the head to the feet, "I have no need for you." No, much rather, those members of the body which seem to be weaker are necessary. Those parts of the body which we think to be less honorable, on those we bestow more abundant honor; and our unpresentable parts have more abundant propriety; whereas our presentable parts have no such need. But God composed the body together, giving more abundant honor to the inferior part, that there should be no division in the body, but that the members should have the same care for one another.*

*Building on Foundations for Eternal Life*

*When one member suffers, all the members suffer with it. Or when one member is honored, all the members rejoice with it.*

*Now you are the body of Christ, and members individually.*
*1Corinthians 12:12-27 WEB*

*Therefore, putting away falsehood, speak truth each one with his neighbor. For we are members of one another.*
*Ephesians 4:25 WEB*

*And let the peace of God rule in your hearts, to which also you were called in one body; and be thankful.*
*Colossians 3:15 WEB*

## Greed / Money

Greed is simply a wrong focus on wanting more money or wealth. Scripture strongly condemns greed repeatedly. Here are some verses to consider:

*"Don't lay up treasures for yourselves on the earth, where moth and rust consume, and where thieves break through and steal; but lay up for yourselves treasures in heaven, where neither moth nor rust consume, and where thieves don't break through and steal; for where your treasure is, there your heart will be also."*
*Matthew 6:19-21 WEB*

*"No one can serve two masters, for either he will hate the one and love the other, or he will be devoted to the one and despise the other. You cannot serve God and money."*
*Matthew 6:24 ESV*

*"Watch out! Be on your guard against all kinds of greed; life does not consist in an abundance of possessions."*
*Luke 12:15 NIV*

*But among you there must not be even a hint of sexual immorality, or of any kind of impurity, or of greed, because these are improper for God's holy people.*
*Ephesians 5:3 NIV*

*For of this you can be sure: No immoral, impure or greedy person—such a person is an idolater—has any inheritance in the kingdom of Christ and of God. Let no one deceive you with empty words, for because of such things God's wrath comes on those who are disobedient.*
                                                              *Ephesians 5:5-6 NIV*

*Put to death, therefore, whatever belongs to your earthly nature: sexual immorality, impurity, lust, evil desires and greed, which is idolatry.*          *Colossians 3:5 NIV*

*But godliness with contentment is great gain. For we brought nothing into the world, and we certainly can't carry anything out. But having food and clothing, we will be content with that. But those who are determined to be rich fall into a temptation and a snare and many foolish and harmful lusts, such as drown men in ruin and destruction. For the love of money is a root of all kinds of evil. Some have been led astray from the faith in their greed, and have pierced themselves through with many sorrows.*                  *1Timothy 6:6-10 WEB*

*But know this, that in the last days, grievous times will come. For men will be lovers of self, lovers of money...*
                                                              *2Timothy 3:1-2 WEB*

*Be free from the love of money, content with such things as you have, for he has said, "I will in no way leave you, neither will I in any way forsake you."*   *Hebrews 13:5 WEB*

A scriptural perspective on money and prosperity will be discussed in more detail in chapter 28 "Prosperity."

## Fear

Fear has to do with self-preservation. We typically become afraid when we think our well-being is threatened in some way. Being afraid of things we shouldn't be afraid of is a form of deception.

Fear of people may lead us into sin, while fear of God keeps us from sin.  Consider these verses:

> *The fear of man proves to be a snare, but whoever puts his trust in Yahweh is kept safe.*  Proverbs 29:25 WEB

> *By mercy and truth iniquity is atoned for.  By the fear of Yahweh men depart from evil.*  Proverbs 16:6 WEB

> *The fear of Yahweh is a fountain of life, turning people from the snares of death.*  Proverbs 14:27 WEB

Here are some examples of *fear of people* leading to problems:

> *The men of the place asked him about his wife. He said, "She is my sister," for he was afraid to say, "My wife," lest, he thought, "the men of the place might kill me for Rebekah, because she is beautiful to look at." ... Abimelech said, "What is this you have done to us? One of the people might easily have lain with your wife, and you would have brought guilt on us!" Genesis 26:7, 10 WEB*

> *Joshua son of Nun and Caleb son of Jephunneh, who were among those who had explored the land, tore their clothes and said to the entire Israelite assembly, "The land we passed through and explored is exceedingly good.  If the LORD is pleased with us, he will lead us into that land, a land flowing with milk and honey, and will give it to us.  Only do not rebel against the LORD. And do not be afraid of the people of the land, because we will devour them.  Their protection is gone, but the LORD is with us.  Do not be afraid of them."*

> *But the whole assembly talked about stoning them.*
> Numbers 14:6-10 NIV

> *Saul said to Samuel, "I have sinned; for I have transgressed the commandment of Yahweh, and your words, because I feared the people, and obeyed their voice."*  1Samuel 15:24 WEB

> *David left his things with the keeper of supplies, ran to*

*the battle lines and asked his brothers how they were. As he was talking with them, Goliath, the Philistine champion from Gath, stepped out from his lines and shouted his usual defiance, and David heard it. Whenever the Israelites saw the man, they all fled from him in great fear.*                    1Samuel 17:22-24 NIV

*There was much murmuring among the multitudes concerning him. Some said, "He is a good man." Others said, "Not so, but he leads the multitude astray." Yet no one spoke openly of him for fear of the Jews.*
                                                    John 7:12-13 WEB

Nehemiah provides a good example of someone who rightly discerned deception associated with fear:

*And I understood and saw that God had not sent him, but he had pronounced the prophecy against me because Tobiah and Sanballat had hired him. For this purpose he was hired, that I should be afraid and act in this way and sin, and so they could give me a bad name in order to taunt me.*                         Nehemiah 6:12-13 ESV

Scripture often encourages us to not fear people. Consider these verses:

*In God, whose word I praise, in God I trust; I shall not be afraid. What can flesh do to me?*          Psalms 56:4 ESV

*I have put my trust in God. I will not be afraid. What can man do to me?*                                Psalms 56:11 WEB

*Yahweh is on my side. I will not be afraid. What can man do to me?*                                     Psalms 118:6 WEB

*"Do not be afraid of those who kill the body but cannot kill the soul. Rather, be afraid of the One who can destroy both soul and body in hell."*     Matthew_10:28 NIV

*"I tell you, my friends, do not be afraid of those who kill the body and after that can do no more. But I will show you whom you should fear: Fear him who, after your*

*body has been killed, has authority to throw you into hell. Yes, I tell you, fear him."* Luke_12:4-5 NIV

*Whatever happens, conduct yourselves in a manner worthy of the gospel of Christ. Then, whether I come and see you or only hear about you in my absence, I will know that you stand firm in the one Spirit, striving together as one for the faith of the gospel without being frightened in any way by those who oppose you. This is a sign to them that they will be destroyed, but that you will be saved—and that by God.* Philippians 1:27-28 NIV

*So that with good courage we say, "The Lord is my helper. I will not fear. What can man do to me?"* Hebrews 13:6 WEB

*But even if you should suffer for righteousness' sake, you are blessed. "Don't fear what they fear, neither be troubled."* 1Peter 3:14 WEB

On the other hand, scripture often encourages us to fear God. Here are just a few of many such verses:

*Let all the earth fear Yahweh. Let all the inhabitants of the world stand in awe of him.* Psalms 33:8 WEB

*Oh fear Yahweh, you his saints, for there is no lack with those who fear him.* Psalms 34:9 WEB

*The fear of Yahweh is the beginning of knowledge; but the foolish despise wisdom and instruction.* Proverbs 1:7 WEB

*"Do not be afraid of those who kill the body but cannot kill the soul. Rather, be afraid of the One who can destroy both soul and body in hell."* Matthew 10:28 NIV

*Having therefore these promises, beloved, let us cleanse ourselves from all defilement of flesh and spirit, perfecting holiness in the fear of God.* 2Corinthians 7:1 WEB

*Honor all men. Love the brotherhood. Fear God.*

**Honor the king.**                                    1Peter 2:17 WEB

However, scripture also talks about not being afraid of God when we are in right relationship with God. Consider these verses:

*"...to grant to us that we, being delivered out of the hand of our enemies, should serve him without fear, in holiness and righteousness before him all the days of our life."*                    Luke 1:74-75 WEB

*For you didn't receive the spirit of bondage again to fear, but you received the Spirit of adoption, by whom we cry, "Abba! Father!"*                    Romans 8:15 WEB

*For God didn't give us a spirit of fear, but of power, love, and self-control.*                    2Timothy 1:7 WEB

*There is no fear in love. But perfect love drives out fear, because fear has to do with punishment. The one who fears is not made perfect in love.*                    1John 4:18 NIV

Here is a verse that appears to promote the fear of God without being afraid of God:

*All the people perceived the thunderings, the lightnings, the sound of the trumpet, and the mountain smoking. When the people saw it, they trembled, and stayed at a distance. They said to Moses, "Speak with us yourself, and we will listen; but don't let God speak with us, lest we die."*

*Moses said to the people, "Don't be afraid, for God has come to test you, and that his fear may be before you, that you won't sin."*                    Exodus 20:18-20 WEB

## Free Will?

Do people really have free will to decide things for themselves, or is everything that happens predestined to happen? Is our apparent ability to make choices a reality, or just an illusion?

222          *Building on Foundations for Eternal Life*

This is one of those topics about which the truth likely lies in the middle somewhere, as discussed in chapter 14, *"Deception Goes Both Ways."* It appears to me that overly simple or extreme views on this subject are not uncommon.

Unfortunately, this is an issue that many believers seem to divide over. Although this is an important issue, which impacts how we view many areas of faith, I believe it is a secondary issue that we should not divide over. I offer my viewpoint here for your prayerful consideration.

First, let's consider a self-evident truth. If we really do have free will to some degree, our choices are limited by our environment and circumstances. For example, we presently can't choose to live on another planet. We can't choose our parents, or the natural color of our skin (other than to "tan" our skin with sunlight or artificial light). We can't choose whether we are born male or female. We can't choose to stay young forever. Some choices we may make may result in us going to jail or prison, and then our choices will be even more limited.

Now, let's look at what scripture says. Consider the numerous verses in scripture that instruct us how we should live. For example:

> ***This day I call the heavens and the earth as witnesses against you that I have set before you life and death, blessings and curses. Now choose life, so that you and your children may live and that you may love the LORD your God, listen to his voice, and hold fast to him. For the LORD is your life, and he will give you many years in the land he swore to give to your fathers, Abraham, Isaac and Jacob.*** *Deuteronomy 30:19-20 NIV*

It appears to me that verses like this (which instruct us how to live) only make sense if we genuinely have a choice, to some degree at least, whether or not we will choose to do such things.

Consider the story of the vineyard, in Isaiah 5.

*I will sing for the one I love a song about his vineyard: My loved one had a vineyard on a fertile hillside. He dug it up and cleared it of stones and planted it with the choicest vines. He built a watchtower in it and cut out a winepress as well. Then he looked for a crop of good grapes, but it yielded only bad fruit.*

*"Now you dwellers in Jerusalem and people of Judah, judge between me and my vineyard. What more could have been done for my vineyard than I have done for it? When I looked for good grapes, why did it yield only bad? Now I will tell you what I am going to do to my vineyard: I will take away its hedge, and it will be destroyed; I will break down its wall, and it will be trampled. I will make it a wasteland, neither pruned nor cultivated, and briers and thorns will grow there. I will command the clouds not to rain on it."*

*The vineyard of the LORD Almighty is the nation of Israel, and the people of Judah are the vines he delighted in. And he looked for justice, but saw bloodshed; for righteousness, but heard cries of distress.*

*Isaiah 5:1-7 NIV*

Israel, God's *vineyard*, had turned away from God. The LORD asks **"What more could have been done for my vineyard than I have done for it?"** This is a rhetorical question; the obvious answer is "Nothing." God had done everything necessary for their success. The failure was on the part of the people; they used their free will to turn away from God.

If God has predestined absolutely everything (implying that free will does not exist at all, or is just an illusion), then the people's failure to follow God is God's own fault. His question **("What more could have been done... than I have done...?")** makes no sense, unless, of course, God is expecting to be blamed for the people's failure to follow him. However, this passage of scripture clearly finds fault with the people, not God. Without free will, this passage makes no sense.

This brings us to the age-old question of good and evil. Where does evil come from? Is God to blame? As I see it, only people's free will provides an explanation that is consistent with scripture and does not blame God for evil.

Another angle to consider is the issue of spiritual slavery. Paul speaks of unbelievers as being slaves to sin, and believers as being slaves to righteousness. For example:

> *But thanks be to God that, though you used to be slaves to sin, you have come to obey from your heart the pattern of teaching that has now claimed your allegiance. You have been set free from sin and have become slaves to righteousness.* Romans 6:17-18 NIV

Does being a slave in either of these senses mean that we have no free will at all? I note that even slaves with human masters still have some choices they appear to decide themselves, even though slaves generally have fewer choices than people who are not slaves. So, it seems to me that being a slave to sin or to righteousness does not negate the existence of genuine choices or free will, we simply have fewer choices than if we weren't slaves.

History is full of examples of people who, though they were slaves to human masters, used their own free will to escape (or try to escape) from slavery. Similarly, I believe those who are still **slaves to sin** can make a choice to repent and have faith in Jesus and thus become **slaves to righteousness**, and thus be transferred from the realm of darkness to the Kingdom of God (Colossians 1:13-14). This is the good news of the Gospel of Jesus, which is available to all people!

Further, let's consider the purpose of creation. Many have proposed that the main purpose of creation is that God wants deep relationships with many people, simply because **"God** *is Love"* (1John 4:8). He wants there to be genuine love between Himself and lots of people. That is partly why Jesus said the greatest commands are to love God and to love each other (Matthew 22:37-40, Mark 12:29-31). It has been proposed by many, and I agree, that true love is only possible in the context of true free will. Love that is coerced or forced is really not love at all.

It appears to me that God so values love and free will that he rarely will override man's free will. This ultimately is a primary source of evil: man's free will used to rebel against God and do things his own way. However, God does sometimes put limits on the evil he will allow people to do. His judgements with the flood (Genesis 6 to 9), against Sodom and Gomorrah (Genesis 18 to 19), and against his own people of Israel (summarized in 2 Chronicles 36:14-21) are examples of God taking action to limit evil. On an individual level, there is this principle in scripture:

**He who is often rebuked and stiffens his neck will be destroyed suddenly, with no remedy.** *Proverbs 29:1 WEB*

So then, how will you use your free will today? Will you choose to follow Jesus today, and build a love relationship with God, or will you choose to go your own way?

## For Further Reflection

- Has selfishness, pride, individualism, or greed been evident in your life?

- Has fear of people caused you to do something, or caused you to not do something, which you now regret?

- Do you believe you have free will to some degree? Why or why not?

\*\*\*\*\*\*\*\*\*\*\*

# Chapter 28
# Prosperity

*"So do not worry, saying, 'What shall we eat?' or 'What shall we drink?' or 'What shall we wear?' For the pagans run after all these things, and your heavenly Father knows that you need them. But seek first his kingdom and his righteousness, and all these things will be given to you as well."*

*Matthew 6:31-33 NIV*

---

You probably already know: There has been a dispute among believers regarding to what degree we should expect and teach that God blesses believers with "prosperity" in this present life, especially regarding health and material wealth.

Many believers appear to have polar opposite beliefs about this subject, rather than finding middle-ground truth. Some people teach rather extreme positions on this subject, leading many people astray. I hope to find some middle ground here, especially regarding the material-wealth aspect of this subject. Let's see what scripture has to say about this topic.

## Gain Is Godliness

Let's start with a verse that can have significantly different meanings, depending on how it is translated:

*...men of corrupt minds, and destitute of the truth, supposing that gain is godliness: from such withdraw thyself.*

*1Timothy 6:5 KJV*

I quoted the King James Version here because it appears to present a more literal translation than most newer translations. *"Supposing that gain is godliness"* may reveal a belief system that equates having more wealth with having more godliness. Or, perhaps these people simply make getting more material wealth their religion. Many people view having wealth to be evidence of their godliness. Put another way, their wealth is evidence of God's blessing in their life. They may never have thought about trying to be godly in order to get wealth, their wealth simply indicates God's blessing and shows that they are godly people. This belief, of course, implies that poor people are not blessed by God.

Many verses appear to speak against this belief that *"gain is godliness."* Here are a few of them:

> *Better is the little that the righteous has than the abundance of many wicked.*  Psalm 37:16 ESV

> *Better is little, with the fear of Yahweh, than great treasure with trouble. Better is a dinner of herbs, where love is, than a fattened calf with hatred.*
>                                                             Proverbs 15:16-17 WEB

> *"Blessed are you who are poor, for yours is the Kingdom of God."*  Luke 6:20 NIV

> *"But woe to you who are rich, for you have already received your comfort."*  Luke 6:24 NIV

> *Come now, you rich, weep and howl for your miseries that are coming on you. Your riches are corrupted and your garments are moth-eaten. Your gold and your silver are corroded, and their corrosion will be for a testimony against you, and will eat your flesh like fire. You have laid up your treasure in the last days. Behold, the wages of the laborers who mowed your fields, which you have kept back by fraud, cry out, and the cries of those who reaped have entered into the ears of the Lord of Armies. You have lived delicately on the earth, and taken your pleasure. You have nourished your hearts as in a day of slaughter.*  James 5:1-5 WEB

So, we see that people who suppose *that gain is godliness* clearly do not have a scriptural viewpoint. Paul instructs us: *"from such withdraw thyself"* (1 Timothy 6:5 KJV).

# Godliness Is a Means of Gain

Now let's look at another way of translating 1 Timothy 6:5:

> *...people of corrupt minds and destitute of the truth, who suppose that godliness is a means of gain. Withdraw yourself from such.*
>
> 1Timothy 6:5 WEB

With this translation (less literal in my opinion), *people of corrupt mind* think that being godly will lead to *gain*, and the context seems to be about gaining material wealth (see verses 6 to 11). These people think that a righteous life will (or normally should) result in a materially prosperous life.

Does scripture condemn this viewpoint elsewhere? What other verses can we find relating to this subject? There are many Old-Testament verses that seem to clearly support the belief that godliness and prosperity are (or were) often linked in scripture. Consider these verses:

> *It shall happen, if you shall listen diligently to my commandments which I command you today, to love Yahweh your God, and to serve him with all your heart and with all your soul, that I will give the rain for your land in its season, the former rain and the latter rain, that you may gather in your grain, your new wine, and your oil. I will give grass in your fields for your livestock, and you shall eat and be full.*
>
> Deuteronomy 11:13-15 WEB

> *For if you shall diligently keep all these commandments which I command you, to do them, to love Yahweh your God, to walk in all his ways, and to cling to him, then Yahweh will drive out all these nations from before you, and you shall dispossess nations greater and mightier than yourselves. Every place on which the sole of your foot treads shall be yours: from the wilderness and Lebanon, from the river, the river Euphrates, even to the western sea shall be your border. No man will be able to stand before you. Yahweh your God will lay the fear of*

*you and the dread of you on all the land that you tread on, as he has spoken to you.*     Deuteronomy 11:22-25 WEB

*Therefore keep the words of this covenant and do them, that you may prosper in all that you do.*
Deuteronomy 29:9 WEB

*"I am going the way of all the earth. You be strong therefore, and show yourself a man; and keep the instruction of Yahweh your God, to walk in his ways, to keep his statutes, his commandments, his ordinances, and his testimonies, according to that which is written in the law of Moses, that you may prosper in all that you do, and wherever you turn yourself."*     1Kings 2:2-3 WEB

If we understand the word *"godliness"* to correlate with *"to love Yahweh your God, and to serve him with all your heart and with all your soul"* (Deuteronomy 11:13), then clearly, for the nation of Israel, under the Mosaic Covenant, their economic success was indeed tied to their godliness. Two of the clearest statements of this correlation are in the extended blessings and curses listed in Leviticus 26 and Deuteronomy 28 (too long to include here).

The above verses show that economic success was indeed dependent on following God in the Old Testament, at least in the context of the nation of Israel.

Let's also look at some similar verses that appear to apply this principle to individual people, rather than applying primarily to the nation of Israel:

*Blessed is the man who doesn't walk in the counsel of the wicked, nor stand on the path of sinners, nor sit in the seat of scoffers; but his delight is in Yahweh's law. On his law he meditates day and night. He will be like a tree planted by the streams of water, that produces its fruit in its season, whose leaf also does not wither. Whatever he does shall prosper.*     Psalm 1:1-3 WEB

*Praise the LORD!  Blessed is the man who fears the LORD, who greatly delights in his commandments!  His offspring will be mighty in the land; the generation of the upright will be blessed.  Wealth and riches are in his house, and his righteousness endures forever.*

*Psalm 112:1-3 ESV*

*Blessed is everyone who fears Yahweh, who walks in his ways.  For you will eat the labor of your hands.  You will be happy, and it will be well with you.*   *Psalm 128:1-2 WEB*

*"I, wisdom, have made prudence my dwelling.  Find out knowledge and discretion.  The fear of Yahweh is to hate evil.  I hate pride, arrogance, the evil way, and the perverse mouth.  Counsel and sound knowledge are mine.  I have understanding and power.  By me kings reign, and princes decree justice.  By me princes rule; nobles, and all the righteous rulers of the earth.  I love those who love me.  Those who seek me diligently will find me.  With me are riches, honor, enduring wealth, and prosperity."*    *Proverbs 8:12-18 WEB*

*Yahweh's blessing brings wealth, and he adds no trouble to it.*    *Proverbs 10:22 WEB*

*The result of humility and the fear of Yahweh is wealth, honor, and life.*    *Proverbs 22:4 WEB*

These verses appear to show a clear connection between godliness and material prosperity on an individual level.

From reviewing all these verses, it seems to me that if **"godliness is a means of gain"** is a legitimate translation of 1 Timothy 6:5, then perhaps the corrupt person's problem lies with their hope of economic gain being their main reason for trying to be godly (rather than hating evil, loving God, and loving others being their main reasons for being godly).

However, there is another possibility we should consider: *Does the New Covenant differ from previous covenants in*

## A New-Covenant Perspective

Does the New Testament and the New Covenant view the link between *godliness* and *prosperity* differently than in Old Testament times? Those same kinds of verses we just saw throughout the Old Testament, linking economic prosperity and godliness, are not so easy to find in the New Testament.

For the sake of comparison, let's look at some New Testament verses that are sometimes put forward to support prosperity teaching:

*Jesus said, "Most certainly I tell you, there is no one who has left house, or brothers, or sisters, or father, or mother, or wife, or children, or land, for my sake, and for the sake of the Good News, but he will receive one hundred times more now in this time: houses, brothers, sisters, mothers, children, and land, with persecutions; and in the age to come eternal life. But many who are first will be last; and the last first."* Mark 10:29-31 WEB

*"The thief only comes to steal, kill, and destroy. I came that they may have life, and may have it abundantly."* John 10:10 WEB

*What then shall we say about these things? If God is for us, who can be against us? He who didn't spare his own Son, but delivered him up for us all, how would he not also with him freely give us all things?* Romans 8:31-32 WEB

*And God is able to make all grace abound to you, so that having all sufficiency in all things at all times, you may abound in every good work. As it is written, "He has distributed freely, he has given to the poor; his righteousness endures forever." He who supplies seed to the sower and bread for food will supply and multiply your seed for sowing and increase the harvest of your righteousness. You will be enriched in every way to be generous in every way, which through us will produce thanksgiving to God.* 2Corinthians 9:8-11 ESV

*You don't have, because you don't ask.* James 4:2 WEB

*Beloved, I pray that you may prosper in all things and be healthy, even as your soul prospers.* 3John 2 WEB

Note that the contexts of these verses are generally not about promoting material prosperity. For example, Mark 10:29-31 was spoken right after Jesus told the rich young ruler to sell everything he had and give the proceeds to the poor. John 10:10 is in the context of Jesus speaking about the Good Shepherd laying down his life for the sheep. Romans 8:31-32 is in the context of God providing salvation through Jesus, and his care for us both presently and in the future. 2 Corinthians 9:8-11 is in the context of an offering being taken to benefit believers in Judea who apparently needed financial help from wealthier believers elsewhere. James 4:2 is in the context of James rebuking people for being selfish. 3 John 2 is a prayer, not a promise or a teaching.

While these verses do speak of God's provision for his people, the general emphasis in the New Testament seems to be significantly different than in the Old Testament. The reward emphasized in the New Testament for following Jesus seems to be *eternal life* and a future *inheritance*, rather than material prosperity in this life. Here are just a few of the verses that seem to me to read that way:

*"This is the will of the one who sent me, that everyone who sees the Son, and believes in him, should have eternal life; and I will raise him up at the last day."*
John 6:40 WEB

*Don't be deceived. God is not mocked, for whatever a man sows, that he will also reap. For he who sows to his own flesh will from the flesh reap corruption. But he who sows to the Spirit will from the Spirit reap eternal*

*life. Let us not be weary in doing good, for we will reap in due season, if we don't give up.*   Galatians 6:7-9 WEB

*Blessed be the God and Father of our Lord Jesus Christ! According to his great mercy, he has caused us to be born again to a living hope through the resurrection of Jesus Christ from the dead, to an inheritance that is imperishable, undefiled, and unfading, kept in heaven for you, who by God's power are being guarded through faith for a salvation ready to be revealed in the last time.*   1Peter 1:3-5 ESV

*But when the kindness of God our Savior and his love toward mankind appeared, not by works of righteousness, which we did ourselves, but according to his mercy, he saved us through the washing of regeneration and renewing by the Holy Spirit, whom he poured out on us richly, through Jesus Christ our Savior; that being justified by his grace, we might be made heirs according to the hope of eternal life.*   Titus 3:4-7 WEB

*And this is the promise that he made to us—eternal life.*   1John 2:25 ESV

Similar to the concept of *eternal life* and a future *inheritance*, the New Testament often speaks of future reward in the next life for those who follow Jesus, rather than reward in this life. Future reward is often contrasted with present suffering. Consider these verses.

*"Blessed are those who have been persecuted for righteousness' sake, for theirs is the Kingdom of Heaven. Blessed are you when people reproach you, persecute you, and say all kinds of evil against you falsely, for my sake. Rejoice, and be exceedingly glad, for great is your reward in heaven. For that is how they persecuted the prophets who were before you."*   Matthew 5:10-12 WEB

*Building on Foundations for Eternal Life*

*For this light momentary affliction is preparing for us an eternal weight of glory beyond all comparison, as we look not to the things that are seen but to the things that are unseen. For the things that are seen are transient, but the things that are unseen are eternal.*

*2Corinthians 4:17-18 ESV*

*But remember the former days, in which, after you were enlightened, you endured a great struggle with sufferings; partly, being exposed to both reproaches and oppressions; and partly, becoming partakers with those who were treated so. For you both had compassion on me in my chains, and joyfully accepted the plundering of your possessions, knowing that you have for yourselves a better possession and an enduring one in the heavens.*

*Hebrews 10:32-34 WEB*

*By faith, Moses, when he had grown up, refused to be called the son of Pharaoh's daughter, choosing rather to share ill treatment with God's people, than to enjoy the pleasures of sin for a time; accounting the reproach of Christ greater riches than the treasures of Egypt; for he looked to the reward.*

*Hebrews 11:24-26 WEB*

*"The nations were angry, and your wrath came, as did the time for the dead to be judged, and to give your bondservants the prophets, their reward, as well as to the saints, and those who fear your name, to the small and the great; and to destroy those who destroy the earth."*

*Revelation 11:18 WEB*

*"Behold, I come quickly. My reward is with me, to repay to each man according to his work."*

*Revelation 22:12 WEB*

Now let's look at some other New Testament verses about wealth that seem to be contrary to some prosperity-gospel teaching. These verses tend to emphasize problems associated with wealth, and that followers of Jesus should not expect an easy time in this present life:

*"Don't lay up treasures for yourselves on the earth, where moth and rust consume, and where thieves break through and steal; but lay up for yourselves treasures in heaven, where neither moth nor rust consume, and where thieves don't break through and steal; for where your treasure is, there your heart will be also."*
Matthew 6:19-21 WEB

*He called the multitude to himself with his disciples, and said to them, "Whoever wants to come after me, let him deny himself, and take up his cross, and follow me. For whoever wants to save his life will lose it; and whoever will lose his life for my sake and the sake of the Good News will save it. For what does it profit a man, to gain the whole world, and forfeit his life?"*  Mark 8:34-36 WEB

*"Blessed are you who are poor, for yours is the Kingdom of God."*
Luke 6:20 NIV

*"But woe to you who are rich, for you have already received your comfort."*
Luke 6:24 NIV

*"Watch out! Be on your guard against all kinds of greed; life does not consist in an abundance of possessions."*
Luke 12:15 NIV

*"Fear not, little flock, for it is your Father's good pleasure to give you the kingdom. Sell your possessions, and give to the needy. Provide yourselves with moneybags that do not grow old, with a treasure in the heavens that does not fail, where no thief approaches and no moth destroys. For where your treasure is, there will your heart be also."*
Luke 12:32-34 ESV

*Yes, and all who desire to live godly in Christ Jesus will suffer persecution.*
2Timothy 3:12 WEB

*But you have dishonored the poor man. Don't the rich oppress you, and personally drag you before the courts? Don't they blaspheme the honorable name by which you are called?*
James 2:6-7 WEB

In the New Covenant, God appears to be much more concerned about our spiritual prosperity than our material prosperity. Material prosperity is often associated with spiritual poverty. Material wealth is often spoken of as something that competes with our allegiance to God. Jesus summarized that problem this way:

> *"No one can serve two masters, for either he will hate the one and love the other, or he will be devoted to the one and despise the other. You cannot serve God and money."* Matthew 6:24 ESV

Those who do have riches are warned to not trust in them, and are encouraged to be generous:

> *As for the rich in this present age, charge them not to be haughty, nor to set their hopes on the uncertainty of riches, but on God, who richly provides us with everything to enjoy. They are to do good, to be rich in good works, to be generous and ready to share, thus storing up treasure for themselves as a good foundation for the future, so that they may take hold of that which is truly life.* 1Timothy 6:17-19 ESV

## Godliness with Contentment

Let's return now to Paul's teaching in 1 Timothy chapter 6. Regardless of which is the better translation for verse 5 (*"gain is godliness,"* or *"godliness is a means to gain"*), starting in verse 6 Paul gives us a preferred way to view godliness, gain, and material wealth:

> *But godliness with contentment is great gain. For we brought nothing into the world, and we certainly can't carry anything out. But having food and clothing, we will be content with that. But those who are determined to be rich fall into a temptation and a snare and many foolish and harmful lusts, such as drown men in ruin and destruction. For the love of money is a root of all*

*kinds of evil. Some have been led astray from the faith in their greed, and have pierced themselves through with many sorrows.*                    *1Timothy 6:6-10 WEB*

Paul warns us here about the dangers of pursuing material wealth. He encourages us to be content having just our basic needs satisfied. A similar perspective is found in the book of Hebrews:

*Keep your life free from love of money, and be content with what you have, for he has said, "I will never leave you nor forsake you."*                    *Hebrews 13:5 ESV*

## A Living Hope

Even with the many promises of prosperity for the righteous in the Old Testament, things did not always appear to correlate well with those promises. It sometimes appeared like the unrighteous prospered while the righteous suffered. Consider these verses:

*Surely God is good to Israel, to those who are pure in heart. But as for me, my feet had almost slipped; I had nearly lost my foothold. For I envied the arrogant when I saw the prosperity of the wicked. They have no struggles; their bodies are healthy and strong. They are free from common human burdens; they are not plagued by human ills. Therefore pride is their necklace; they clothe themselves with violence.*
*Psalm 73:1-6 NIV*

The writer later concludes that he must wait for a future time for God to make all things right:

*Yet I am always with you; you hold me by my right hand. You guide me with your counsel, and afterward you will take me into glory.*          *Psalm 73:23-24 NIV*

That seems to parallel what we often see taught in the New Testament: present suffering; future glory.

Let's conclude with a verse that is well-known and cherished by many:

*The LORD is my shepherd; I shall not want.*

*Psalm 23:1 KJV*

God does provide for those who follow him. What does that verse mean for each of us in this life? I think that is a matter between each of us and God. Does scripture guarantee that godliness will lead to material prosperity in this life? I don't think so. However, we do have a promise of a future *inheritance* in the life to come:

*Blessed be the God and Father of our Lord Jesus Christ! According to his great mercy, he has caused us to be born again to a living hope through the resurrection of Jesus Christ from the dead, to an inheritance that is imperishable, undefiled, and unfading, kept in heaven for you, who by God's power are being guarded through faith for a salvation ready to be revealed in the last time.* 1Peter 1:3-5 ESV

## For Further Reflection

- Are you expecting material reward in this life for following Jesus, or reward in the life to come?

\*\*\*\*\*\*\*\*\*\*\*\*

# Chapter 29
# Science

*It is the glory of God to conceal things,*
*but the glory of kings is to search things out.*
Proverbs 25:2 ESV

*Science* is often spoken of as though it is unaffected by religion and philosophy. *Science* is often promoted as something that should not be questioned. In this section we'll look at how *science* can be involved with deception.

## Hard and Soft Science

When discussing science, I find it helpful to try to understand how reliable and certain the science is that is being discussed. Some areas of science have a long history of very solid evidence supporting them, including directly observable evidence, consistently repeatable experimental evidence, and widely accepted results. That's what I call *"hard science."*

One example of *hard science,* in my opinion at least, is Newtonian Mechanics. Newtonian Mechanics was originally developed by Isaac Newton, as described in his book "Mathematical Principles of Natural Philosophy" (originally published in 1687 in Latin). Newtonian Mechanics mathematically describes how forces and objects interact. It may not apply to subatomic particles, the vastness of space, or speeds approaching that of light, but, for most practical purposes on earth, it provides a mathematically precise way of relating forces and motion. Our modern society would not be possible if Newtonian Mechanics were not consistently valid. Airplanes would not fly, cars would not run, factories would not produce.

On the other side is what is referred to as *"soft science."* The evidence associated with *soft science* is generally not as directly observable, consistently repeatable, or as widely accepted as that of *hard science*. Typically, social sciences are often considered to be *soft science*, and natural sciences to be *hard science*.

A common deception is for soft science to be promoted as though it is hard science, and therefore should not be questioned. People may be deceived into believing a falsehood by the claim that "science" has proven it.

An example of soft science, which is often promoted as hard science, is the theory of macroevolution. I have not heard of any directly observable or repeatable experiments associated with macroevolution, only conjecture based on disputable fossil evidence. Yet macroevolution is often promoted as though it is hard science that should not be questioned. Whatever your views on this subject are, please don't be deceived into thinking it is hard science that shouldn't be questioned. It is not directly observable or repeatable. It is soft science at best.

Science relating to the origin of the universe and the earth is also often promoted as though it involves only *hard science*. But, again, I have not heard of any directly observable or repeatable experiments associated with this kind of science. Whether someone is promoting a naturalistic view, or creationism, or arguing for intelligent design, these all involve *soft science*, not *hard science*.

It should be noted that "*hard science*" and "*soft science*" are subjective terms without a clear dividing line between them. A lot of science falls into a grey area between these terms. Some aspects of a particular scientific subject may be closer to hard science, while other aspects of the same subject may be soft science. This is an area that is often difficult to discern. As you gain understanding and wisdom in this area, do not expect others to readily agree with you.

# Naturalism

Is Naturalism a religion? As I understand it, Naturalism is a belief system that claims there are no supernatural forces at work in the universe. Naturalism holds that everything can be explained by natural scientific laws. Since *God*, by most definitions, involves supernatural power that influences the universe in supernatural ways, Naturalism claims that *God* does not exist.

Likewise, since a supernatural realm, by most definitions, is outside of what natural science can deal with, the existence of a supernatural realm is also denied.

Please note that holding a Naturalistic viewpoint involves a lot of faith. I have previously defined *"faith"* (in the book *"Beneath Foundations for Eternal Life,"* chapter 18 *"About Faith"*) in a broad and simple way:

> **Faith:** Belief in something that has not been directly observed.

There are a huge number of things in the universe that natural science is not yet able to explain with natural scientific laws, and there are many things scientists have not been able to duplicate, even with modern high-tech laboratories. It takes a lot of faith to believe that they are all explainable by natural scientific laws. Here are just a few examples of things science presently has no good explanation for:

- How any living thing (even a single cell) can come into existence from inorganic matter without supernatural help.

- How the complex coding in DNA came into existence without supernatural help.

- How photosynthesis developed without supernatural help.

These things are exceptionally complex. To believe that all

these things developed without supernatural help takes a lot of faith. For that reason, I consider Naturalism to be a religion, not simply a viewpoint based strictly on science.

Some people claim to know that there is no God, often claiming that science supports their claim. Don't be deceived. Such claims involve religious conviction and faith, not just science.

## Microevolution and Macroevolution

A few more words are in order regarding the topic of evolution. For clarity on this subject, it is necessary to make a distinction between *microevolution* and *macroevolution*.

*Microevolution* involves small changes within a species. Microevolution is observable in both plants and animals. Some examples of microevolution include:

- Plants developing resistance to herbicides.
- Insects developing resistance to insecticides.
- The color/pattern of an animal changing to become more similar to its environment, thereby helping it avoid predators.

As these examples show, some types of microevolution are readily observable and repeatable. In this sense, some aspects of microevolution can be said to be relatively *hard science*.

On the other hand, *macroevolution* involves new species developing from other species. A key claim of macroevolution is that more-advanced species have developed over time from less-advanced species, simply based on natural selection, mutations, and lots of time.

I am not aware of any examples of macroevolution happening today. Mutations are not observed to result in more advanced animals, but rather less-advanced animals. Natural selection and mutations observable today only appear to support microevolution, not macroevolution.

Many people claim that fossils prove macroevolution. However, I have never seen any fossil evidence that clearly supports such a claim (have you?). The study of macroevolution is NOT based on directly observable or repeatable experimental evidence. Macroevolution is therefore, in my opinion, *soft science*, not *hard science*.

This is important, since many people claim that the science of macroevolution proves the Bible to be false, since, they claim, macroevolution shows the creation account in the book of Genesis to be false. Many people readily believe these assertions, largely based on the claim that "science says so." *Soft science* generally does not prove anything. Beware of claims based on *soft science*.

In summary, the existence of microevolution does not prove the existence of macroevolution. Macroevolution is not *hard science*. Be cautious with claims to the contrary.

## Creation or Evolution?

The first book of the Bible, Genesis, begins with these words:

> *In the beginning God created the heavens and the earth. Now the earth was formless and empty. Darkness was on the surface of the deep and God's Spirit was hovering over the surface of the waters.*
>
> *God said, "Let there be light," and there was light. God saw the light, and saw that it was good. God divided the light from the darkness. God called the light "day," and the darkness he called "night." There was evening and there was morning, the first day.*      Genesis 1:1-5 WEB

Chapter 1 continues with 5 more days of creation, and then there is a day of rest spoken of in chapter 2.

It is likely no surprise to you that believers hold widely differing viewpoints regarding how literally this chapter should be understood. It is not appropriate to try to resolve those differences in just a few paragraphs. However, I will make a few comments that I hope will be helpful to some.

The two major areas of debate appear to me to be:

- Are the earth and universe very young, or very old? Some claim Genesis shows they are both only several thousand years old.

- The account in Genesis appears to be contrary to macroevolution. How should this be resolved?

Much of the debate on the first point seems to hinge on a belief that a literal interpretation of Genesis chapter 1 requires a "young earth" and "young universe" conclusion. I don't see it that way. There is no indication of the amount of time that may have occurred between verse 1 and verse 2. Or, some may reason that verse 1 may refer just to the earth and the "heavens" around the earth, not the entire universe as we understand it today. One can hold to a literal understanding of Genesis 1 without holding to a young earth or a young universe position. It seems to me that allowing for a lot of time between verses 1 and 2 may resolve most difficulties in this area for many people. (Note that this is a disputable matter, in my opinion; please don't condemn me if you believe differently!)

Regarding macroevolution, Genesis 1 is clearly not written from a macroevolution perspective, but rather emphasizes creation by God. I personally am not aware of any *hard science* (or any science that is not very *soft*) that contradicts a literal view of this creation account.

Our beliefs about creation and evolution affect a lot of other beliefs. I can understand why some believers may hold that beliefs in this area are primary, and are worth dividing over. However, I believe these are secondary issues that believers should avoid being divisive about. Please consider prayerfully whether this issue is really worth dividing over, before being divisive about this subject yourself. Where you land on the issue of causing division may involve deception that is greater than not having right beliefs about creation. (The importance of avoiding division over secondary issues will be discussed in the next chapter.)

Salvation is about trusting and following Jesus, who is the Christ, the Son of God, Lord of all. It's not about having right beliefs about creation and evolution. However, it does appear to me that accepting macroevolution as hard science does hinder many people from coming to Jesus and being saved.

## Science, Philosophy, or Religion?

Unfortunately, the divisions between science, religion, and philosophy are often not clear. Scientists are inevitably influenced by their own religious viewpoints and philosophical viewpoints, often without realizing it. Beliefs that are based partly on philosophy or religion are often put forward as science. Scripture provides us some warnings:

> *See to it that no one takes you captive by philosophy and empty deceit, according to human tradition, according to the elemental spirits of the world, and not according to Christ.* *Colossians 2:8 ESV*

> *O Timothy, guard the deposit entrusted to you. Avoid the irreverent babble and contradictions of what is falsely called "knowledge," for by professing it some have swerved from the faith. Grace be with you.* *1Timothy 6:20-21 ESV*

## For Further Reflection

- Have you ever been deceived into believing something to be true, which is actually false, by a claim that "science proves it?"

\*\*\*\*\*\*\*\*\*\*\*\*

# Chapter 30
# Division

*"Not for these only do I pray, but for those also who will believe in me through their word, that they may all be one; even as you, Father, are in me, and I in you, that they also may be one in us; that the world may believe that you sent me."*
*John 17:20-21 WEB*

*Now there are various kinds of gifts, but the same Spirit. There are various kinds of service, and the same Lord. There are various kinds of workings, but the same God, who works all things in all...*

*...that there should be no division in the body, but that the members should have the same care for one another.*
*1Corinthians 12:4-6, 25 WEB*

---

We have already seen how false teachers seek to cause division in chapter 11 *"Deceivers Among Us."* Recall Peter's warning to us about false teachers:

*But false prophets also arose among the people, just as there will be false teachers among you, who will secretly bring in destructive heresies, even denying the Master who bought them, bringing upon themselves swift destruction. And many will follow their sensuality, and because of them the way of truth will be blasphemed. And in their greed they will exploit you with false words.*
*2Peter 2:1-3 ESV*

Paul instructs us to *turn away* from such people:

*Now I beg you, brothers, look out for those who are causing the divisions and occasions of stumbling, contrary to the doctrine which you learned, and turn away from them. For those who are such don't serve our Lord, Jesus Christ, but their own belly; and by their smooth and flattering speech, they deceive the hearts of the innocent.* Romans 16:17-18 WEB

So, in the case of false teachers, the proper response for believers is to **turn away from them**, or, we might say, to divide from them.

Paul also instructs us to turn away from people who reject morality:

> *But know this, that in the last days, grievous times will come. For men will be lovers of self, lovers of money, boastful, arrogant, blasphemers, disobedient to parents, unthankful, unholy, without natural affection, unforgiving, slanderers, without self-control, fierce, not lovers of good, traitors, headstrong, conceited, lovers of pleasure rather than lovers of God; holding a form of godliness, but having denied its power. Turn away from these, also.* 2Timothy 3:1 WEB

However, all too often true believers divide from each other over disputable matters or secondary issues. The unity of believers, the one body of Christ, is a huge issue in scripture. Yet, what does the world often see today? Division among believers. Dear friends, this should not be.

We will look for some middle ground between two extreme viewpoints. First, the viewpoint that unity is based on agreement on a large assortment of doctrines. Without complete doctrinal agreement on many subjects, some people think there can be no unity. A second extreme viewpoint is that beliefs and right doctrine shouldn't matter at all; we should avoid doctrinal issues and simply all just get along.

## What Is Unity Based On?

What is our unity based on? It seems to me that maybe we ought to go back to the early church and look at what was important then. One summary of important beliefs of early believers is found in the Apostles' Creed. Its origins are rather obscure, but it is often attributed to the first Apostles (as its title suggests). Here is one version of it:

> *I believe in God, the Father Almighty,*
> *maker of heaven and earth;*
> *and in Jesus Christ his only Son, our Lord;*
> *who was conceived by the Holy Spirit,*
> *born of the Virgin Mary,*
> *he suffered under Pontius Pilate,*
> *he was crucified, he died, and was buried;*
> *the third day he rose from the dead;*
> *he ascended into heaven,*
> *and sits at the right hand of God the Father Almighty;*
> *from there he shall come to judge the living and the dead.*
> *I believe in the Holy Spirit,*
> *one holy universal church,*
> *the communion of saints,*
> *the forgiveness of sins,*
> *the resurrection of the body,*
> *and life everlasting.  Amen.*

It may be helpful to note that over half of this creed focuses on Jesus: who he is, what he has done, and what he will do in the future.  Keep in mind that the early believers did not have the New Testament to refer to regarding these things.  So, it was necessary and good to provide a minimal outline about Jesus within a creed.  Clearly, *who Jesus is,* as understood and recorded by his early followers, is a primary issue.  I find that the outline about Jesus in the Apostles' Creed is still valuable today.

Now let's look briefly at the other beliefs mentioned in the Apostles' Creed:

- *"I believe in God, the Father Almighty, maker of heaven and earth."*  Clearly, belief in God the Father is foundational to our faith.  Belief that God created heaven and earth is also foundational.

- *"The Holy Spirit."* There is no divisive doctrine here; it just indicates the existence and the importance of the Holy Spirit.

- *"One holy universal church."* Believers are part of one body, the body of Christ. Man-made divisions between believers are not promoted here.

- *"The communion of saints."* There should be fellowship between true believers, and love for one another.

- *"The forgiveness of sins."* This is not as closely tied to Jesus' crucifixion as I would like, but it is clearly an important belief. Without forgiveness of sins, there can be no salvation.

- *"The resurrection of the body."* As Paul wrote: ***"For if the dead aren't raised, neither has Christ been raised. If Christ has not been raised, your faith is vain; you are still in your sins"*** (1 Corinthians 15:16-17 WEB).

- *"Life everlasting."* This is a primary goal of our faith.

These all appear to me to be primary issues, about which there is widespread agreement among believers.

However, it seems to me that many subsequent creeds and various church councils tended to deal with secondary issues, and sometimes promoted division based on those secondary issues, rather than promoting the unity of all believers. The main purpose of some subsequent creeds appears to be to force conformity to majority opinion regarding secondary issues, rather than promoting true unity. I question how various doctrines, which first-century believers weren't even aware of, and which are not clearly revealed in scripture, somehow became beliefs that many people and churches claim are necessary for salvation.

Some hold that even the Apostles' Creed is too much. A

more basic set of beliefs is provided by Paul in his letter to the believers in the city of Corinth:

> *Now I declare to you, brothers, the Good News which I preached to you, which also you received, in which you also stand, by which also you are saved, if you hold firmly the word which I preached to you—unless you believed in vain. For I delivered to you first of all that which I also received: that Christ died for our sins according to the Scriptures, that he was buried, that he was raised on the third day according to the Scriptures, and that he appeared to Cephas, then to the twelve. Then he appeared to over five hundred brothers at once, most of whom remain until now, but some have also fallen asleep.* 1Corinthians 15:1-6 WEB

The emphasis here is on the death, burial, and resurrection of Jesus, who is the "*Christ.*" Surely, at the heart of our faith is that Jesus is the Christ (the long-awaited Messiah), that he died for our sins, was buried, and rose again. Those who deliberately reject these fundamental truths are surely not one with us. Those who genuinely embrace these truths, who genuinely seek to follow Jesus, are fellow believers with us.

John affirms that genuine belief in Jesus as the Christ, the Son of God, is key:

> *And we have seen and testify that the Father has sent his Son to be the Savior of the world. Whoever confesses that Jesus is the Son of God, God abides in him, and he in God.* 1John 4:14-15 ESV

> *Everyone who believes that Jesus is the Christ has been born of God, and everyone who loves the Father loves whoever has been born of him.* 1John 5:1 ESV

## One Body

We should keep in mind that salvation is not about mental

agreement with particular doctrines, but is rather about coming to Jesus for salvation, trusting in Jesus, and following Jesus. If we do these things, we are each a member of his one body. Jesus is our head, our Savior, and our Lord. We are one in him. Consider these verses:

> *For just as each of us has one body with many members, and these members do not all have the same function, so in Christ we, though many, form one body, and each member belongs to all the others.* Romans 12:4-5 NIV

> *For as the body is one, and has many members, and all the members of the body, being many, are one body; so also is Christ. For in one Spirit we were all baptized into one body, whether Jews or Greeks, whether bond or free; and were all given to drink into one Spirit.*
> 1Corinthians 12:12-13 WEB

> *This mystery is that the Gentiles are fellow heirs, members of the same body, and partakers of the promise in Christ Jesus through the gospel.* Ephesians 3:6 ESV

> *There is one body, and one Spirit, even as you also were called in one hope of your calling; one Lord, one faith, one baptism, one God and Father of all, who is over all, and through all, and in us all.* Ephesians 4:4-6 WEB

> *There is neither Jew nor Greek, there is neither slave nor free, there is no male and female, for you are all one in Christ Jesus.* Galatians 3:28 ESV

We are members of one body, because God, through Jesus, has made all true believers members of one body.

## Disputable Matters

Typically, we tend to find fault with others who understand things differently than we do. If the subject we differ on is spiritual in nature, we tend to think of others as less mature spiritually, or less knowledgeable, or weak in faith (whether or not any of those things are actually true). Consider Paul's words to the believers in Rome:

*Accept the one whose faith is weak, without quarreling over disputable matters. One person's faith allows them to eat anything, but another, whose faith is weak, eats only vegetables. The one who eats everything must not treat with contempt the one who does not, and the one who does not eat everything must not judge the one who does, for God has accepted them. Who are you to judge someone else's servant? To their own master, servants stand or fall. And they will stand, for the Lord is able to make them stand. One person considers one day more sacred than another; another considers every day alike. Each of them should be fully convinced in their own mind. Whoever regards one day as special does so to the Lord. Whoever eats meat does so to the Lord, for they give thanks to God; and whoever abstains does so to the Lord and gives thanks to God.* Romans 14:1-6 NIV

Paul mentions two examples here of *disputable matters:* our diets (vegetarian or not), and special days. He could have given a much longer list, but that would likely not be helpful, as a longer list might lead us to think the list was a complete list of all the things that are disputable. In reality, there seems to be no limit to the things people can dispute over. I think it is safe to say that many of the issues that believers have divided over throughout history are disputable matters. How much better it would have been for believers to have accepted their differences rather than to have divided over them.

Paul continues discussing this issue through the rest of Romans 14 and into chapter 15 (it may be helpful to take a break here to read it in full). Here are some of Paul's concluding thoughts on the subject:

*We who are strong ought to bear with the failings of the weak and not to please ourselves. Each of us should please our neighbors for their good, to build them up.*

*For even Christ did not please himself but, as it is written: "The insults of those who insult you have fallen on me."*
Romans 15:1-3 NIV

*May the God who gives endurance and encouragement give you the same attitude of mind toward each other that Christ Jesus had, so that with one mind and one voice you may glorify the God and Father of our Lord Jesus Christ. Accept one another, then, just as Christ accepted you, in order to bring praise to God.*
Romans 15:5-7 NIV

## Secondary Issues

"Secondary issues" perhaps go deeper than "disputable matters" (some people do not make a distinction between them; scripture does not directly mention "secondary issues"). We see things in scripture that don't appear to us to be disputable, and scripture doesn't clearly call them disputable. Yet other people who claim faith in Jesus view those things much differently. What should we do?

I believe Paul's advice about not **quarreling over disputable matters** (Romans 14:1 NIV) also applies to what I am calling "secondary issues." Let's avoid being divisive about such things. Surely many of the existing divisions between believers are **not** God's will for us. Surely our witness to unbelievers is weakened by our many divisions over secondary issues. Dear friends, this should not be.

On an individual level, some believers seem to believe that promoting and defending their beliefs about secondary issues is more important than preserving relationships with other believers. They seem to put doctrinal purity above the command to love others. Or perhaps they think that forcing their beliefs on others is a loving thing to do. If this describes you, please prayerfully reconsider how important unity is, and how easily unity is damaged by disagreements over secondary issues.

Division over secondary issues obviously also occurs on a larger scale than between individual people. Many local churches (and entire denominations) require members to believe a particular way on many secondary issues. In many cases, those who believe otherwise are not allowed to become members (unless they are not honest about their beliefs). Division seems to be preferred over allowing diverse perspectives. Dear friends, this should not be.

Of course, a simple solution would be for churches to allow members to have diverse perspectives on secondary issues. However, if that is not thought to be a good option regarding some secondary issues, then an alternative would be to merely require that members respect that the church holds a particular perspective, and members should not openly speak against the church's perspective on those secondary issues.

Consider Paul's words:

> *Now I beg you, brothers, through the name of our Lord, Jesus Christ, that you all speak the same thing and that there be no divisions among you, but that you be perfected together in the same mind and in the same judgment. For it has been reported to me concerning you, my brothers, by those who are from Chloe's household, that there are contentions among you. Now I mean this, that each one of you says, "I follow Paul," "I follow Apollos," "I follow Cephas," and, "I follow Christ." Is Christ divided? Was Paul crucified for you? Or were you baptized into the name of Paul?*
>
> *1Corinthians 1:10-13 WEB*

As in Paul's time, so it is in our present time. Different theological viewpoints are often labeled with the names of people who initially promoted them. Paul admonishes us here not to divide over those kinds of things.

## Heresy

We previously discussed different understandings of *heresy* in chapter 15 *"Heresy."* We saw that the original meaning of *"heresy"* has more to do with causing division among God's people, rather than believing wrong doctrine (though promoting wrong doctrine may contribute to divisions). Focusing on the correctness of secondary beliefs is often a primary source of division. Calling questionable beliefs "heresy," and calling those who may have wrong beliefs "heretics," is a well-established way of dividing believers. Dear friends, this should not be.

## Our Way Is the Only Way!

Ungodly division is often promoted as righteousness. Some people, groups, denominations, and so-called "cults" promote their beliefs as being the only right way to believe, and they condemn all other beliefs and practices. Some go so far as to say that one's salvation is dependent on being part of their group. If you aren't part of their group, or if you leave their group, they claim you are "not saved."

Now let's be clear here. From the world's perspective all of us, all who truly follow Jesus, are such a group or cult. We do believe that following Jesus is the only way to eternal life. Apart from following Jesus there is no other way to be saved. Here are a couple verses commonly referenced regarding this exclusive nature of salvation:

> *Jesus said to him, "I am the way, the truth, and the life. No one comes to the Father, except through me."*
> *John 14:6 WEB*

> *"And there is salvation in no one else, for there is no other name under heaven given among men by which we must be saved."* *Acts 4:12 ESV*

So, when we discuss this issue, it is good to realize that it is one of those issues about which *deception goes both ways* (as discussed in chapter 14). Those who claim that faith in Jesus is **not** necessary for salvation clearly do not hold to a scriptural perspective. However, those who claim that it is necessary to be part of their group to be saved, based on some other set of criteria, are likely promoting ungodly division. Don't fall for that deception. As Paul wrote:

> *There is one body, and one Spirit, even as you also were called in one hope of your calling; one Lord, one faith, one baptism, one God and Father of all, who is over all, and through all, and in us all.*      *Ephesian 4:4-6 WEB*

All of God's people, all who truly follow Jesus, throughout the world, are members of our *one body*. People belonging to various organized groups may be part of our *one body*, but their groups don't define the limits of our *one body*.

So, beware of groups who claim to be the only true body of Christ, or the only true followers of Jesus.

## Division or Love?

History is full of divisions between people who claim to be believers in our Lord Jesus. Many of those divisions have their roots in different beliefs about disputable matters and secondary issues. Division often occurs when people's different beliefs are greater than their love for one another. A failure to deeply love one another results in a tendency to divide over relatively minor issues. Often, where there is division, there has been a failure to love.

Those who promote division often appear to disregard Jesus' instructions for us to love one another:

> *"A new commandment I give to you, that you love one another. Just as I have loved you, you also love one another. By this everyone will know that you are my disciples, if you have love for one another."*
> *John 13:34-35 WEB*

> *"This is my commandment, that you love one another, even as I have loved you. Greater love has no one than this, that someone lay down his life for his friends."*
> *John 15:12-13 WEB*

*For this is the message that you have heard from the beginning, that we should love one another.*

*1John 3:11 ESV*

Knowing truth, understanding truth, and living by truth is important. However, we should do so without being divisive about secondary issues. Jesus calls us to *love one another.* Let us humble ourselves, throw off divisive attitudes and practices, and serve one another and build one another up. Consider Jesus' words again:

*"A new commandment I give to you, that you love one another. Just as I have loved you, you also love one another. By this everyone will know that you are my disciples, if you have love for one another."*

*John 13:34-35 WEB*

And let's remember what John wrote to all believers:

*Beloved, let us love one another, for love is from God, and whoever loves has been born of God and knows God. Anyone who does not love does not know God, because God is love.*
*1John 4:7-8 ESV*

*If anyone says, "I love God," and hates his brother, he is a liar; for he who does not love his brother whom he has seen cannot love God whom he has not seen. And this commandment we have from him: whoever loves God must also love his brother.*
*1John 4:20-21 ESV*

## For Further Reflection

- Have you observed believers wrongly dividing? If so, what could have been done to prevent the division?

\*\*\*\*\*\*\*\*\*\*\*\*

# Chapter 31
# Do Not Judge

*"Don't judge, so that you won't be judged.*
*For with whatever judgment you judge, you will be judged;*
*and with whatever measure you measure,*
*it will be measured to you."*
Matthew 7:1-2 WEB

---

In the previous chapter we saw the importance of unity, and the need to avoid division among believers. While this is important, there is a deception that is often associated with this: a belief that we shouldn't judge anything.

It has become common for both believers and unbelievers to quote scripture verses about not judging others, while ignoring the many verses that call us to avoid sin or confront sin. Indeed, it has become fashionable to not talk about *sin* at all, and those who do are often accused of judging others.

To understand this issue properly, there are several key principles to be aware of:

- **Right Distinctions:** Scripture repeatedly calls us to make right distinctions between things: whether something is good or bad, right or wrong, clean or unclean.

- **We Condemn Ourselves:** We tend to judge others for the same things we are guilty of, thereby condemning ourselves.

- **Don't Judge Motives:** We are unable to rightly judge people's hearts or motives. So, we should not judge people's hearts or motives!

- **Only Judge Actions:** Sometimes it is appropriate to judge people's actions. When doing so we must be careful to use clear scriptural standards, and realize that we may be bringing judgment on ourselves in doing so, and may be tempted toward similar sin.

- **Discern Evil and Avoid Evil:**  We should discern what is evil, hate evil, and avoid evil.

- **Jesus will Judge:**  Jesus has been appointed to judge everyone (in the future), and he will repay each person according to what he has done. Jesus is able to judge both motives and actions righteously.

- **Don't Take Revenge:**  We are not to take revenge, but rather leave that to God.

Let's look at what scripture says about each of these points.

## Right Distinctions

In chapter 25 of the book *"Beneath Foundations for Eternal Life,"* I concluded that "God makes distinctions between things that are good and things that are bad." This was found to be a self-evident truth that is not dependent on scripture to be known. I would like to expand on that thought some, as I believe that a failure to make proper distinctions is an important form of deception.

Throughout scripture we see God making many distinctions between things that are good and bad, clean and unclean, righteous and unrighteous, holy and not holy. Distinctions are also made between things that are good, such as when God made people: "male and female he created them." He calls his people to similarly make right distinctions. Here are a few related verses:

> *You are to make a distinction between the holy and the common, and between the unclean and the clean.*
> *Leviticus_10:10 WEB*

> *"But when the Son of Man comes in his glory, and all the holy angels with him, then he will sit on the throne of his glory. Before him all the nations will be gathered, and he will separate them one from another, as a*

*shepherd separates the sheep from the goats. He will set the sheep on his right hand, but the goats on the left."*
*Matthew 25:31-33 WEB*

*"You hypocrites! You know how to interpret the appearance of the earth and the sky, but how is it that you don't interpret this time? Why don't you judge for yourselves what is right?"*
*Luke 12:56-57 WEB*

*Test all things, and hold firmly that which is good. Abstain from every form of evil.* *1Thessalonians 5:21-22 WEB*

Equally important is to NOT make distinctions when they should not be made. For example, many things that divide people in the world should not divide believers:

*For you are all children of God, through faith in Christ Jesus. For as many of you as were baptized into Christ have put on Christ. There is neither Jew nor Greek, there is neither slave nor free man, there is neither male nor female; for you are all one in Christ Jesus.*
*Galatians 3:26-28 WEB*

Making right distinctions between things that are different is important. Where God makes distinctions, it appears to me that the unrighteous often promote no distinctions. Where God makes no distinction, is seems that the unrighteous often promote distinctions.

The most obvious application here is that we should make right distinctions between things that are good and bad, or right and wrong.

## We Condemn Ourselves

We tend to judge others for the same things we are guilty of, thereby condemning ourselves. Consider these verses:

*"Don't judge, so that you won't be judged. For with whatever judgment you judge, you will be judged; and with whatever measure you measure, it will be measured*

*to you.  Why do you see the speck that is in your brother's eye, but don't consider the beam that is in your own eye?  Or how will you tell your brother, 'Let me remove the speck from your eye;' and behold, the beam is in your own eye?  You hypocrite!  First remove the beam out of your own eye, and then you can see clearly to remove the speck out of your brother's eye."*

Matthew 7:1-5 WEB

*Therefore you are without excuse, O man, whoever you are who judge.  For in that which you judge another, you condemn yourself.  For you who judge practice the same things.  We know that the judgment of God is according to truth against those who practice such things.  Do you think this, O man who judges those who practice such things, and do the same, that you will escape the judgment of God?*

Romans 2:1-3 WEB

## Don't Judge Motives

You may have noticed how some scriptures appear to say *"don't judge,"* while other scriptures appear to say *"do judge."*  The difference has to do with the context.  The *"don't judge"* verses are generally referring to people's hearts and motives, or people's actions that are disputable matters.  The *"do judge"* verses are generally referring to people's actions that are clearly unrighteous.  Consider these *"don't judge"* verses:

*I care very little if I am judged by you or by any human court; indeed, I do not even judge myself.  My conscience is clear, but that does not make me innocent.  It is the Lord who judges me.  Therefore judge nothing before the appointed time; wait until the Lord comes.  He will bring to light what is hidden in darkness and will expose the motives of the heart. At that time each will receive their praise from God.*  1Corinthians 4:3-5 NIV

*Don't speak against one another, brothers.  He who*

*speaks against a brother and judges his brother, speaks against the law and judges the law. But if you judge the law, you are not a doer of the law, but a judge. Only one is the lawgiver, who is able to save and to destroy. But who are you to judge another?* James 4:11-12 WEB

*Therefore do not let anyone judge you by what you eat or drink, or with regard to a religious festival, a New Moon celebration or a Sabbath day. These are a shadow of the things that were to come; the reality, however, is found in Christ.* Colossians 2:16-17 NIV

*Accept the one whose faith is weak, without quarreling over disputable matters. One person's faith allows them to eat anything, but another, whose faith is weak, eats only vegetables. The one who eats everything must not treat with contempt the one who does not, and the one who does not eat everything must not judge the one who does, for God has accepted them. Who are you to judge someone else's servant? To their own master, servants stand or fall. And they will stand, for the Lord is able to make them stand.* Romans 14:1-4 NIV

## Only Judge Actions

Now let's look at some verses that call us to judge unrighteous actions, especially actions of those who claim to follow Jesus. Consider these verses:

*"If your brother sins against you, go, show him his fault between you and him alone. If he listens to you, you have gained back your brother. But if he doesn't listen, take one or two more with you, that at the mouth of two or three witnesses every word may be established. If he refuses to listen to them, tell it to the assembly. If he refuses to hear the assembly also, let him be to you as a Gentile or a tax collector."* Matthew 18:15-17 WEB

*For anyone who eats and drinks without discerning the*

*body eats and drinks judgment on himself. That is why many of you are weak and ill, and some have died. But if we judged ourselves truly, we would not be judged.*

1Corinthians 11:29-31 ESV

*I wrote to you in my letter not to associate with sexually immoral people—not at all meaning the sexually immoral of this world, or the greedy and swindlers, or idolaters, since then you would need to go out of the world. But now I am writing to you not to associate with anyone who bears the name of brother if he is guilty of sexual immorality or greed, or is an idolater, reviler, drunkard, or swindler—not even to eat with such a one. For what have I to do with judging outsiders? Is it not those inside the church whom you are to judge? God judges those outside. "Purge the evil person from among you."*

1Corinthians 5:9-13 ESV

*Dare any of you, having a matter against his neighbor, go to law before the unrighteous, and not before the saints? Don't you know that the saints will judge the world? And if the world is judged by you, are you unworthy to judge the smallest matters? Don't you know that we will judge angels? How much more, things that pertain to this life?*

1Corinthians 6:1-3 WEB

*Brothers, if anyone is caught in any transgression, you who are spiritual should restore him in a spirit of gentleness. Keep watch on yourself, lest you too be tempted.*

Galatians 6:1 ESV

When judging actions, we must be careful to use clear scriptural standards, and realize that we may be bringing judgment on ourselves in doing so, and we may be tempted toward similar sin.

## Discern Evil and Avoid Evil

We should discern what is evil, hate evil, and avoid evil. This involves making judgments about what is right and what is wrong. Consider these verses:

*He said to the multitudes also, "When you see a cloud rising from the west, immediately you say, 'A shower is coming,' and so it happens. When a south wind blows, you say, 'There will be a scorching heat,' and it happens. You hypocrites! You know how to interpret the appearance of the earth and the sky, but how is it that you don't interpret this time? Why don't you judge for yourselves what is right?"* Luke 12:54-57 WEB

*Let love be without hypocrisy. Abhor that which is evil. Cling to that which is good.* Romans 12:9 WEB

*But solid food is for the mature, for those who have their powers of discernment trained by constant practice to distinguish good from evil.* Hebrews 5:14 ESV

*Test all things, and hold firmly that which is good. Abstain from every form of evil.* 1Thessalonians 5:21-22 WEB

## Jesus Will Judge

Jesus will eventually judge all people, and punish or reward all people according to what they have done. Consider these verses:

*"For the Father judges no one, but he has given all judgment to the Son, that all may honor the Son, even as they honor the Father. He who doesn't honor the Son doesn't honor the Father who sent him."* John 5:22-23 WEB

*"The times of ignorance therefore God overlooked. But now he commands that all people everywhere should repent, because he has appointed a day in which he will judge the world in righteousness by the man whom he has ordained; of which he has given assurance to all men, in that he has raised him from the dead."*
Acts 17:30-31 WEB

*For we must all appear before the judgment seat of*

*Christ, so that each of us may receive what is due us for the things done while in the body, whether good or bad.*
*2Corinthians 5:10 NIV*

*"Look, I am coming soon! My reward is with me, and I will give to each person according to what they have done."*
*Revelation 22:12 NIV*

## Don't Take Revenge

It's natural to want to take revenge against those who have hurt us, but God calls us to not do that. Rather, we are to love our enemies (Matthew 5:44) and wait for God to repay people for the wrong they have done. Consider these verses:

*"You have heard that it was said, 'An eye for an eye, and a tooth for a tooth.' But I tell you, don't resist him who is evil; but whoever strikes you on your right cheek, turn to him the other also. If anyone sues you to take away your coat, let him have your cloak also. Whoever compels you to go one mile, go with him two."*
*Matthew 5:38-41 WEB*

*Repay no one evil for evil. Respect what is honorable in the sight of all men.*
*Romans 12:17 WEB*

*Don't seek revenge yourselves, beloved, but give place to God's wrath. For it is written, "Vengeance belongs to me; I will repay, says the Lord." Therefore "If your enemy is hungry, feed him. If he is thirsty, give him a drink; for in doing so, you will heap coals of fire on his head."*
*Romans 12:19-20 WEB*

## For Further Reflection

- Have you brought judgment on yourself by wrongly judging others?

- Have you not judged some things that you should have judged?

\*\*\*\*\*\*\*\*\*\*\*\*

# Chapter 32
# The Holy Spirit

*For the kingdom of God*
*is not a matter of eating and drinking*
*but of righteousness and peace and joy in the Holy Spirit.*
Romans 14:17 ESV

---

We have seen, back in chapter 19 *"The Spirit,"* what a great blessing the Holy Spirit is. God has chosen to dwell within his people! We believers are, as Paul said, temples of the Holy Spirit:

> **Don't you know that you are a temple of God, and that God's Spirit lives in you?** *1Corinthians 3:16 WEB*

The Holy Spirit plays a key part in our salvation, being involved in both cleansing us of sin and renewing us spiritually. As Paul also said:

> **But when the kindness of God our Savior and his love toward mankind appeared, not by works of righteousness which we did ourselves, but according to his mercy, he saved us through the washing of regeneration and renewing by the Holy Spirit, whom he poured out on us richly, through Jesus Christ our Savior, so that being justified by his grace we might be made heirs according to the hope of eternal life.** *Titus 3:4-7 WEB*

There is wide agreement among believers that the Holy Spirit plays a critical role in our salvation, and in equipping us for ministry. There should be great unity among us over that truth. Unfortunately, that is often not the case.

Few things divide believers today as much as different understandings about the Holy Spirit. It is a sad state of affairs that a topic that should be a strong source of unity is associated with so much division. In this chapter, I present a middle-ground perspective which will hopefully reduce the division, not add to it. Please try to read this chapter with that goal in mind.

Our beliefs about the Holy Spirit ought to be consistent with scripture. However, it seems to me that many people put popular teachings ahead of scripture when it comes to the Holy Spirit.

To better understand scripture in this area, let's first explore the intended meanings of some important phrases in scripture associated with the Holy Spirit. Here are three questions to consider:

- What does it mean to *receive the Holy Spirit*?

- What does it mean to *be filled with the Holy Spirit*?

- What does it mean to *be baptized in the Holy Spirit*?

## Receive the Holy Spirit

Let's look at our first question:

- What does it mean to *receive the Holy Spirit*?

Prior to the New Covenant, the Holy Spirit is said to dwell in relatively few people. However, under the New Covenant the Holy Spirit is given to all believers. This is clear from Peter's preaching at Pentecost:

> *Peter said to them, "Repent, and be baptized, every one of you, in the name of Jesus Christ for the forgiveness of sins, and you will receive the gift of the Holy Spirit. For the promise is to you, and to your children, and to all who are far off, even as many as the Lord our God will call to himself."*　　　　　*Acts 2:38-39 WEB*

Please note that Peter says *"you will receive the gift of the Holy Spirit."* He doesn't say that receiving the Holy Spirit is optional or may happen, but that if they repent and are baptized they *"will receive the gift of the Holy Spirit."*

Peter also says that this is a promise that applies *"to you, and to your children, and to all who are far off, even as many as the Lord our God will call to himself."* The gift of the Holy Spirit is given to all true believers.

The word *receive* here is translated from the Greek word *"limbano."* Most English translations seem to be fairly consistent in translating *limbano* (and its variations) as *receive* (and its variations) when speaking about the Holy Spirit. I am fairly certain that all of the verses that I reference in this section which speak of *receiving* the Holy Spirit have variations of *limbano* in the original Greek.

Let's look at some other verses that support this understanding that believers *receive* the Holy Spirit at the point of true salvation. Notice the sense in most of these verses that receiving (or having) the Holy Spirit is normal for all believers. For clarity, I have underlined variations of the word *"receive"* (in each case translated from the Greek word *"limbano"*):

> *On the last day of the feast, the great day, Jesus stood up and cried out, "If anyone thirsts, let him come to me and drink. Whoever believes in me, as the Scripture has said, 'Out of his heart will flow rivers of living water.'" Now this he said about the Spirit, whom those who believed in him were to <u>receive</u>, for as yet the Spirit had not been given, because Jesus was not yet glorified.*
> John 7:37-39 ESV

> *"If you love me, you will keep my commandments. And I will ask the Father, and he will give you another Helper, to be with you forever, even the Spirit of truth, whom the world cannot <u>receive</u>, because it neither sees him nor knows him. You know him, for he dwells with you and will be in you. I will not leave you as orphans; I will come to you."*
> John 14:15-18 ESV

> *Jesus answered him, "If anyone loves me, he will keep my word, and my Father will love him, and we will come*

*to him and make our home with him."*     *John 14:23 ESV*

*Not only this, but we also rejoice in our sufferings, knowing that suffering produces perseverance; and perseverance, proven character; and proven character, hope: and hope doesn't disappoint us, because God's love has been poured out into our hearts through the Holy Spirit who was given to us.*     *Romans 5:3-5 WEB*

*But you are not in the flesh but in the Spirit, if it is so that the Spirit of God dwells in you. But if any man doesn't have the Spirit of Christ, he is not his.*
*Romans 8:9 WEB*

*For as many as are led by the Spirit of God, these are children of God. For you didn't <u>receive</u> the spirit of bondage again to fear, but you <u>received</u> the Spirit of adoption, by whom we cry, "Abba! Father!"*
*Romans 8:14-15 WEB*

*But we <u>received</u>, not the spirit of the world, but the Spirit which is from God, that we might know the things that were freely given to us by God.*     *1Corinthians 2:12 WEB*

*Don't you know that you are a temple of God, and that God's Spirit lives in you?*     *1Corinthians 3:16 WEB*

*Or don't you know that your body is a temple of the Holy Spirit who is in you, whom you have from God?*
*1Corinthians 6:19 WEB*

*Examine yourselves to see whether you are in the faith; test yourselves. Do you not realize that Christ Jesus is in you—unless, of course, you fail the test?*
*2Corinthians 13:5 NIV*

*Let me ask you only this: Did you <u>receive</u> the Spirit by works of the law or by hearing with faith? Are you so foolish? Having begun by the Spirit, are you now being perfected by the flesh?*     *Galatians 3:2-3 ESV*

*But when the fullness of the time came, God sent out his*

*Son, born to a woman, born under the law, that he might redeem those who were under the law, that we might receive the adoption of children. And because you are children, God sent out the Spirit of his Son into your hearts, crying, "Abba, Father!"* Galatians 4:4-6 WEB

It may be helpful to note that the eleven apostles apparently *received* the Holy Spirit shortly after Jesus' resurrection (before Pentecost):

*When therefore it was evening, on that day, the first day of the week, and when the doors were locked where the disciples were assembled, for fear of the Jews, Jesus came and stood in the middle, and said to them, "Peace be to you."*

*When he had said this, he showed them his hands and his side. The disciples therefore were glad when they saw the Lord. Jesus therefore said to them again, "Peace be to you. As the Father has sent me, even so I send you." When he had said this, he breathed on them, and said to them, "<u>Receive</u> the Holy Spirit!"*

John 20:19-22 WEB

So, the Holy Spirit was apparently *received* by the eleven apostles without much external evidence of that happening. However, they were not *baptized in the Holy Spirit* or *filled with the Holy Spirit* until the day of Pentecost (in Acts 2).

From all this, I conclude that *receiving the Holy Spirit* is what normally happens when believers are first saved: the Holy Spirit enters them to dwell in them; they *receive the Holy Spirit*.

## Filled with the Holy Spirit

Now let's look at our second question:

- What does it mean to *be filled with the Holy Spirit*?

We have already seen that all true believers have *received* the Holy Spirit, and therefore have the Holy Spirit dwelling in them. Now we look at what it means to be *filled with* the Holy Spirit, which partly has to do with whether or not a person is strongly influenced by the Holy Spirit.

Though there is little teaching in the New Testament *letters* about this subject, we see several examples in the book of Acts where various people are said to be *filled with the Holy Spirit*, or are said to be *full of the Holy Spirit*. As we review those various passages, I think it is helpful to consider them from these possible different perspectives:

- **God's Initiative:**  Being *filled with the Holy Spirit* may primarily be associated with God choosing to *fill* a person, to empower them for a particular situation. Here the focus is on God's particular purpose in a person's life or in a particular situation.

- **Our Initiative:**  Being *filled with the Holy Spirit* may primarily be associated with a person allowing the Holy Spirit to *fill* every part of them, or to inhabit or influence every part of their life. Here the focus is on our cooperation with God and our openness to being *filled*. In this case, God has already made provision to be *filled*, and it is up to us to satisfy the conditions of being *filled*.

- **A Combination:**  Being *filled with the Holy Spirit* may be influenced both by God's initiative and our initiative.

Scripture speaks of being filled with the Spirit as something that believers may experience from time-to-time (or possibly to varying degrees), rather than being an automatic continual state. Scripture records some people being *filled with the Spirit* before Pentecost. Here are all the clear examples I find in Scripture:

> **Yahweh spoke to Moses, saying, "Behold, I have called by name Bezalel the son of Uri, the son of Hur, of the**

*tribe of Judah. I have filled him with the Spirit of God, in wisdom, and in understanding, and in knowledge, and in all kinds of workmanship, to devise skillful works, to work in gold, and in silver, and in brass, and in cutting of stones for setting, and in carving of wood, to work in all kinds of workmanship."* Exodus 31:1-5 WEB

*But the angel said to him, "Don't be afraid, Zacharias, because your request has been heard, and your wife, Elizabeth, will bear you a son, and you shall call his name John. You will have joy and gladness; and many will rejoice at his birth. For he will be great in the sight of the Lord, and he will drink no wine nor strong drink. He will be filled with the Holy Spirit, even from his mother's womb."* Luke 1:13-15 WEB

*When Elizabeth heard Mary's greeting, the baby leaped in her womb, and Elizabeth was filled with the Holy Spirit. She called out with a loud voice, and said, "Blessed are you among women, and blessed is the fruit of your womb!"* Luke 1:41-42 WEB

*His father, Zacharias, was filled with the Holy Spirit, and prophesied, saying...* Luke 1:67 WEB

Similarly, there are numerous times in the Old Testament where the Holy Spirit *"came on,"* or *"came upon"* various people. For those interested in the details, here are some references: Numbers 24:2; Judges 3:10, 6:34, 11:29, 14:6, 14:19, 15:14; 1 Samuel 10:10, 11:6, 16:13, 19:20, 19:23; 1 Chronicles 12:18; 2 Chronicles 15:1, 20:14, 24:20.

Here are examples of people being *filled with the Spirit,* starting at Pentecost:

*They were all filled with the Holy Spirit, and began to speak with other languages, as the Spirit gave them the ability to speak.* Acts 2:4 WEB

*Then Peter, filled with the Holy Spirit, said to them,*

*"You rulers of the people, and elders of Israel..."*
                                                    *Acts 4:8 WEB*

**When they had prayed, the place was shaken where they were gathered together. They were all filled with the Holy Spirit, and they spoke the word of God with boldness.** *Acts 4:31 WEB*

**Ananias departed, and entered into the house. Laying his hands on him, he said, "Brother Saul, the Lord, who appeared to you on the road by which you came, has sent me, that you may receive your sight, and be filled with the Holy Spirit."** *Acts 9:17 WEB*

**But Saul, who was also called Paul, filled with the Holy Spirit, looked intently at him and said, "You son of the devil, you enemy of all righteousness, full of all deceit and villainy, will you not stop making crooked the straight paths of the Lord?"** *Acts 13:9-10 ESV*

**And the disciples were filled with joy and with the Holy Spirit.** *Acts 13:52 ESV*

A similar phrase to consider is *"full of the Holy Spirit."* This phrase appears to be associated with people who are consistently strongly influenced by the Holy Spirit. Here are all the verses I find in the New Testament that use that phrase:

**Jesus, full of the Holy Spirit, returned from the Jordan, and was led by the Spirit into the wilderness for forty days, being tempted by the devil.** *Luke 4:1-2 WEB*

**The twelve summoned the multitude of the disciples and said, "It is not appropriate for us to forsake the word of God and serve tables. Therefore select from among you, brothers, seven men of good report, full of the Holy Spirit and of wisdom, whom we may appoint over this business.** *Acts 6:2-3 WEB*

**These words pleased the whole multitude. They chose**

*Stephen, a man full of faith and of the Holy Spirit, Philip, Prochorus, Nicanor, Timon, Parmenas, and Nicolaus, a proselyte of Antioch; whom they set before the apostles.*                                   Acts 6:5-6 WEB

*Now when they heard these things, they were cut to the heart, and they gnashed at him with their teeth. But he, being full of the Holy Spirit, looked up steadfastly into heaven, and saw the glory of God, and Jesus standing on the right hand of God, and said, "Behold, I see the heavens opened, and the Son of Man standing at the right hand of God!"*               Acts 7:54-56 WEB

*They sent out Barnabas to go as far as Antioch, who, when he had come, and had seen the grace of God, was glad. He exhorted them all, that with purpose of heart they should remain near to the Lord. For he was a good man, and full of the Holy Spirit and of faith, and many people were added to the Lord.*             Acts 11:22-24 WEB

It may be helpful to consider some related terms, which appear to me to mean the same as being *filled with the Holy Spirit*. Recall Jesus' words to the apostles before Pentecost:

*"But you will receive power when the Holy Spirit comes on you; and you will be my witnesses in Jerusalem, and in all Judea and Samaria, and to the ends of the earth."*
                                                Acts 1:8 NIV

At Pentecost, *"they were all filled with the Holy Spirit"* (Acts 2:4, above), and Peter boldly preached to the people, and about 3000 people were saved (Acts 2:41). This clearly correlates with what Jesus said would happen in Acts 1:8. Since the apostles had previously *received* the Holy Spirit (John 20:22), it appears that Jesus' words *"when the Holy Spirit comes on you"* (Acts 1:8) correlate with the believers being *"filled with the Holy Spirit"* in Acts 2:4.

A similar filling of the Spirit occurred when the Gentiles first believed, in Acts 10. However, in this case the people also *received* the Holy Spirit (as new believers), and scripture says the Holy Spirit *"fell on"* them (some translations say *"came on"* them):

> **While Peter was still speaking these words, the Holy Spirit _fell on_ all those who heard the word.** *Acts 10:44 WEB*

> **"Can anyone forbid these people from being baptized with water? They have _received_ the Holy Spirit just like us."** *Acts 10:47 WEB*

> **As I began to speak, the Holy Spirit _fell on_ them, even as on us at the beginning. I remembered the word of the Lord, how he said, 'John indeed baptized in water, but you will be baptized in the Holy Spirit.' If then God gave to them the same gift as us, when we believed in the Lord Jesus Christ, who was I, that I could withstand God?"** *Acts 11:15-17 WEB*

Here it appears that the phrase *"the Holy Spirit fell on"* correlates with the new believers both *receiving the Holy Spirit* and being *filled with the Holy Spirit.*

Now let's look at what the *letters* of the New Testament say about being *filled with the Holy Spirit.* I find only one verse that uses a phrase similar to *"filled with the Holy Spirit"*:

> **Don't be drunken with wine, in which is dissipation, but be filled with the Spirit, speaking to one another in psalms, hymns, and spiritual songs; singing, and making melody in your heart to the Lord; giving thanks always concerning all things in the name of our Lord Jesus Christ, to God, even the Father; subjecting yourselves one to another in the fear of Christ.** *Ephesians 5:18-21 WEB*

We can learn several important things from these verses:

- We should all make it our goal to be consistently *filled with the Spirit*.

- Being *filled with the Spirit* does not happen

automatically, since Paul instructs the people at Ephesus to *be filled with the Spirit.* Being *filled with the Spirit* appears to require our cooperation with God.

- We can choose, to some degree at least, to be *drunken with wine* or *filled with the Spirit.* Just as being drunk with wine involves ongoing drinking of wine, so being filled with the Spirit usually involves ongoing spiritual focus, in accordance with the next point.

- Being *filled with the Spirit* is associated with singing spiritual songs to one another, singing to the Lord, giving thanks to God, and subjecting ourselves to one another, and doing all these things *in the fear of Christ.*

From all this, I conclude that being *filled with the Holy Spirit* involves being strongly influenced by the Holy Spirit. It is often associated with spiritual power for ministry. It may be a temporary experience, or a long-term experience. Some aspects of being filled with the Holy Spirit are dependent on our cooperation with God.

Here are some additional thoughts on being *filled with the Holy Spirit*, which are not directly based on scripture, but which I believe are consistent with scripture, and which may be helpful to some:

- Becoming *full of the Holy Spirit* involves humbly submitting ourselves to God, and having a thankful heart.

- Becoming *full of the Holy Spirit* involves loving God and loving others.

- Some have said that we must empty ourselves of selfishness in order to be *full of the Holy Spirit.*

- Being *full of the Holy Spirit* may involve the Holy Spirit having more of us, rather than us having more of the Holy Spirit.

- Paul wrote: **"Don't quench the Spirit"** (1 Thessalonians 5:19 WEB) and **"Don't grieve the Holy Spirit of God, in whom you were sealed for the day of redemption"** (Ephesians 4:30 WEB). *Quenching* or *grieving* the Holy Spirit results in not being *full of the Holy Spirit.*

- Referring to the Holy Spirit, Jesus said ***"He who believes in me, as the Scripture has said, from within him will flow rivers of living water"*** (John 7:38 WEB). This implies a continual flow of the Holy Spirit in our lives. Yesterday's flow is not adequate for today; we need fresh flow continually.

## "Baptize"

Now let's begin to look at our third question:

- What does it mean to *be baptized in the Holy Spirit?*

Let's start by considering the origins of the word *"baptize."* What did John the Baptist and Jesus mean when they said people would be *baptized in the Holy Spirit?* Before dealing with that specific subject, let's first try to understand what the words *baptize* and *baptism* meant before people were *baptized in the Holy Spirit.*

"Baptize" is now an English word derived from the New Testament Greek word *baptizo*. In English it generally carries religious meaning, usually being associated with either baptism in water or baptism in the Holy Spirit. However, in New Testament Greek it had a broader meaning, more along the lines of meaning to *immerse* or *dip* in a liquid, and was associated with washing people or things. The sense that baptism in the New Testament normally involved immersing in water (rather than sprinkling or pouring water) is supported by these verses:

> *Jesus, when he was baptized, went up directly from the water: and behold, the heavens were opened to him. He*

*saw the Spirit of God descending as a dove, and coming on him.*
*Matthew 3:16 WEB*

*In those days, Jesus came from Nazareth of Galilee, and was baptized by John in the Jordan. Immediately coming up from the water, he saw the heavens parting, and the Spirit descending on him like a dove.*
*Mark 1:9-10 WEB*

*Now John also was baptizing at Aenon near Salim, because there was plenty of water, and people were coming and being baptized.*
*John 3:23 NIV*

The following verses show that the Greek word *baptizo* may include a sense of washing something (*baptizo* is translated as "<u>wash</u>" in these verses):

*Now when the Pharisees gathered to him, with some of the scribes who had come from Jerusalem, they saw that some of his disciples ate with hands that were defiled, that is, unwashed. (For the Pharisees and all the Jews do not eat unless they wash their hands properly, holding to the tradition of the elders, and when they come from the marketplace, they do not eat unless they <u>wash.</u> And there are many other traditions that they observe, such as the washing of cups and pots and copper vessels and dining couches.)*
*Mark 7:1-4 ESV*

*While Jesus was speaking, a Pharisee asked him to dine with him, so he went in and reclined at table. The Pharisee was astonished to see that he did not first <u>wash</u> before dinner.*
*Luke 11:37-38 ESV*

Similarly, in Mark 7:4 (above), the word "*washing*" (*of cups and pots...*) is translated from a related Greek word, *baptismos*, which is usually translated as "*baptisms*" in Hebrews 6:2. *Baptismos* is also used in Hebrews 9:10, where it is usually translated as *"washings."*

A connection between ceremonial washing and being *baptized* (Greek word *baptizo*) is made fairly directly in the

Septuagint. (The Septuagint is a Greek translation of the Old Testament that was completed more than a century before Jesus' time on earth; it was widely used by the Jews in New Testament times.) The connection is made in the account of Naaman the leper:

> *So Naaman came with his horses and with his chariots, and stood at the door of the house of Elisha. Elisha sent a messenger to him, saying, "Go and wash in the Jordan seven times, and your flesh shall come again to you, and you shall be clean."*

> *But Naaman was angry, and went away, and said, "Behold, I thought, 'He will surely come out to me, and stand, and call on the name of Yahweh his God, and wave his hand over the place, and heal the leper.' Aren't Abanah and Pharpar, the rivers of Damascus, better than all the waters of Israel? Couldn't I wash in them, and be clean?" So he turned and went away in a rage.*

> *His servants came near, and spoke to him, and said, "My father, if the prophet had asked you do some great thing, wouldn't you have done it? How much rather then, when he says to you, 'Wash, and be clean?'"*

> *Then went he down, and dipped himself seven times in the Jordan, according to the saying of the man of God; and his flesh was restored like the flesh of a little child, and he was clean.*     2Kings 5:9-14 WEB

The word **"wash"**, which is used three times in these verses, correlates with the Greek word *"louo"* (Strong's Exhaustive Concordance reference number G3068), and this is the same Greek word translated as *"bathe"* in Leviticus 14:8 and 15:27 and Numbers 19:19 (discussed below under "Jewish Baptisms"). However, when Naaman **dipped himself seven times in the Jordan**, the word **"dipped"** correlates with the Greek word *"baptizo"* (Strong's G907) in the Septuagint.

So, per the Septuagint, Naaman *"baptized"* himself seven times in the Jordan. This strengthens the correlation I see between being *baptized* in the New Testament and ceremonial washing in the Old Testament.

Likewise, water baptism of believers in the New Testament is associated with a physical washing associated with spiritual washing, a cleansing of sins. Consider these verses:

> *An argument developed between some of John's disciples and a certain Jew over the matter of ceremonial washing. They came to John and said to him, "Rabbi, that man who was with you on the other side of the Jordan—the one you testified about—look, he is baptizing, and everyone is going to him."*
>
> *John 3:25-26 NIV*

> *Peter said to them, "Repent, and be baptized, every one of you, in the name of Jesus Christ for the forgiveness of sins, and you will receive the gift of the Holy Spirit."*
>
> *Acts 2:38 WEB*

> *"Now why do you wait? Arise, be baptized, and wash away your sins, calling on the name of the Lord."*
>
> *Acts 22:16 WEB*

Note that, in John 3:25-26, *"ceremonial washing"* appears to correlate with *"he is baptizing."* In Acts 2:38 *"be baptized"* is associated with *"forgiveness of sins."* In Acts 22:16, *"be baptized"* correlates with *"wash away your sins."*

So, when we consider what it means to be *"baptized in the Holy Spirit,"* it seems appropriate to keep in mind that a common meaning of *"baptize"* was to wash something to make it clean.

## Jewish Baptisms

Now let's look more closely at how Jewish people in New Testament times, before Jesus died and rose, understood the concept of *"baptism,"* and explore how baptism may have roots in Old Testament requirements for ceremonial washing.

The first time we see the words *"baptize"* or *"baptism"* used in scripture, in most English translations, is in Matthew 3, where John the Baptist is introduced:

> **In those days, John the Baptizer came, preaching in the wilderness of Judea, saying, "Repent, for the Kingdom of Heaven is at hand!"**
> *Matthew 3:1-2 WEB*

> **Then people from Jerusalem, all of Judea, and all the region around the Jordan went out to him. They were baptized by him in the Jordan, confessing their sins.**
> *Matthew 3:5-6 WEB*

> **I indeed baptize you in water for repentance, but he who comes after me is mightier than I, whose shoes I am not worthy to carry. He will baptize you in the Holy Spirit.**
> *Matthew 3:11 WEB*

The Gospels of Mark and Luke have similar accounts. Mark summarizes John's ministry this way:

> **John appeared, baptizing in the wilderness and proclaiming a baptism of repentance for the forgiveness of sins. And all the country of Judea and all Jerusalem were going out to him and were being baptized by him in the river Jordan, confessing their sins.**
> *Mark 1:4-5 ESV*

Scripture makes little effort in the New Testament to explain where this idea of being *"baptized"* **for the forgiveness of sins** came from. The people seem to understand that it's a good thing to do, and they come to John to be baptized, in response to his call to do so. This implies that baptism was already a part of their culture, and John was simply bringing a new emphasis to it.

It appears that baptism in the New Testament developed from the Old Testament requirement for people to wash themselves as part of the process of being cleansed of ritual uncleanness. Many verses in the Law of Moses, especially in the book of Leviticus, require washing in water. For example:

> *Yahweh spoke to Moses, saying, "This shall be the law of the leper in the day of his cleansing. He shall be brought to the priest... He who is to be cleansed shall wash his clothes, and shave off all his hair, and bathe himself in water; and he shall be clean."*
>
> *Leviticus 14:1-2, 8 WEB*

> *"Whoever touches these things shall be unclean, and shall wash his clothes and bathe himself in water, and be unclean until the evening."*    *Leviticus 15:27 WEB*

> *"Whoever in the open field touches one who is slain with a sword, or a dead body, or a bone of a man, or a grave, shall be unclean seven days. ... He shall wash his clothes and bathe himself in water, and shall be clean at evening."*
>
> *Numbers 19:16, 19 WEB*

Some English translations read *"with water"* rather than *"in water."* Apparently the original Hebrew is not clear on this point, leaving some uncertainty regarding how the washing was to be done. Speaking practically, some options *may* include washing with a wet cloth, sprinkling or splashing or pouring water onto the body, or by immersion in water. Just what was acceptable might depend on the circumstances and local culture.

There is historical evidence that accepted practices in Israel for this kind of ceremonial washing became narrower over time. By the time of Jesus' ministry on earth, the preferred practice of ritual washing was by immersion in water, as evidenced by "mikvah" washing pools in Israel that date back to that time period. Jewish tradition often required immersion in water, as indicated in the Talmud (ancient Jewish writings). Consider this passage in the Talmud, which is referring to the *washing* required in Leviticus 15:16:

*"The definite article in the phrase 'in the water' indicates that this bathing is performed in water mentioned elsewhere, i.e., specifically in the water of a ritual bath, and not in just any water. And the phrase "all his flesh" indicates that it must be in water into which all of his body can enter."* (Talmud Bavli, The William Davidson Talmud, Eruvin 4b; available at www.sefaria.org.)

Further, Jewish tradition requires that a convert to Judaism be ritually immersed in a ritual bath as a final step in becoming a Jew. That ceremony carries the sense of being cleansed of a former life and being born again. *"Once he has immersed and emerged, he is like a born Jew in every sense."* (Talmud Bavli, The William Davidson Talmud, Yevamot 47b; available at www.sefaria.org.)

Here we see that baptism in water is associated with conversion from one religion to another. Baptism was the final step for a non-Jewish person to become a Jew *"like a born Jew in every sense."* This may shed some light on what Jesus meant when he told Nicodemus:

> **"Most certainly I tell you, unless one is born of water and spirit, he can't enter into God's Kingdom."**
>
> *John 3:5 WEB*

In summary, we have seen how baptism in water appears to be related to ceremonial washing required by the Law of Moses. It also appears to have ties to religious conversion ceremonies, such as Jewish converts being immersed in water as a final step of their conversion, with implications of being cleansed of an old life and being made new. These correlations lead me to conclude that baptism, in New Testament times, was at least partly about ritual cleansing, being washed clean of a physical or a spiritual problem. When John came **proclaiming a baptism of repentance for the forgiveness of sins** (Mark 1:4 ESV), it was partly about an outward washing associated with a spiritual cleansing, the forgiveness of sins. It was also about **repentance**, which involves a change in thinking, a change in direction. John's baptism, some would say, involved a religious *conversion*.

So, when we consider what it means to be *"baptized in the Holy Spirit,"* it seems appropriate to keep in mind that, during the time of John the Baptist, baptism in water was associated with physical cleansing, spiritual cleansing, and religious conversion.

## Baptized in the Holy Spirit

Now, with all that background about baptism, let's look at our third question more directly:

- What does it mean to *be baptized in the Holy Spirit*?

Verses in the four gospels which refer to being *baptized in* (or *with*) *the Holy Spirit* are all quotes of John the Baptist, and all appear to speak of what Jesus will do for all believers in the future, in contrast to John baptizing in water for repentance and forgiveness of sins. I find only these four verses in the four gospels that speak of being baptized in, or with, the Holy Spirit:

> *"I indeed baptize you in water for repentance, but he who comes after me is mightier than I, whose shoes I am not worthy to carry. He will baptize you in the Holy Spirit."*
> Matthew 3:11 WEB

> *"I baptized you in water, but he will baptize you in the Holy Spirit."*
> Mark 1:8 WEB

> *John answered them all, saying, "I baptize you with water, but he who is mightier than I is coming, the strap of whose sandals I am not worthy to untie. He will baptize you with the Holy Spirit and fire."* Luke 3:16 ESV

> *"I myself did not know him, but he who sent me to baptize with water said to me, 'He on whom you see the Spirit descend and remain, this is he who baptizes with the Holy Spirit.'"*
> John 1:33 ESV

In all these verses, the main point seems to be that John merely baptized with water, but Jesus will baptize with the Holy Spirit!

In the above verses, consider replacing the word *"baptize"* with the word *"wash."* Does thinking of *"baptism"* as a *"washing"* help you understand what it means for Jesus to *baptize* us in (or with) the Holy Spirit? I thank God, the Holy Spirit has cleansed me of sin!! I have been *washed* by the Holy Spirit! I have been *baptized* in the Holy Spirit! If you are saved, the same is true of you!

John's baptism in water was about repentance and forgiveness of sins. People went to John *"confessing their sins"* (Matthew 3:6, Mark 1:5) for forgiveness of sins:

> **And he went into all the region around the Jordan, proclaiming a baptism of repentance for the forgiveness of sins.** *Luke 3:3 ESV*

However, forgiveness of past sins is different than being delivered from the power of sin. People baptized by John had to wait for washing in the Holy Spirit (done later by Jesus after he ascended to heaven) to actually be delivered from the power of sin so they could live a righteous life.

I am not saying that spiritual washing is the only thing involved in being *baptized in the Holy Spirit*, but I think it is an important aspect that should be considered. The sense of baptism signifying a religious conversion should also be considered. Paul clarifies in Romans 6 that being **baptized into Christ Jesus** involves dying with Christ and being resurrected with Christ. That reinforces the sense that baptism is not just about *spiritual cleansing*, but is also about *spiritual conversion*. Consider again Paul's words to Titus:

> **...he saved us through the washing of regeneration and renewing by the Holy Spirit, whom he poured out on us richly, through Jesus Christ our Savior...** *Titus 3:5-6 WEB*

The cleansing done by the Holy Spirit involves **the washing** *of regeneration and renewing by the Holy Spirit.* I thank God, I have been regenerated and renewed by the Holy Spirit! The Holy Spirit has converted me from being a slave to sin into a child of God! I have been *baptized* by Jesus *in the Holy Spirit*! I am now a follower of Jesus!

Now let's look at the only other verses I find in the New Testament that talk about being **baptized in the Holy Spirit:**

> *"For John indeed baptized in water, but you will be baptized in the Holy Spirit not many days from now."*
>
> Acts 1:5 WEB

> *"And I remembered the word of the Lord, how he said, 'John baptized with water, but you will be baptized with the Holy Spirit.'"*
>
> Acts 11:16 ESV

In these verses, *"baptized in the Holy Spirit"* is used to refer to the initial pouring out of the Spirit at Pentecost (Acts 2), and the initial pouring out of the Holy Spirit on the Gentiles at Joppa (Acts 10 to 11). Again, being baptized in the Holy Spirit is simply contrasted with John baptizing in water, and it makes sense to think of being baptized in the Holy Spirit as involving spiritual washing and spiritual conversion.

The six verses listed above are the only verses I find in the New Testament that directly speak of being *baptized in the Holy Spirit.* That phrase, or a similar phrase, does not appear to be in any of the *letters* of the New Testament. It may be helpful to prayerfully consider the significance of that with regard to your own beliefs about what it means to be *"baptized in the Holy Spirit."*

Now let's consider the subject of *spiritual power*, how that is related to the Holy Spirit being poured out at Pentecost, and how it may be related to being *baptized in the Holy Spirit.* Spiritual power is a strong theme in scripture, and is usually associated with the Holy Spirit living in us. Consider these verses, both spoken by Jesus, both of which look forward to what would happen at Pentecost:

*"Behold, I send out the promise of my Father on you. But wait in the city of Jerusalem until you are clothed with power from on high."* Luke 24:49 WEB

*But you will receive power when the Holy Spirit has come upon you. You will be witnesses to me in Jerusalem, in all Judea and Samaria, and to the uttermost parts of the earth."* Acts 1:8 WEB

Clearly, receiving *spiritual power* is a major theme associated with Pentecost, and is clearly associated with the Holy Spirit. But is receiving *spiritual power* part of being baptized in the Holy Spirit? Many people make that connection, and perhaps rightly so. However, I think it is worth noting that scripture usually makes the connection of *spiritual power* with being *filled with the Holy Spirit*, not with being *baptized in the Holy Spirit*.

This raises a question: Is being *baptized in the Holy Spirit* the same as being *filled with the Holy Spirit*? I don't think so, simply because I don't see anywhere that scripture clearly makes that correlation, and those phrases appear to have significantly different meanings:

- We have seen that the word *"baptism"* is normally associated with spiritual washing and spiritual conversion. That doesn't correlate well with how the phrase *"filled with the Holy Spirit"* is normally used in scripture.

- The phrase *"baptize in the Holy Spirit"* literally refers to being *immersed* in the Holy Spirit. That has to do with a person being in the Holy Spirit. Being *filled with the Holy Spirit* rather seems to involve the Holy Spirit being in a person.

Is this just semantics? Why am I being so careful with this subject? Simply because a huge amount of division has occurred among believers due to people making various claims about what *baptism in the Holy Spirit* means. Such claims are hard to verify or refute, simply because scripture says almost nothing directly about being *baptized in the Holy Spirit*, except that it is done by Jesus, and it happened starting at Pentecost in Acts 2. When people strongly promote doctrines which have only weak scriptural support, division is usually a result, rather than unity.

This brings us to some difficult issues. Many different teachings have arisen around the phrase *"baptism in the Holy Spirit"* (and similar phrases). Many people seem to use the phrase *"baptism in the Holy Spirit"* (and similar phrases) to promote their particular spiritual experience as something that all believers should experience. Indeed, many groups of believers today seem to largely define themselves by how they define and promote *"baptism in the Holy Spirit."*

Is *"baptism in the Holy Spirit"* more than spiritual cleansing and regeneration received by all true believers when they are first saved? Is *"baptism in the Holy Spirit"* something many believers first experience long after salvation? Is *baptism in the Holy Spirit* something believers should seek? Let's look at scripture for some possible answers to these questions.

We previously saw that a phrase similar to *"baptize in the Holy Spirit"* is only used in six places in scripture, and four of those places are simply similar quotes of John the Baptist by the four different authors of the four accounts of Jesus' life (Matthew 3:11, Mark 1:8, Luke 3:16, John 1:33). All six occurrences simply contrast John baptizing people in water with what Jesus would do in the future: Jesus would baptize people in the Holy Spirit. There are no direct references to *"baptize in the Holy Spirit"* in any of the letters of the New Testament. The phrases "baptism in the Holy Spirit" and "Spirit Baptism" (and similar noun phrases which include the words "baptism" and "Spirit") do not occur anywhere in scripture (except possibly in some paraphrased translations). There are no verses that instruct us to seek *baptism in the Holy Spirit* or to be *baptized in the Holy Spirit*. While the

Holy Spirit is a huge topic in scripture, being *baptized in the Holy Spirit* is a minor topic in scripture.

Now let's look at this question more closely: Is *baptism in the Holy Spirit* something believers should seek? While scripture does instruct us to be *filled with the Holy Spirit* (Ephesians 5:18), I do not find any verses that instruct us to be *baptized in the Holy Spirit* or to seek a *baptism in the Holy Spirit*. While there are many examples in the book of Acts of believers who are said to be *filled with the Holy Spirit* or *full of the Holy Spirit*, I don't see any examples of believers who are said to be *baptized in the Holy Spirit* (distinct from believers who are not). There are no references in scripture to anyone being *baptized in the Holy Spirit* other than at Pentecost (Acts 1:5 looking ahead to Acts 2) or at the point of being saved (Acts 11:16 looking back on Acts 10).

Why are there no references to being *baptized in the Holy Spirit* in the letters of the New Testament, and only two mentions of it in the book of Acts (which are both quotes of Jesus)? I think it is simply because the early church associated being *baptized in the Holy Spirit* with what normally happens when a person is saved, and they preferred to use other vocabulary to refer to various aspects of salvation and the Holy Spirit.

So, when considering spiritual power for life and ministry, keep in mind that the focus of scripture is on the simple concept of being *filled with the Holy Spirit*. Clearly, all believers should aim to be *full of the Holy Spirit*, as already discussed above under the heading *"Filled with the Holy Spirit."* Wouldn't being full of the Holy Spirit provide us with all the power and anointing we need? Why look for spiritual power in some other experience?

Let's not make spiritual experiences, spiritual progress, and spiritual power more complicated than scripture does. Each person is unique. Let's allow the Holy Spirit to deal with each person uniquely. Let's not assume that our own spiritual experiences should be duplicated in all believers. Let's simply do as scripture does, and encourage one another to be *filled with the Holy Spirit* (Ephesians 5:18-21).

Much of the confusion today about *baptism in the Holy Spirit* may be the result of neglecting a simple concept: God is free to do as he pleases, differently in every situation if he so chooses. Just because he chooses to do things one way in a particular situation does not obligate him to do the same in other situations. We should not expect the Holy Spirit to fit neatly inside of our theological boxes. We ought to embrace the gift of the Holy Spirit without limiting him by our own ideas of how he should work in our own life and in the lives of others.

As you consider your own beliefs about this topic, please keep in mind how little scripture actually says about being *baptized in the Holy Spirit,* and do not be misled into unscriptural beliefs. Holding to a neutral attitude about things that aren't clear may be helpful (per chapter 13 *"A Neutral Attitude"*).

Although there is no direct mention of being *baptized in the Holy Spirit* in any of the *letters* of the New Testament, I think it is indirectly mentioned. Based on a common meaning of *baptize* being to wash something, I understand these verses to be referring to being *baptized in the Holy Spirit*:

> *And such were some of you. But you were washed, you were sanctified, you were justified in the name of the Lord Jesus Christ and by the Spirit of our God.*
>
> *1Corinthians 6:11 ESV*

> *But when the kindness of God our Savior and his love toward mankind appeared, not by works of righteousness, which we did ourselves, but according to his mercy, he saved us through the washing of regeneration and renewing by the Holy Spirit, whom he*

*poured out on us richly, through Jesus Christ our Savior...* *Titus 3:4-6 WEB*

While these verses do not use the Greek word *"baptizo"* or *"baptismo"* for *"wash"* or *"washing,"* the message is similar: the Holy Spirit within us is associated with *washing* us clean, and renewing and sanctifying us spiritually.

In conclusion, I understand that Jesus is the one who *baptizes in the Holy Spirit* (Matthew 3:11, Mark 1:8, Luke 3:16, John 1:33), and that involves **the washing of regeneration and renewing by the Holy Spirit** (Titus 3:5). This normally happens at the point of salvation, but may also be a progressive work over time. I prefer to think of being *filled with the Holy Spirit* as being distinct from being *baptized in the Holy Spirit*, though beliefs about this vary widely.

Here is the only other verse I am aware of in the New Testament that mentions *Spirit* along with *baptism* or *baptize*:

**For in one Spirit we were all baptized into one body— Jews or Greeks, slaves or free—and all were made to drink of one Spirit.** *1Corinthians 12:13 ESV*

Here the word *baptize* appears to have the meaning of being *immersed* into something. In this case, all believers are *immersed* into one body, the body of Christ. Here the emphasis is on the unity of all believers, and the one Spirit we all have, not on any doctrine that divides believers into various groups based on spiritual experiences some have had and others haven't had.

By way of review, here are the three questions that we set out to answer at the beginning of this chapter:

- What does it mean to *receive the Holy Spirit*?

- What does it mean to *be filled with the Holy Spirit*?

- What does it mean to *be baptized in the Holy Spirit*?

And here is a summary of how I have answered these questions:

- We *receive the Holy Spirit* when we first truly come to Jesus and are saved. The Holy Spirit enters us and dwells within us. Generally speaking, those who do not have the Holy Spirit dwelling in them are not yet saved.

- Being *filled with the Holy Spirit* involves being strongly influenced by the Holy Spirit. It is often associated with spiritual power for ministry. It may be a temporary experience, or a long-term experience. Some aspects of being filled with the Holy Spirit are dependent on our cooperation with God.

- Jesus is the one who *baptizes in the Holy Spirit* (Matthew 3:11, Mark 1:8, Luke 3:16, John 1:33), and that involves **the washing of regeneration and renewing by the Holy Spirit** (Titus 3:5). This normally happens at the point of salvation, but may also be a progressive work over time.

## Spiritual Gifts

Now, let's turn our attention to spiritual gifts. There is wide agreement that the *"fruit of the Spirit"* should be the experience of all believers:

*But the fruit of the Spirit is love, joy, peace, patience, kindness, goodness, faith, gentleness, and self-control. Against such things there is no law.*

*Galatians 5:22-23 WEB*

However, the Holy Spirit also imparts particular gifts to people, as Paul explains in these verses:

*Now there are various kinds of gifts, but the same Spirit. There are various kinds of service, and the same Lord. There are various kinds of workings, but the same God, who works all things in all. But to each one is given the manifestation of the Spirit for the profit of all. For to one is given through the Spirit the word of wisdom, and to another the word of knowledge, according to the same Spirit; to another faith, by the same Spirit; and to another gifts of healings, by the same Spirit; and to another workings of miracles; and to another prophecy; and to another discerning of spirits; to another different kinds of languages; and to another the interpretation of languages. But the one and the same Spirit produces all of these, distributing to each one separately as he desires.* 1Corinthians 12:4-11 WEB

Paul gives a similar list of spiritual gifts in his letter to the Romans:

*For just as each of us has one body with many members, and these members do not all have the same function, so in Christ we, though many, form one body, and each member belongs to all the others. We have different gifts, according to the grace given to each of us. If your gift is prophesying, then prophesy in accordance with your faith; if it is serving, then serve; if it is teaching, then teach; if it is to encourage, then give encourage-ment; if it is giving, then give generously; if it is to lead, do it diligently; if it is to show mercy, do it cheerfully.* Romans 12:4-8 NIV

Paul's statements *"to each one is given the manifestation of the Spirit for the profit of all"* (1 Corinthians 12:7) and *"We have different gifts, according to the grace given to each of us"* (Romans 12:6) seem to indicate that *all* believers are given some kind of spiritual gift. However, it is God who distributes spiritual gifts *"to each one separately as he desires."* Paul clarifies this further:

*God has set some in the assembly: first apostles, second prophets, third teachers, then miracle workers, then gifts of healings, helps, governments, and various kinds of languages. Are all apostles? Are all prophets? Are all*

*teachers? Are all miracle workers? Do all have gifts of healings? Do all speak with various languages? Do all interpret? But earnestly desire the best gifts.*

1Corinthians 12:28-31 WEB

God works differently in different people. Those who expect others to experience the Holy Spirit in the same way they have don't seem to understand this. Those who promote a particular spiritual gift as being normal for all appear to me to be speaking contrary to scripture.

In 1 Corinthians 12:12-27, Paul emphasizes that believers have been given diverse gifts for the purpose of edifying one another and building up the body of Christ, similar to how the different members of our physical bodies work together for the benefit of the whole body (as also mentioned in Romans 12:4-8 above). While some parts of our bodies appear to be more important than others, all the parts are necessary for a properly functioning body. Likewise, we are each part of one body, the body of Christ, and we each have a different role to fill:

*For as the body is one, and has many members, and all the members of the body, being many, are one body; so also is Christ. For in one Spirit we were all baptized into one body, whether Jews or Greeks, whether bond or free; and were all given to drink into one Spirit. For the body is not one member, but many. If the foot would say, "Because I'm not the hand, I'm not part of the body," it is not therefore not part of the body.*

1Corinthians 12;13-15 WEB

*The eye can't tell the hand, "I have no need for you," or again the head to the feet, "I have no need for you." No, much rather, those members of the body which seem to be weaker are necessary. Those parts of the body which we think to be less honorable, on those we bestow more abundant honor; and our unpresentable parts have more abundant propriety; whereas our presentable*

*Building on Foundations for Eternal Life*        *295*

*parts have no such need. But God composed the body together, giving more abundant honor to the inferior part, that there should be no division in the body, but that the members should have the same care for one another.* 1Corinthians 12:21-25 WEB

Note the purpose in how God distributes spiritual gifts: *"...that there should be no division in the body, but that the members should have the same care for one another."* Our beliefs and practices regarding spiritual gifts should result in *care for one another* and *no division*. As Paul writes in the following chapter (1 Corinthians 13), we must have love for one another as we serve one another with the gifts God has given us. Otherwise our gifts and service profit nothing.

A wrong understanding of spiritual gifts can lead to pride and division. Some people seem to equate having a particular spiritual gift with being spiritual or being spiritually mature. Note the situation in Corinth. Paul indicates that they were not lacking any gift:

*I always thank my God for you because of his grace given you in Christ Jesus. For in him you have been enriched in every way—with all kinds of speech and with all knowledge—God thus confirming our testimony about Christ among you. Therefore you do not lack any spiritual gift as you eagerly wait for our Lord Jesus Christ to be revealed.* 1Corinthians 1:4-7 NIV

However, they were not spiritual or spiritually mature; they were still fleshly:

*Brothers, I couldn't speak to you as to spiritual, but as to fleshly, as to babies in Christ. I fed you with milk, not with meat; for you weren't yet ready. Indeed, not even now are you ready, for you are still fleshly. For insofar as there is jealousy, strife, and factions among you, aren't you fleshly, and don't you walk in the ways of men?* 1Corinthians 3:1-3 WEB

So, we see that having spiritual gifts is not an indication of being spiritual or having spiritual maturity. Rather, God gives various gifts to various people as he chooses, for the purpose of believers serving one another in love. As Peter wrote:

> *Each of you should use whatever gift you have received to serve others, as faithful stewards of God's grace in its various forms. If anyone speaks, they should do so as one who speaks the very words of God. If anyone serves, they should do so with the strength God provides, so that in all things God may be praised through Jesus Christ. To him be the glory and the power for ever and ever. Amen.*
> *1Peter 4:10-11 NIV*

## Speaking in Tongues

Unfortunately, there has been a great deal of misunderstanding and division over the gift of various languages (often referred to as the gift of *"tongues"* or *"speaking in tongues"*). People on different sides of this issue have often taken extreme positions that have little support in scripture, thereby turning a minor secondary issue into a major source of division. Dear friends, this should not be.

To try to put this subject into right perspective, let's look at some verses about this topic.

First, Mark records Jesus saying:

> *"These signs will accompany those who believe: in my name they will cast out demons; they will speak with new languages; they will take up serpents; and if they drink any deadly thing, it will in no way hurt them; they will lay hands on the sick, and they will recover."*
> *Mark 16:17-18 WEB*

*"Will speak with new languages"* was at least partly fulfilled at Pentecost when the Holy Spirit was first poured out. This served as a supernatural sign to foreigners when they heard

believers praising God in their own languages:

> *They were all filled with the Holy Spirit, and began to speak with other languages, as the Spirit gave them the ability to speak. Now there were dwelling in Jerusalem Jews, devout men, from every nation under the sky. When this sound was heard, the multitude came together, and were bewildered, because everyone heard them speaking in his own language. They were all amazed and marveled, saying to one another, "Behold, aren't all these who speak Galileans? How do we hear, everyone in our own native language? Parthians, Medes, Elamites, and people from Mesopotamia, Judea, Cappadocia, Pontus, Asia, Phrygia, Pamphylia, Egypt, the parts of Libya around Cyrene, visitors from Rome, both Jews and proselytes, Cretans and Arabians: we hear them speaking in our languages the mighty works of God!" They were all amazed, and were perplexed, saying one to another, "What does this mean?"*
>
> *Acts 2:4-12 WEB*

While it appears that all of the 120 original believers (Acts 1:15, 2:1) spoke about *the mighty works of God* in the languages of the foreigners who were present, there is no indication that the 3000 people saved later that day (Acts 2:41) did anything similar.

When some Gentiles were first saved, something similar happened:

> *While Peter was still speaking these words, the Holy Spirit fell on all those who heard the word. They of the circumcision who believed were amazed, as many as came with Peter, because the gift of the Holy Spirit was also poured out on the Gentiles. For they heard them speaking in other languages and magnifying God.*
>
> *Acts 10:44-46 WEB*

The disciples Paul found in Ephesus also spoke in other languages after the Holy Spirit *came on them*:

***When Paul had laid his hands on them, the Holy Spirit
came on them, and they spoke with other languages and
prophesied.***

*Acts 19:6 WEB*

Somewhat surprising, given the enormity of this subject in
some circles, those four passages (one in Mark, three in
Acts) appear to me to be the only locations in scripture that
speak about this subject, other than what Paul wrote in 1
Corinthians chapters 12 to 14. If this subject were truly an
important key to spirituality, one would expect it to be
spoken of frequently in the various letters of the New
Testament. Instead we find it spoken of in only one letter (1
Corinthians).

It may be worth noting that the ***other languages*** said to be
spoken in Acts 10 and Acts 19 do not completely correlate
with what happened in Acts 2. In Acts 2, all the people
speaking were ***"Galileans"*** (Acts 2:7) who presumably all
had the same native language, and there was a clear impact
on unsaved foreigners who were there, who understood what
was being said in their ***"own native language"*** (Acts 2:8
WEB). In Acts 10 and Acts 19 the people speaking all likely
had native languages that were different from Peter's and
Paul's native language. It is not stated clearly in those
accounts whether the people were miraculously speaking
languages unknown to them (as in Acts 2), or simply broke
out praising God in their own native languages because they
had been saved and had received the gift of the Holy Spirit.
Praising God is a natural result of being saved, and doing so
in one's own native language is a natural way to do so.
However, Peter's statement ***"As I began to speak, the Holy
Spirit fell on them, even as on us at the beginning"*** (Acts
11:15 WEB) implies the ***other languages*** spoken were
supernatural, as was the case at Pentecost in Acts 2.
Likewise, in Acts 19, Luke's statement ***"When Paul had
laid his hands on them, the Holy Spirit came on them, and
they spoke with other languages and prophesied"*** (Acts
19:6 WEB) implies the ***other languages*** spoken then were

also supernatural.

Now let's consider a few points from Paul's first letter to the Corinthians.

In chapter 12, Paul talks about spiritual gifts in a general way, and simply lists the gift of other languages as one of the gifts of the Holy Spirit (1 Corinthians 12:10, 28). At the end of the chapter he asks some rhetorical questions, including: *"Do all speak with various languages?"* (1 Corinthians 12:30 WEB). The implied answer seems to be "No."

He also emphasizes the diversity of spiritual gifts, while emphasizing that the unity of all believers is based on us all serving the same Spirit, Lord, and God. He also says that the purpose of diverse spiritual gifts is *for the profit of all*:

> *Now there are various kinds of gifts, but the same Spirit. There are various kinds of service, and the same Lord. There are various kinds of workings, but the same God, who works all things in all. But to each one is given the manifestation of the Spirit for the profit of all.*
>
> *1 Corinthians 12:4-7*

In chapter 13, Paul emphasizes the importance of doing all things in love. He indicates that speaking in any language can be just meaningless noise if it is not done in love:

> *If I speak with the languages of men and of angels, but don't have love, I have become sounding brass, or a clanging cymbal.*          *1 Corinthians 13:1 WEB*

In Chapter 14, Paul speaks in some detail about the importance of using spiritual gifts to build up the assembly of believers, and he seems to focus on how the gift of other languages doesn't do that, unless there is an interpreter. At Pentecost, in Acts 2, the languages spoken were known languages, which were understood by the foreigners who were present. However, in 1 Corinthians 14, Paul refers to languages being spoken that are not generally understood by other people, but only by God. The primary benefit is the *edification* of the person who is speaking to God, not the *edification* of other people:

> **For he who speaks in another language speaks not to men, but to God; for no one understands; but in the Spirit he speaks mysteries. But he who prophesies speaks to men for their edification, exhortation, and consolation. He who speaks in another language edifies himself, but he who prophesies edifies the assembly.**
>
> *1Corinthians 14:2-4 WEB*

Paul promotes the use of other gifts as normally being better suited for building up the assembly of believers:

> **Now I desire to have you all speak with other languages, but rather that you would prophesy. For he is greater who prophesies than he who speaks with other languages, unless he interprets, that the assembly may be built up. But now, brothers, if I come to you speaking with other languages, what would I profit you, unless I speak to you either by way of revelation, or of knowledge, or of prophesying, or of teaching?**
>
> *1Corinthians 14:5-6 WEB*

The gift of other languages involves a person's own spirit speaking, not the Holy Spirit speaking directly. This is clear from these verses:

> **For if I pray in another language, my spirit prays, but my understanding is unfruitful. What is it then? I will pray with the spirit, and I will pray with the understanding also. I will sing with the spirit, and I will sing with the understanding also.**
>
> *1Corinthians 14:14-15 WEB*

Paul himself claimed to speak in tongues more than all the people in Corinth. This shows that Paul considered the gift to be of significant value. However, he apparently used it only in his private prayer life, preferring to speak a few words with understanding to an assembly rather than thousands of words in an unknown language:

> *I thank my God, I speak with other languages more than you all. However in the assembly I would rather speak five words with my understanding, that I might instruct others also, than ten thousand words in another language.*
> *1Corinthians 14:18-19 WEB*

Paul gave instructions that the gift of other languages is not to be used in an assembly of believers, unless there is an interpreter:

> *If any man speaks in another language, let it be two, or at the most three, and in turn; and let one interpret. But if there is no interpreter, let him keep silent in the assembly, and let him speak to himself, and to God.*
> *1Corinthians 14:27-28 WEB*

Lastly, Paul instructs us to not forbid speaking in other languages:

> *Therefore, brothers, desire earnestly to prophesy, and don't forbid speaking with other languages.*
> *1Corinthians 14:39 WEB*

## Controlling or Empowering?

Now let's turn our attention to another important question:

- Does a right relationship with the Holy Spirit result in the Holy Spirit controlling us?

I don't see anywhere in scripture that the Holy Spirit is intended to control us. We have already discussed this some in chapter 12 *"Passivity."* We saw that God calls us to actively follow him, to **not** be passive, and **not** expect him to control us. Part of the *fruit of the Spirit* is *"self-control"* (Galatians 5:22-23).

Unfortunately, some Bible translations (and some Bible paraphrases) promote a misunderstanding in this area. Consider Romans 8:9. A fairly literal translation reads like this:

> *But you are not in the flesh but in the Spirit, if it is so that the Spirit of God dwells in you. But if any man doesn't have the Spirit of Christ, he is not his.*
>
> *Romans 8:9 WEB*

We have discussed at some length the importance of understanding the difference between the flesh and the Spirit (in Part 3 *"Flesh or Spirit"*). However, many people do not have much understanding in this area, so some modern translations try to avoid phrases like *"in the flesh"* and *"in the Spirit."* Such phrases may be unfamiliar to many people, and may result in confusion; so translations that make readability a priority may avoid using these phrases. Consider how the 1984 version of the New International Version (NIV) translated that same verse:

> *You, however, are controlled not by the sinful nature but by the Spirit, if the Spirit of God lives in you. And if anyone does not have the Spirit of Christ, he does not belong to Christ.*
>
> *Romans 8:9 NIV '84*

Here there is a clear inference that the Holy Spirit controls us, an inference that is not in the original language. It appears that the translation team was influenced by the very misunderstanding we are discussing in this section. In this case, the New International Version was revised in 2011, and that problem was fixed. The newer 2011 version of the NIV translates that same verse this way:

> *You, however, are not in the realm of the flesh but are in the realm of the Spirit, if indeed the Spirit of God lives in you. And if anyone does not have the Spirit of Christ, they do not belong to Christ.*
>
> *Romans 8:9 NIV*

Unfortunately, many other translations and paraphrases use the word *"control"* in this verse, as well as in Romans 8:4-6, in reference to the Holy Spirit.

This is a good example of why we should not rely on only a

single translation when dealing with important subjects like this. It is not reasonable to expect that the theological leanings of translators will not impact a translation (and especially a paraphrase). Comparing more than one translation will often reveal these kinds of translation weaknesses.

So, I conclude that the Holy Spirit empowers us to follow Jesus; the Holy Spirit does **not** normally control us. Please refer back to chapter 12 *"Passivity"* for a more complete discussion of this topic.

## A Second Blessing?

As already discussed in chapter 19 "The Spirit," the Holy Spirit dwelling in us is a huge blessing. We have already seen that genuine believers *receive* the Holy Spirit when they are saved. However, some people teach the importance of having a second experience of the Holy Spirit, subsequent to salvation, in order to have spiritual power for righteous living and effective ministry. This is sometimes referred to as a *"second blessing,"* or *"baptism in the Holy Spirit."*

Please note that I am not questioning the validity of various spiritual experiences in this section (this has already been dealt with some in Part 2 *"Understanding Deception"*). Rather the focus now is on how we should *understand* various spiritual experiences, which may appear to be a kind of *"second blessing."*

Scripture encourages us to grow in our faith. There is wide agreement that following Jesus involves spiritual growth and change. The change that happens at the time we are saved, when we first genuinely choose to follow Jesus and *receive* the Holy Spirit, is the beginning of a new life of spiritual growth and change.

Growth and change may be gradual, or it may be more sudden if we arrive at some kind of spiritual breakthrough, or receive a new filling or gifting from the Holy Spirit. Growth and change tends to be somewhat unique to each person. No two people are alike, and each of us will likely experience growth in our spiritual life differently. Likewise, we may each experience being *filled with the Holy Spirit* differently (as previously discussed). Problems can develop when we expect others to experience spiritual growth and the Holy Spirit in the same way we have.

We have discussed how scripture encourages us to be *filled with the Holy Spirit*, and how that may be something that happens long after salvation. Some believers may never experience being full of the Holy Spirit if they remain *fleshly*, as the believers in Corinth initially did (1 Corinthians 3:1-3 WEB). Being *filled with the Holy Spirit* may not be a permanent state, but may depend on our cooperation with God, and on our willingness to yield all of ourselves to the Holy Spirit.

The question at hand is not about whether new experiences of the Holy Spirit subsequent to salvation are legitimate and good. Rather, the question is whether there is a second experience of the Holy Spirit, with similar characteristics, that all believers should experience subsequent to salvation (referred to by some as *a second blessing* or *baptism in the Holy Spirit*).

Alternatively, some may teach that a particular experience of the Holy Spirit should happen at salvation, and only if that particular experience didn't happen is a second experience of the Holy Spirit necessary.

Some may say that the difference between being *filled with the Holy Spirit* and being *baptized in the Holy Spirit* is just semantics, and perhaps for them it is just semantics. However, there is a huge difference between understanding spiritual power for life and ministry to be dependent on our present relationship with God (*being full of the Holy Spirit*, as I intend its meaning), or understanding it to be dependent on a one-time previous event in a person's life (*a second blessing* or *baptism in the Holy Spirit,* as some have defined it).

I will approach this subject from three angles:

1. What does scripture teach?
2. What does scripture show by example?
3. What is the impact on believers?

First, let's look at what scripture teaches on this subject. I am not aware of any verses that directly teach about a universal second blessing, subsequent to salvation, or a particular experience at the point of salvation being normal (other than receiving the Holy Spirit and being washed clean in the Holy Spirit). Rather, scripture emphasizes the unity of believers and the fullness of what has been given to all true believers. Consider these verses:

> *There is one body and one Spirit—just as you were called to the one hope that belongs to your call—one Lord, one faith, one baptism, one God and Father of all, who is over all and through all and in all. But grace was given to each one of us according to the measure of Christ's gift.*
> *Ephesians 4:4-7 ESV*

> *For just as the body is one and has many members, and all the members of the body, though many, are one body, so it is with Christ. For in one Spirit we were all baptized into one body—Jews or Greeks, slaves or free—and all were made to drink of one Spirit.*
> *1Corinthians 12:12-13 ESV*

> *His divine power has granted to us all things that pertain to life and godliness, through the knowledge of him who called us to his own glory and excellence, by which he has granted to us his precious and very great promises, so that through them you may become partakers of the divine nature, having escaped from the corruption that is in the world because of sinful desire.*
> *2Peter 1:3-4 ESV*

Regarding a common experience of the Holy Spirit that all believers should have, I find these verses that seem to apply:

> *On the last day of the feast, the great day, Jesus stood up and cried out, "If anyone thirsts, let him come to me and drink. Whoever believes in me, as the Scripture has said, 'Out of his heart will flow rivers of living water.'" Now this he said about the Spirit, whom those who believed in him were to receive, for as yet the Spirit had not been given, because Jesus was not yet glorified.*
>
> *John 7:37-39 ESV*

> *The Spirit himself testifies with our spirit that we are God's children.*
>
> *Romans 8:16 NIV*

> *For the kingdom of God is not a matter of eating and drinking but of righteousness and peace and joy in the Holy Spirit.*
>
> *Romans 14:17 ESV*

> *Now the Lord is the Spirit, and where the Spirit of the Lord is, there is freedom.*
>
> *2Corinthians 3:17 ESV*

> *But when the kindness of God our Savior and his love toward mankind appeared, not by works of righteousness, which we did ourselves, but according to his mercy, he saved us through the washing of regeneration and renewing by the Holy Spirit, whom he poured out on us richly, through Jesus Christ our Savior; that, being justified by his grace, we might be made heirs according to the hope of eternal life.*
>
> *Titus 3:4-7 WEB*

From these verses we see that all believers should experience such things as:

- *"Rivers of living water"* flowing out of them.

- An inner testimony *"that we are God's children."*

- *"Righteousness and peace and joy in the Holy Spirit."*

- *"Freedom."*

- *"The washing of regeneration and renewing by the Holy Spirit."*

None of the verses listed appear to me to promote a second experience of the Holy Spirit in order to experience such things. Rather, these are all things that all true believers, all who have received the Holy Spirit, should experience. However, those who are *full of the Holy Spirit* may have a much deeper or more consistent experience of these things than those who are not *full of the Holy Spirit*.

Second, let's look at what scripture shows by example. Let's look at some situations in the book of Acts that are sometimes used to support second-blessing beliefs.

Consider what happened with Jesus' first disciples. The disciples apparently *received* the Holy Spirit before Jesus ascended (John 20:22), but were not *filled with* the Holy Spirit until Pentecost (Acts 2:4). They weren't filled with the Holy Spirit until Pentecost because the Holy Spirit was not *poured out* until after Jesus was glorified, and Pentecost was the day Jesus did so. This is in accordance with these verses:

*Now on the last and greatest day of the feast, Jesus stood and cried out, "If anyone is thirsty, let him come to me and drink! He who believes in me, as the Scripture has said, from within him will flow rivers of living water." But he said this about the Spirit, which those believing in him were to receive. For the Holy Spirit was not yet given, because Jesus wasn't yet glorified.*

*John 7:37-39 WEB*

*Nevertheless I tell you the truth: It is to your advantage that I go away, for if I don't go away, the Counselor won't come to you. But if I go, I will send him to you.*

*John 16:7 WEB*

*"This Jesus God raised up, to which we all are witnesses. Being therefore exalted by the right hand of*

*God, and having received from the Father the promise of the Holy Spirit, he has poured out this, which you now see and hear."*
*Acts 2:32-33 WEB*

The Holy Spirit has been *"poured out"* on believers ever since Pentecost. At Pentecost, Peter said that what happened at Pentecost would now be normal for all believers:

*"But this is what has been spoken through the prophet Joel: 'It will be in the last days, says God, that I will pour out my Spirit on all flesh. Your sons and your daughters will prophesy. Your young men will see visions. Your old men will dream dreams. Yes, and on my servants and on my handmaidens in those days, I will pour out my Spirit, and they will prophesy.'"*
*Acts 2:16-18 WEB (quoting Joel 2:28-29)*

*Peter said to them, "Repent, and be baptized, every one of you, in the name of Jesus Christ for the forgiveness of sins, and you will receive the gift of the Holy Spirit. For the promise is to you, and to your children, and to all who are far off, even as many as the Lord our God will call to himself."*
*Acts 2:38-39 WEB*

Believers should not be waiting for Pentecost to happen again. Rather, believers should seek to be *filled with the Holy Spirit* day by day, based on the grace God has already made available. Might that involve waiting on God? Yes, it may. Might that involve asking God to fill us? Yes, it may. However, the focus should not be on receiving a one-time *second-blessing* experience, but on being continually *filled with the Holy Spirit*, who has already been *poured out,* who is already dwelling in every true believer. The focus should be on humbling ourselves and submitting ourselves to God to allow the Holy Spirit to fill us more completely and more consistently.

So, while Pentecost in Acts 2 was certainly a deeper experience of the Holy Spirit, and was apparently subsequent to receiving the Holy Spirit, this should not be understood to be a normal two-step experience for believers today. If there is a lack of Holy Spirit power in our lives today, it is likely due to a failure on our part to fully embrace what God has already made available to us. Spiritual growth associated with more fully embracing the Holy Spirit, more fully yielding our lives to God, should be viewed as normal progressive spiritual growth; not a one-time second blessing.

Now let's consider what happened when some Samaritans first believed:

> *Now when the apostles who were at Jerusalem heard that Samaria had received the word of God, they sent Peter and John to them, who, when they had come down, prayed for them, that they might receive the Holy Spirit; for as yet he had fallen on none of them. They had only been baptized in the name of Christ Jesus. Then they laid their hands on them, and they received the Holy Spirit.*  Acts 8:14-17 WEB

Consider the uniqueness of this situation:

- This was the first time that a non-Jewish group of people came to faith in Jesus.

- There were huge cultural divisions between the Samaritans and Jewish believers.

- They did not *receive* the Holy Spirit when they believed, even though they were *baptized in the name of Christ Jesus.*

These verses speak of the first time that a group of people who were **not** properly Jewish (some Samaritans) believed in Jesus and were baptized. For some reason these new believers had not *received* the Holy Spirit; the Holy Spirit was not yet dwelling in any of them; their salvation was not complete. Why was this? Scripture doesn't say. I conjecture that it was important to God that they have a strong connection with the believers in Judea, rather than allowing historical divisions to divide believers. Apparently, the Samaritans had been baptized in water (*baptized in the name of Christ Jesus*), but the Holy Spirit was withheld from them until a strong connection was made with the believers in Judea. Note here that this is not a second experience of the Holy Spirit, but rather a first experience, for scripture says that they *prayed for them, that they might <u>receive</u> the Holy Spirit.*

The Holy Spirit not *falling on* any of them was taken as evidence that the Samaritans had not yet *received* the Holy Spirit (Acts 8:14-16). The Samaritans did not receive the Holy Spirit, and the Holy Spirit did not *fall on* any of them until Peter and John came and prayed for them. It appears to me that the Holy Spirit was withheld initially from the Samaritans to ensure that they would not remain culturally separated from the church in Jerusalem.

In summary, the situation with the Samaritans in Acts 8 is a unique situation. It is not a *second blessing* experience, but rather a first encounter with the Holy Spirit. They *received* the Holy Spirit, and the Holy Spirit may have *fallen on* them (or *filled* them) at the same time, after Peter and John prayed for them.

Now let's consider what happened with some *disciples* in Ephesus:

> *While Apollos was at Corinth, Paul, having passed through the upper country, came to Ephesus, and found certain disciples. He said to them, "Did you receive the Holy Spirit when you believed?" They said to him, "No, we haven't even heard that there is a Holy Spirit." He said, "Into what then were you baptized?" They said, "Into John's baptism." Paul said, "John indeed baptized with the baptism of repentance, saying to the people that they should believe in the one who would come after him, that is, in Jesus." When they heard this, they were baptized in the name of the Lord Jesus.*

*When Paul had laid his hands on them, the Holy Spirit came on them, and they spoke with other languages and prophesied.* Acts 19:1-6 WEB

Here the problem appears to be that the people Paul found had not been taught well, they had only received John's baptism of repentance, they said they had not *received* the Holy Spirit, and they did not even know about the Holy Spirit. They apparently knew little about Jesus.

There is some disagreement about whether these *"disciples"* were actually saved when Paul found them. Evidence in favor of them being saved is Paul's question: **"Did you receive the Holy Spirit when you believed?"** Paul seems to indicate that they *"believed,"* and this is said to be evidence of their salvation.

Evidence against seems to me to be threefold:

- They said they had not received the Holy Spirit.

- They had not been baptized in the name of Jesus.

- They apparently knew little about Jesus. Just what they **"believed"** is not clear.

Consider with me the basic criteria for *receiving* the Holy Spirit. When the Holy Spirit was first poured out at Pentecost, these were some of Peter's words to the crowd that had gathered:

**Peter said to them, "Repent, and be baptized, every one of you, in the name of Jesus Christ for the forgiveness of sins, and you will receive the gift of the Holy Spirit."**
Acts 2:38 WEB

Here we see that *receiving* the Holy Spirit is said to be associated with two things: repentance, and being baptized in the Name of Jesus. The disciples that Paul found in Ephesus had not been baptized in the name of Jesus. This is a further reason to understand that they had not previously received the Holy Spirit (beyond the disciples saying themselves that they had not received the Holy Spirit).

As previously discussed, receiving the Holy Spirit is foundational to being a saved follower of Jesus. So, I see the issue in Acts 19 as being about obtaining true salvation through faith in Jesus, being baptized in the name of the Lord Jesus for the first time, and receiving the Holy Spirit for the first time, not about obtaining a *second* experience of the Holy Spirit.

However, even if you look at these "disciples" as already being saved, this still appears to be a first experience of the Holy Spirit for them, not a second experience of the Holy Spirit. In this case, their salvation appears to be very substandard, since they apparently had not been baptized in the name of Jesus, had not *received* the Holy Spirit, and didn't even know about the Holy Spirit.

Either way, this raises an important issue: There may be many people today who are religious, but who have been poorly taught. They may not have been baptized in the name of Jesus (when or after they first turned to Jesus and repented of their sins), and may not have received the Holy Spirit, and they may not be genuinely saved. Dear friend, have you been baptized in the name of Jesus? Have you received the Holy Spirit? Have you been washed clean by the Holy Spirit? Do you have an inner testimony that you are a child of God?

> ***The Spirit himself testifies with our spirit that we are children of God; and if children, then heirs; heirs of God, and joint heirs with Christ; if indeed we suffer with him, that we may also be glorified with him.***
>
> *Romans 8:16-17 WEB*

If not, please get right with God today. You may want to consider chapter 16 in the book *"Foundations for Eternal Life,"* entitled *"What Must I do to be Saved?"* along with chapter 17 *"Be Baptized."* Or, go to someone who is genuinely saved, and ask them for help in truly coming to

Jesus and receiving the Holy Spirit.

A clarification is in order. Is baptism in water in the name of Jesus a strict requirement for receiving the Holy Spirit? When the gentiles were first saved in Acts 10, the order was clearly reversed. They received the Holy Spirit and then they were baptized (Acts 10:45-48). So, the answer to that question is clearly "No." However, I think Peter's instructions in Acts 2:38 show what should be normal. Repentance, baptism in water, and receiving the Holy Spirit should all normally happen close together. The situation with the disciples in Ephesus (Acts 19:1-6) shows that a serious problem can result when understanding and practice are poor.

In the book of Acts, baptism in water is consistently done shortly after a person believes in Jesus (Acts 2:41, 8:12-13, 8:38, 9:17-18, 10:43-48, 16:14-15, 16:30-33, 18:8, 19:4-5, 22:12-16). Repentance, baptism in water, and receiving the Holy Spirit appear to be intended to be a package deal. Unfortunately, in many churches baptism in water in the name of Jesus (or *"in the name of the Father, and of the Son and of the Holy Spirit"* per Matthew 28:19) is often delayed due to a poor understanding of its importance in the normal salvation process. Fortunately, God is often willing to extend his grace even when our practices are substandard. Many, including myself, can testify to receiving the Holy Spirit at the point of true repentance and faith, even though baptism in water in the name of Jesus did not happen until weeks, months, or years later. (However, in my case I have been told that I was sprinkle-baptized as an infant; I'm not sure how God views that).

Summarizing the second point, we have looked at some situations in the book of Acts that are sometimes used to support *second-blessing* beliefs. We have seen that each of those passages can be understood in ways that do not support *second-blessing* beliefs.

Third, let's look at the impact of *second-blessing* teachings. I see three main impacts, one positive, and two negative.

On the positive side, many people have been encouraged to go deeper in their faith and experience the Holy Spirit in ways they previously had not.

On the negative side, some people who believe they have had a *second blessing* experience seem to think they have become spiritually mature as a result, and have become lax in their faith, and make little effort to grow further.

Also on the negative side, huge division has occurred between various believers due to this teaching, since it divides believers into two classes of people: those who believe they have received the *second blessing*, and everyone else.

These negative impacts have been hugely detrimental to the body of Christ.

Can we encourage people to go deeper in their faith, and to experience the Holy Spirit in ways they previously have not, without promoting a particular "second blessing" experience? Each person is unique, and God may deal with each person in unique ways. We shouldn't presume that other people's experiences of the Holy Spirit should be the same as our own experience. We should be encouraging everyone to grow in their faith and experience with the Holy Spirit in ways that don't divide the body of Christ.

I am not saying that people can't be *"filled with the Holy Spirit"* separate from salvation, or receive a new spiritual gift from the Holy Spirit separate from salvation. But these should not be looked at as a one-time *"second-blessing"* which people either have or don't have. Rather, these are things that depend on the unique relationship that God has with each person.

Promoting a particular *second-blessing* experience as something all believers should experience is not beneficial.

Doing so has caused huge divisions in the body of Christ. Dear friends, this should not be.

## Benefits of the Holy Spirit

The Holy Spirit was given to unite us, not divide us. Let us humbly seek to be filled with the Holy Spirit day by day, as we seek to serve one another in love with the gifts and strength he provides. As Peter wrote:

*Each of you should use whatever gift you have received to serve others, as faithful stewards of God's grace in its various forms. If anyone speaks, they should do so as one who speaks the very words of God. If anyone serves, they should do so with the strength God provides, so that in all things God may be praised through Jesus Christ. To him be the glory and the power for ever and ever. Amen.* 1Peter 4:10-11 NIV

Let's close this chapter with a few verses that remind us of some of the benefits of the Holy Spirit.

*On the last day of the feast, the great day, Jesus stood up and cried out, "If anyone thirsts, let him come to me and drink. Whoever believes in me, as the Scripture has said, 'Out of his heart will flow rivers of living water.'" Now this he said about the Spirit, whom those who believed in him were to receive, for as yet the Spirit had not been given, because Jesus was not yet glorified.* John 7:37-39 ESV

*"But you will receive power when the Holy Spirit has come upon you. You will be witnesses to me in Jerusalem, in all Judea and Samaria, and to the uttermost parts of the earth."* Acts 1:8 WEB

*The Spirit himself testifies with our spirit that we are God's children.* Romans 8:16 NIV

*For the kingdom of God is not a matter of eating and drinking but of righteousness and peace and joy in the*

*Now we have received not the spirit of the world, but the Spirit who is from God, that we might understand the things freely given us by God.*          *1Corinthians 2:12 ESV*

*And such were some of you. But you were washed, you were sanctified, you were justified in the name of the Lord Jesus Christ and by the Spirit of our God.*
*1Corinthians 6:11 ESV*

*Now the Lord is the Spirit, and where the Spirit of the Lord is, there is freedom.*          *2Corinthians 3:17 ESV*

*But I say, walk by the Spirit, and you won't fulfill the lust of the flesh.*          *Galatians 5:16 WEB*

*For this cause, I bow my knees to the Father of our Lord Jesus Christ, from whom every family in heaven and on earth is named, that he would grant you, according to the riches of his glory, that you may be strengthened with power through his Spirit in the inward man...*          *Ephesians 3:14-16 WEB*

*But when the kindness of God our Savior and his love toward mankind appeared, not by works of righteousness, which we did ourselves, but according to his mercy, he saved us through the washing of regeneration and renewing by the Holy Spirit, whom he poured out on us richly, through Jesus Christ our Savior; that, being justified by his grace, we might be made heirs according to the hope of eternal life.*
*Titus 3:4-7 WEB*

## For Further Reflection

- Has your understanding of the Holy Spirit changed over time? If so, how?

\*\*\*\*\*\*\*\*\*\*\*

# Chapter 33
# God Told Me...

*Yahweh spoke to Moses face to face,*
*as a man speaks to his friend.*
Exodus 33:11 WEB

---

Does God communicate with each of us individually? Should we expect God to speak directly to us with audible words? Should we expect God to speak to us in some other way? Does God's Holy Spirit within us communicate directly to us? With words? If not with words, how does God communicate with each of us?

## Ways God Has Spoken

Let's start to answer these questions by considering the many ways that God may communicate with people. Note that I am not claiming here that God presently does all of these things, I am just trying to clarify the possibilities. Here is a list of many of the ways God has communicated with people in the past.

**Through Creation:** The created universe reveals a lot about God, and we should consider that creation itself is one way that God communicates with people. Consider these verses:

*The heavens declare the glory of God. The expanse shows his handiwork. Day after day they pour out speech, and night after night they display knowledge. There is no speech nor language, where their voice is not heard. Their voice has gone out through all the earth, their words to the end of the world.*
Psalm 19:1-4 WEB

*For what can be known about God is plain to them, because God has shown it to them. For his invisible attributes, namely, his eternal power and divine nature, have been clearly perceived, ever since the creation of the world, in the things that have been made. So they are without excuse.*                   *Romans 1:19-20 ESV*

**Face to Face Audibly:** God has appeared to some people as a person and spoken with them face to face and audibly, just as people often speak to each other. This occurred regularly with Moses:

*When Moses entered into the Tent, the pillar of cloud descended, stood at the door of the Tent, and spoke with Moses. All the people saw the pillar of cloud stand at the door of the Tent, and all the people rose up and worshiped, everyone at their tent door. Yahweh spoke to Moses face to face, as a man speaks to his friend.*
*Exodus 33:9-11 WEB*

Some other people have had briefer experiences, in which God seems to have appeared to them as a person and spoken to them face to face. Here are some examples:

*The men turned from there, and went toward Sodom, but Abraham stood yet before Yahweh.*   *Genesis 18:22 WEB*

*When Joshua was by Jericho, he lifted up his eyes and looked, and behold, a man stood in front of him with his sword drawn in his hand. ... Yahweh said to Joshua, "Behold, I have given Jericho into your hand, with its king and the mighty men of valor."*   *Joshua 5:13, 6:2 WEB*

*Yahweh's angel came and sat under the oak which was in Ophrah, that belonged to Joash the Abiezrite. His son Gideon was beating out wheat in the wine press, to hide it from the Midianites. Yahweh's angel appeared to him, and said to him, "Yahweh is with you, you mighty man of valor!"*   *Judges 6:11-12 WEB*

**Audibly:** Sometimes God speaks to people audibly, but not face-to-face. Here are some examples:

*The angel of Yahweh appeared to him in a flame of fire*

*out of the middle of a bush. He looked, and behold, the bush burned with fire, and the bush was not consumed. Moses said, "I will go now, and see this great sight, why the bush is not burned." When Yahweh saw that he came over to see, God called to him out of the middle of the bush, and said, "Moses! Moses!" He said, "Here I am."*
                                                    *Exodus 3:2-4 WEB*

*Then the LORD called Samuel, and he said, "Here I am!" and ran to Eli and said, "Here I am, for you called me." But he said, "I did not call; lie down again." So he went and lay down. And the LORD called again, "Samuel!" and Samuel arose and went to Eli and said, "Here I am, for you called me." But he said, "I did not call, my son; lie down again."*
                                                    *1Samuel 3:4-6 ESV*

*Behold, a voice out of the heavens said, "This is my beloved Son, with whom I am well pleased."*
                                                    *Matthew 3:17 WEB*

*Behold, a voice came out of the cloud, saying, "This is my beloved Son, in whom I am well pleased. Listen to him."*
                                                    *Matthew 17:5 WEB*

*"Father, glorify your name." Then a voice came from heaven: "I have glorified it, and I will glorify it again."*
                                                    *John 12:28 ESV*

*As he traveled, he got close to Damascus, and suddenly a light from the sky shone around him. He fell on the earth, and heard a voice saying to him, "Saul, Saul, why do you persecute me?"*
                                                    *Acts 9:3-4 WEB*

**Through Prophets:** Throughout the Old Testament, God often spoke to the people through prophets. God spoke to a prophet (typically through dreams or visions, per Numbers 12:6), and the prophet passed the messages along to the people. Peter describes *the prophetic word* this way:

*And we have the prophetic word more fully confirmed, to which you will do well to pay attention as to a lamp shining in a dark place, until the day dawns and the morning star rises in your hearts, knowing this first of all, that no prophecy of Scripture comes from someone's own interpretation. For no prophecy was ever produced by the will of man, but men spoke from God as they were carried along by the Holy Spirit.*   2Peter 1:19-21 ESV

All of the Old Testament books from Isaiah to Malachi are examples of God speaking through prophets.  Here is an example of a New Testament prophet:

*While we were staying for many days, a prophet named Agabus came down from Judea.  And coming to us, he took Paul's belt and bound his own feet and hands and said, "Thus says the Holy Spirit, 'This is how the Jews at Jerusalem will bind the man who owns this belt and deliver him into the hands of the Gentiles.'"*

Acts 21:10-11 ESV

**Dreams:**  God can speak to us through our dreams.  Here are a couple of the many examples in scripture:

*But God came to Abimelech in a dream of the night, and said to him, "Behold, you are a dead man, because of the woman whom you have taken.  For she is a man's wife."*   Genesis 20:3 WEB

*Now when they had departed, behold, an angel of the Lord appeared to Joseph in a dream, saying, "Arise and take the young child and his mother, and flee into Egypt, and stay there until I tell you, for Herod will seek the young child to destroy him."*   Matthew 2:13 WEB

**Visions:**  Visions are usually understood to differ from dreams in that they may occur while a person is awake.  Here are some examples:

*He said, "Now hear my words.  If there is a prophet among you, I, Yahweh, will make myself known to him in a vision.  I will speak with him in a dream."*

Numbers 12:6 WEB

*In the third year of the reign of king Belshazzar a vision appeared to me, even to me, Daniel, after that which appeared to me at the first.*  *Daniel 8:1 WEB*

*Peter went up on the housetop to pray at about noon. He became hungry and desired to eat, but while they were preparing, he fell into a trance. He saw heaven opened and a certain container descending to him, like a great sheet let down by four corners on the earth, in which were all kinds of four-footed animals of the earth, wild animals, reptiles, and birds of the sky. A voice came to him, "Rise, Peter, kill and eat!"*  *Acts 10:9-13 WEB*

*I must go on boasting. Though there is nothing to be gained by it, I will go on to visions and revelations of the Lord. I know a man in Christ who fourteen years ago was caught up to the third heaven—whether in the body or out of the body I do not know, God knows.*
*2Corinthians 12:1-2 ESV*

**Miracles:**  Supernatural works are a form of communication. Consider these verses:

*The Jews therefore came around him and said to him, "How long will you hold us in suspense? If you are the Christ, tell us plainly."*

*Jesus answered them, "I told you, and you don't believe. The works that I do in my Father's name, these testify about me. But you don't believe, because you are not of my sheep, as I told you. My sheep hear my voice, and I know them, and they follow me."*  *John 10:24-27 WEB*

*They went out, and preached everywhere, the Lord working with them, and confirming the word by the signs that followed. Amen.*  *Mark 16:20 WEB*

*This salvation, which was first announced by the Lord, was confirmed to us by those who heard him. God also testified to it by signs, wonders and various miracles, and by gifts of the Holy Spirit distributed according to*

***his will.***

**Answered Prayer:** Similar to miracles, answered prayer is a form of communication from God. Answered prayer can take many forms, many of which may not appear miraculous. Here are some examples of answered prayer in scripture:

*And she vowed a vow and said, "O LORD of hosts, if you will indeed look on the affliction of your servant and remember me and not forget your servant, but will give to your servant a son, then I will give him to the LORD all the days of his life, and no razor shall touch his head."*

*And in due time Hannah conceived and bore a son, and she called his name Samuel, for she said, "I have asked for him from the LORD."*    *1Samuel 1:11, 20 ESV*

*Then he stretched himself upon the child three times and cried to the LORD, "O LORD my God, let this child's life come into him again." And the LORD listened to the voice of Elijah. And the life of the child came into him again, and he revived.*    *1Kings 17:21-22 ESV*

*"Now therefore, Yahweh our God, save us, I beg you, out of his hand, that all the kingdoms of the earth may know that you, Yahweh, are God alone." . . .*

*That night, Yahweh's angel went out, and struck one hundred eighty-five thousand in the camp of the Assyrians. When men arose early in the morning, behold, these were all dead bodies.*    *2Kings 19:19, 35 WEB*

*"Now, Lord, look at their threats, and grant to your servants to speak your word with all boldness, while you stretch out your hand to heal; and that signs and wonders may be done through the name of your holy Servant Jesus." When they had prayed, the place was shaken where they were gathered together. They were all filled with the Holy Spirit, and they spoke the word of God with boldness.*    *Acts 4:29-31 WEB*

**Various "Signs":** Here are some examples:

*"I set my rainbow in the cloud, and it will be for a sign of a covenant between me and the earth."*
*Genesis 9:13 WEB*

*He gave a sign the same day, saying, "This is the sign which Yahweh has spoken: Behold, the altar will be split apart, and the ashes that are on it will be poured out."*
*1Kings 13:3 WEB*

*Hezekiah said to Isaiah, "What will be the sign that Yahweh will heal me, and that I will go up to Yahweh's house the third day?"*

*Isaiah said, "This will be the sign to you from Yahweh, that Yahweh will do the thing that he has spoken: should the shadow go forward ten steps, or go back ten steps?"*
*2Kings 20:8-9 WEB*

*"I will show wonders in the sky above, and signs on the earth beneath; blood, and fire, and billows of smoke. The sun will be turned into darkness, and the moon into blood, before the great and glorious day of the Lord comes."*
*Acts 2:19-20 WEB*

**Urim and Thummim:** In the Old Testament, the breastpiece of the priestly garment included a way for God to communicate with the priest, called the "Urim and Thummim." Precisely how this worked is not clear in scripture, but here are some verses that show that it was a way that God communicated with the priest:

*"Also put the Urim and the Thummim in the breastpiece, so they may be over Aaron's heart whenever he enters the presence of the LORD. Thus Aaron will always bear the means of making decisions for the Israelites over his heart before the LORD."*
*Exodus 28:30 NIV*

*"He is to stand before Eleazar the priest, who will obtain decisions for him by inquiring of the Urim before the*

**LORD.** *At his command he and the entire community of the Israelites will go out, and at his command they will come in."*

Numbers 27:21 NIV

*When Saul inquired of Yahweh, Yahweh didn't answer him by dreams, by Urim, or by prophets.*

1Samuel 28:6 WEB

**A Cloud:** After God led his people out of Egypt, he used a cloud to communicate when the people should move, and where they should camp:

*On the day that the tabernacle was raised up, the cloud covered the tabernacle, even the Tent of the Testimony: at evening it was over the tabernacle, as it were the appearance of fire, until morning. So it was continually. The cloud covered it, and the appearance of fire by night. Whenever the cloud was taken up from over the Tent, then after that the children of Israel traveled; and in the place where the cloud remained, there the children of Israel encamped. At the commandment of Yahweh, the children of Israel traveled, and at the commandment of Yahweh they encamped.*

Numbers 9:15-18 WEB

**Casting Lots:** "Casting lots" is another way that God may provide direction to people. Here are a few of the many occasions scripture records **lots** being used:

- The Law of Moses required that lots be cast to determine which goat would be *a sin offering*, and which would be *the scapegoat* (Leviticus 16:8-9).

- The Promised Land was to be divided *by lot* (Numbers 26:53-56).

- Followers of Jesus used *lots* to determine who would replace Judas and join the eleven apostles (Acts 1:21-26).

The book of Proverbs indicates that God is involved decisions made this way:

*The lot is cast into the lap, but its every decision is from Yahweh.*                                      *Proverbs 16:33 WEB*

**Writing on the Wall:** In the book of Daniel, *fingers of a man's hand* wrote on the wall in front of King Belshazzar; apparently a message from God:

*They drank wine, and praised the gods of gold, and of silver, of bronze, of iron, of wood, and of stone.*

*In the same hour, the fingers of a man's hand came out and wrote near the lamp stand on the plaster of the wall of the king's palace. The king saw the part of the hand that wrote. Then the king's face was changed in him, and his thoughts troubled him; and the joints of his thighs were loosened, and his knees struck one against another.*                                      *Daniel 5:4-6 WEB*

**Through People (other than prophets):** Many people come to faith in Jesus, or are encouraged to deeper faith, through a message, a word of encouragement, or a rebuke from other people. In this case, God is partly using people to communicate truth to other people. Many people's testimonies include something about God speaking to them through other people. Here are some examples which I think fit this category:

*But Peter, standing up with the eleven, lifted up his voice, and spoke out to them, "You men of Judea, and all you who dwell at Jerusalem, let this be known to you, and listen to my words. . . .*

*"Let all the house of Israel therefore know certainly that God has made him both Lord and Christ, this Jesus whom you crucified."*

*Now when they heard this, they were cut to the heart, and said to Peter and the rest of the apostles, "Brothers, what shall we do?"*

*Peter said to them, "Repent, and be baptized, every one*

*of you, in the name of Jesus Christ for the forgiveness of sins, and you will receive the gift of the Holy Spirit."*

Acts 2:14, 36-38 WEB

*With great power, the apostles gave their testimony of the resurrection of the Lord Jesus. Great grace was on them all.*

Acts 4:33 WEB

*Peter opened his mouth and said, "Truly I perceive that God doesn't show favoritism; but in every nation he who fears him and works righteousness is acceptable to him. ... All the prophets testify about him, that through his name everyone who believes in him will receive remission of sins."*

*While Peter was still speaking these words, the Holy Spirit fell on all those who heard the word.*

Acts 10:34-35, 43-44 WEB

**Inaudibly, to a Person's Mind or Spirit:** Some people testify to hearing God speak directly to their mind or spirit. This communication is not audible (not sound heard with their ears), but sometimes is said to be as clear, or more clear, than audible speech. We need to be careful here, for there are many possible sources of thoughts or impressions other than God, and many people appear to have been deceived in this area. Also, this is a subject that scripture is not very clear about (in my opinion). However, this is a possible way that God can communicate with us, and we should not ignore it (more will be said about this later). Here are some verses that *may* fit into this category:

*Behold, there was a man in Jerusalem whose name was Simeon. This man was righteous and devout, looking for the consolation of Israel, and the Holy Spirit was on him. It had been revealed to him by the Holy Spirit that he should not see death before he had seen the Lord's Christ.*

Luke 2:25-26 WEB

*"But the Counselor, the Holy Spirit, whom the Father will send in my name, he will teach you all things, and*

*will remind you of all that I said to you."*   John 14:26 WEB

*"However when he, the Spirit of truth, has come, he will guide you into all truth, for he will not speak from himself; but whatever he hears, he will speak.  He will declare to you things that are coming.  He will glorify me, for he will take from what is mine, and will declare it to you.  All things whatever the Father has are mine; therefore I said that he takes of mine, and will declare it to you."*   John 16:13-15 WEB

*The Spirit said to Philip, "Go near, and join yourself to this chariot."*   Acts 8:29 WEB

*While Peter was pondering the vision, the Spirit said to him, "Behold, three men seek you.  But arise, get down, and go with them, doubting nothing; for I have sent them."*   Acts 10:19-20 WEB

*As they served the Lord and fasted, the Holy Spirit said, "Separate Barnabas and Saul for me, for the work to which I have called them."*   Acts 13:2 WEB

**Giving Knowledge and Understanding:**   We previously saw how God often plays a part in us acquiring knowledge, understanding, and wisdom (in chapter 5 *"Growing in Understanding & Wisdom"*).   Here are a few verses to consider:

*Then he opened their minds, that they might understand the Scriptures.*   Luke 24:45 WEB

*Consider what I say, and may the Lord give you understanding in all things.*   2Timothy 2:7 WEB

*"For this is the covenant that I will make with the house of Israel.  After those days," says the Lord; "I will put my laws into their mind, I will also write them on their heart.  I will be their God, and they will be my people."*   Hebrews 8:10 WEB (quoting Jeremiah 31:33)

*I write these things to you about those who are trying to*

*deceive you. But the anointing that you received from him abides in you, and you have no need that anyone should teach you. But as his anointing teaches you about everything, and is true, and is no lie—just as it has taught you, abide in him.* 1John 2:26-27 ESV

*And we know that the Son of God has come and has given us understanding, so that we may know him who is true; and we are in him who is true, in his Son Jesus Christ. He is the true God and eternal life.* 1John 5:20 ESV

**Revelations:** Similar to giving knowledge and understanding, God may impart knowledge or understanding to people so vividly or suddenly that it may be referred to as a *revelation.* Here are some examples:

*Let the prophets speak, two or three, and let the others discern. But if a revelation is made to another sitting by, let the first keep silent.* 1Corinthians 14:29-30 WEB

*For this reason I, Paul, a prisoner for Christ Jesus on behalf of you Gentiles—assuming that you have heard of the stewardship of God's grace that was given to me for you, how the mystery was made known to me by revelation, as I have written briefly.* Ephesians 3:1-3 ESV

*But I make known to you, brothers, concerning the Good News which was preached by me, that it is not according to man. For neither did I receive it from man, nor was I taught it, but it came to me through revelation of Jesus Christ.* Galatians 1:11-12 WEB

**Opened Eyes:** Similar to giving us understanding, God sometimes enables people to see directly into the spiritual realm. Here are some examples:

*Then Yahweh opened the eyes of Balaam, and he saw Yahweh's angel standing in the way, with his sword drawn in his hand; and he bowed his head, and fell on his face.* Numbers 22:31 WEB

*Elisha prayed, and said, "Yahweh, Please open his eyes, that he may see." Yahweh opened the eyes of the young man; and he saw: and behold, the mountain was full of horses and chariots of fire around Elisha.*
2Kings 6:17 WEB

*But he, full of the Holy Spirit, gazed into heaven and saw the glory of God, and Jesus standing at the right hand of God. And he said, "Behold, I see the heavens opened, and the Son of Man standing at the right hand of God."*
Acts 7:55-56 ESV

**Stirred up Spirit:** There are several places where scripture indicates that God *"stirred up the spirit"* of various people to motivate them to do his will. Here are some examples:

*Now in the first year of Cyrus king of Persia, that the word of Yahweh by the mouth of Jeremiah might be accomplished, Yahweh stirred up the spirit of Cyrus king of Persia, so that he made a proclamation throughout all his kingdom, and put it also in writing, saying...*
2Chronicles 36:22 WEB

*Then the heads of fathers' households of Judah and Benjamin, the priests, and the Levites, all whose spirit God had stirred to go up, rose up to build Yahweh's house which is in Jerusalem.*
Ezra 1:5 WEB

*Yahweh stirred up the spirit of Zerubbabel, the son of Shealtiel, governor of Judah, and the spirit of Joshua, the son of Jehozadak, the high priest, and the spirit of all the remnant of the people; and they came and worked on the house of Yahweh of Armies, their God...*
Haggai 1:14 WEB

**Through Affliction:** Throughout the Old Testament, we see God bringing affliction on the people of Israel when they stubbornly refused to follow him. These afflictions were a severe form of communication from God. God may also deal with individuals in a similar way, as these verses show:

*It is good for me that I have been afflicted, that I may learn your statutes.*                                          *Psalm 119:71 WEB*

*Yahweh, I know that your judgments are righteous, that in faithfulness you have afflicted me.*          *Psalm 119:75 WEB*

*Let a person examine himself, then, and so eat of the bread and drink of the cup. For anyone who eats and drinks without discerning the body eats and drinks judgment on himself. That is why many of you are weak and ill, and some have died. But if we judged ourselves truly, we would not be judged. But when we are judged by the Lord, we are disciplined so that we may not be condemned along with the world.* *1Corinthians 11:28-32 ESV*

*And have you forgotten the exhortation that addresses you as sons? "My son, do not regard lightly the discipline of the Lord, nor be weary when reproved by him. For the Lord disciplines the one he loves, and chastises every son whom he receives." It is for discipline that you have to endure. God is treating you as sons. For what son is there whom his father does not discipline? If you are left without discipline, in which all have participated, then you are illegitimate children and not sons. Besides this, we have had earthly fathers who disciplined us and we respected them. Shall we not much more be subject to the Father of spirits and live? For they disciplined us for a short time as it seemed best to them, but he disciplines us for our good, that we may share his holiness. For the moment all discipline seems painful rather than pleasant, but later it yields the peaceful fruit of righteousness to those who have been trained by it.*                                          *Hebrews 12:5-11 ESV*

**Living as a Person Among Us:** There was a time when God revealed himself through a person living among us. I am, of course, referring to Jesus. Through Jesus, God spoke directly to people while Jesus walked on the earth, as recorded in the Gospels. The opening verses in the book of

Hebrews seems to be making this point:

> *God, having in the past spoken to the fathers through the prophets at many times and in various ways, has at the end of these days spoken to us by his Son, whom he appointed heir of all things, through whom also he made the worlds.*
>
> *Hebrews 1:1-2 WEB*

## Has God Stopped Speaking?

Some people teach that God no longer speaks to people, other than through scripture. This is usually based on a traditional belief that God stopped doing miracles and other supernatural things after various scriptures were compiled into the Bible as we know it today (it was compiled roughly in the fourth century AD). I do not find support for this belief anywhere in scripture, though 1 Corinthians 13:8-10 is sometimes referenced by others to support this belief:

> *Love never fails. But where there are prophecies, they will be done away with. Where there are various languages, they will cease. Where there is knowledge, it will be done away with. For we know in part, and we prophesy in part; but when that which is complete has come, then that which is partial will be done away with.*
>
> *1Corinthians 13:8-10 WEB*

It may be a valid point that, where scripture is readily available, there is less need for supernatural communication, so it may happen less frequently. However, it seems to me to be stretching scripture to claim, based on scripture, that God no longer does anything supernatural, that he never communicates anything with anyone anymore (other than through scripture). The testimonies of countless believers today seem to be clear evidence against that viewpoint.

Consider also Jesus' words:

> *"Most certainly, I tell you, one who doesn't enter by the door into the sheep fold, but climbs up some other way,*

*the same is a thief and a robber. But one who enters in by the door is the shepherd of the sheep. The gatekeeper opens the gate for him, and the sheep listen to his voice. He calls his own sheep by name, and leads them out. Whenever he brings out his own sheep, he goes before them, and the sheep follow him, for they know his voice. They will by no means follow a stranger, but will flee from him; for they don't know the voice of strangers."*

*John 10:1-5 WEB*

*"I am the good shepherd. I know my own, and I'm known by my own; even as the Father knows me, and I know the Father. I lay down my life for the sheep. I have other sheep, which are not of this fold. I must bring them also, and they will hear my voice. They will become one flock with one shepherd."* *John 10:14-16 WEB*

Clearly, the "*sheep*" represent true followers of Jesus. Jesus indicates his sheep "*listen to his voice*," "*know his voice*," and "*hear my voice*." It is not clear in these verses what form Jesus' voice takes (of the many options listed above), but it is clear that his sheep are able to hear his voice.

Consider also God's words in Psalm 91:

*"Because he holds fast to me in love, I will deliver him; I will protect him, because he knows my name. When he calls to me, I will answer him; I will be with him in trouble; I will rescue him and honor him. With long life I will satisfy him and show him my salvation."*

*Psalm 91:14-16 ESV*

Consider the middle part of those verses: *"When he calls to me, I will answer him."* Are we to think that verses like this no longer apply to God's people? Are we to think that God never answers when a righteous person calls to him? I don't think so.

I conclude that God has not stopped speaking to his people.

# What Is Normal and Common?

This is an important question to consider:

- Is there a normal and common way that God communicates with believers?

The above list of different ways that God has communicated to people in the past is not necessarily very helpful with this question, as it doesn't directly deal with the question of *what is normal and common?* Most of the scriptural examples listed above deal with unusual and uncommon circumstances, and it is difficult to determine what is normal and common just from such examples. If there is a normal and common way that God communicates with believers, I would expect to see it spoken of as normal and common in scripture; not just see occasional examples in unusual circumstances.

As was mentioned earlier in this chapter, *God giving us knowledge and understanding* is one way that God communicates with us. I believe scripture shows that this is a *normal and common* way that God communicates with believers. This method of communication appears to be what Jeremiah foretold would be normal and common:

*"Behold, the days come," says Yahweh, "that I will make a new covenant with the house of Israel, and with the house of Judah: not according to the covenant that I made with their fathers in the day that I took them by the hand to bring them out of the land of Egypt; which covenant of mine they broke, although I was a husband to them", says Yahweh. "But this is the covenant that I will make with the house of Israel after those days," says Yahweh: "I will put my law in their inward parts, and I will write it in their heart. I will be their God, and they shall be my people. They will no longer each teach his neighbor, and every man teach his brother, saying, 'Know Yahweh;' for they will all know me, from their*

*least to their greatest," says Yahweh: "for I will forgive their iniquity, and I will remember their sin no more."*

*Jeremiah 31:31-34 WEB*

How does God communicate with all believers under the New Covenant? He says *"I will put my law in their inward parts, and I will write it in their heart."* This correlates with what I am referring to as *"God giving knowledge and understanding."*

Some may question whether the words of Jeremiah 31:31-34 apply today, or to a future time. However, those verses are quoted in the New Testament, in Hebrews 8:8-12, in such a way that it seems clear that they apply to us today, at least to some degree.

Moreover, God giving believers knowledge and understanding is often associated with having the Holy Spirit living in us. Consider these verses that point to knowledge and understanding given through the Holy Spirit:

*But the Counselor, the Holy Spirit, whom the Father will send in my name, he will teach you all things, and will remind you of all that I said to you.* John 14:26 WEB

*However when he, the Spirit of truth, has come, he will guide you into all truth, for he will not speak from himself; but whatever he hears, he will speak. He will declare to you things that are coming.* John 16:13 WEB

*But as it is written, "Things which an eye didn't see, and an ear didn't hear, which didn't enter into the heart of man, these God has prepared for those who love him." But to us, God revealed them through the Spirit. For the Spirit searches all things, yes, the deep things of God. For who among men knows the things of a man, except the spirit of the man, which is in him? Even so, no one knows the things of God, except God's Spirit. But we received, not the spirit of the world, but the Spirit which is from God, that we might know the things that were freely given to us by God.*     *1Corinthians 2:9-12 WEB*

*Now the natural man doesn't receive the things of God's Spirit, for they are foolishness to him, and he can't know them, because they are spiritually discerned. But he who is spiritual discerns all things, and he himself is judged by no one. "For who has known the mind of the Lord, that he should instruct him?" But we have Christ's mind.*     *1Corinthians 2:14-16 WEB*

*You have an anointing from the Holy One, and you all have knowledge. I have not written to you because you don't know the truth, but because you know it, and because no lie is of the truth.*     *1John 2:20-21 WEB*

*I write these things to you about those who are trying to deceive you. But the anointing that you received from him abides in you, and you have no need that anyone should teach you. But as his anointing teaches you about everything, and is true, and is no lie—just as it has taught you, abide in him.*     *1John 2:26-27 ESV*

All of these verses point toward knowledge and understanding given through the Holy Spirit. While some may reason that John 14:26 and 16:13 may apply only to the original disciples, the other verses are not limited in that way.

Consider the following prayers by Paul for believers. Notice that Paul does not pray for people to clearly hear God's voice, but rather for God to give them knowledge and understanding, that they may walk uprightly:

*For this cause, we also, since the day we heard this, don't cease praying and making requests for you, that you may be filled with the knowledge of his will in all spiritual wisdom and understanding, that you may walk worthily of the Lord, to please him in all respects, bearing fruit in every good work...*     *Colossians 1:9-10 WEB*

*And it is my prayer that your love may abound more and*

*more, with knowledge and all discernment, so that you may approve what is excellent, and so be pure and blameless for the day of Christ, filled with the fruit of righteousness that comes through Jesus Christ, to the glory and praise of God.*     *Philippians 1:9-11 ESV*

These prayers for all the believers in Colossae and Philippi support that giving knowledge and understanding is a *normal and common* way that God communicates with believers.

Consider also Paul's letter to the Ephesians. He prays for them to be able *to comprehend* and *to know Christ's love.* In this verse, Paul is praying to God for this to happen for all the believers in Ephesus, not just people with special gifting:

*...that Christ may dwell in your hearts through faith; to the end that you, being rooted and grounded in love, may be strengthened to comprehend with all the saints what is the width and length and height and depth, and to know Christ's love which surpasses knowledge, that you may be filled with all the fullness of God.*
*Ephesians 3:17-19 WEB*

Paul's prayer indicates that *"to comprehend"* and *"to know"* are the result of *"Christ may dwell in your hearts."* Paul's reference to Christ dwelling in their hearts is often understood to be a reference to the Holy Spirit.

So, we see that giving knowledge and understanding is a normal and common way that God communicates with believers under the New Covenant.

Note, however, that giving knowledge and understanding through the Holy Spirit is not something that happens only once and is finished. Paul's prayers show that it is something we should continue to ask God for, and it is something that God may continue to give new measures of. This is consistent with these verses:

*But if any of you lacks wisdom, let him ask of God, who gives to all liberally and without reproach; and it will be given to him.* *James 1:5 WEB*

*"Ask, and it will be given you. Seek, and you will find. Knock, and it will be opened for you. For everyone who asks receives. He who seeks finds. To him who knocks it will be opened."* *Matthew 7:7-8 WEB*

While true believers are given knowledge and understanding by God, the opposite may happen for those who reject truth. God may send a strong delusion to those who reject truth:

*They perish because they refused to love the truth and so be saved. For this reason God sends them a powerful delusion so that they will believe the lie and so that all will be condemned who have not believed the truth but have delighted in wickedness.* *2Thessalonians 2:10-12 NIV*

## Clarity and Certainty

I find it helpful to make distinctions regarding the *clarity* and *certainty* associated with various ways that God may speak to people. For example, consider the differences between how God spoke to Moses and how he typically spoke to other people in Old Testament times:

*Miriam and Aaron spoke against Moses because of the Cushite woman whom he had married; for he had married a Cushite woman. They said, "Has Yahweh indeed spoken only with Moses? Hasn't he spoken also with us?" And Yahweh heard it.*

*Now the man Moses was very humble, above all the men who were on the surface of the earth. Yahweh spoke suddenly to Moses, to Aaron, and to Miriam, "You three come out to the Tent of Meeting!"*

*The three of them came out. Yahweh came down in a pillar of cloud, and stood at the door of the Tent, and called Aaron and Miriam; and they both came forward. He said, "Now hear my words. If there is a prophet among you, I Yahweh will make myself known to him in a vision. I will speak with him in a dream. My servant Moses is not so. He is faithful in all my house. With him I will speak mouth to mouth, even plainly, and not in riddles; and he shall see Yahweh's form. Why then were you not afraid to speak against my servant, against Moses?"*                                        *Numbers 12:1-8 WEB*

In these verses we see four different ways that God spoke to people:

- **To Moses:** God spoke to Moses *"mouth to mouth, even plainly, and not in riddles; and he shall see Yahweh's form"* (this is referred to as *face to face* in Exodus 33:11).

- **To other Prophets:** With visions and dreams.

- **To People through Moses:** God spoke to the people through Moses. The people saw the cloud descend on the tent of meeting (Exodus 33:8-10), and this was strong evidence to the people that God was actually speaking to Moses.

- **To People through other Prophets:** God often used prophets to communicate his messages to many people, often without any supernatural evidence that God had spoken to the prophet.

Each of these ways of communicating has a different level of *clarity* and/or *certainty*. God speaking face to face with Moses has the highest level of *clarity* and *certainty*. Next in line may be how the prophets heard from God through visions and dreams. Next, how the people heard God's message through Moses. Least *certain* would be people hearing God's message from various prophets (other than Moses).

In each case, the people who heard God's message may make a judgment as to the validity of the message, and whether or not they will accept it and obey it. Consider each case:

- **God Speaking to Moses:** The clarity and certainty of these face-to-face messages appear to be beyond question, but even Moses could have rejected the message as being from a god he didn't want to follow.

- **God Speaking to Prophets:** In Numbers 12:1-8 (above), God seems to be making a distinction between how he spoke to Moses, and how he typically spoke to prophets. His point to Miriam and Aaron seems to be that his relationship with Moses was uniquely close. So, Aaron and Miriam should have had greater respect for Moses, and not considered their own prophetic experiences so highly.

  However, there was clarity and certainty regarding how God spoke to the prophets. I don't see any of the prophets ever questioning what God's word to them was. Jonah may not have wanted to hear God's word, and he tried to flee from God, but God's word appears to have been clear and certain even to him. Peter discusses the certainty of God's words to the prophets:

  > *And we have the prophetic word more fully confirmed, to which you will do well to pay attention as to a lamp shining in a dark place, until the day dawns and the morning star rises in your hearts, knowing this first of all, that no prophecy of Scripture comes from someone's own interpretation. For no prophecy was ever produced by the will of man, but men spoke from God as they were carried along by the Holy Spirit.*    *2Peter 1:19-21 ESV*

- **God Speaking to People through Moses:** When people heard Moses tell them what God said, it was second-hand information. People could question whether or not Moses was accurately passing on what God said, or whether or not God was actually speaking to him. Even though the cloud at the tent of meeting was evidence of God's presence, the people could still reject Moses and his message, as Aaron and Miriam apparently did in the verses above (Numbers 12:1-8). So, I consider that the words Moses spoke to the people, regarding what God said, were messages from God that were less *certain* (and perhaps less *clear*) than what Moses experienced hearing directly from God.

- **God Speaking to People through Prophets:** The messages from God that people heard through the prophets were also second-hand information. From the people's perspective, these messages were less certain than messages through Moses, since the prophets generally didn't have supernatural evidence that God was speaking to them (other than the words they spoke). People hearing from a prophet had to discern whether the prophet's message was actually from God or not. For example, Micaiah's prophecy to King Jehoshaphat and the King of Israel was not accepted partly because of uncertainty caused by many false prophets who were prophesying differently than Micaiah (1 Kings 22).

Likewise today, there are different levels of clarity and certainty associated with the various ways God may speak to people. For example, there are many different degrees of clarity and certainty regarding how God may give each of us knowledge and understanding. It may often be so subtle that we don't even realize it has happened, or we may question its source, since it may come to us in a way that is hard to differentiate from our own knowledge and understanding. At other times, the knowledge or understanding given may be clearly supernatural, and may rightly be referred to as "revelation." However, it appears that Satan and his angels also can give people knowledge and understanding, so we shouldn't automatically assume that any supernatural knowledge or understanding we may receive is from God. Consider these verses:

*But even if we or an angel from heaven should preach to you a gospel contrary to the one we preached to you, let him be accursed. As we have said before, so now I say again: If anyone is preaching to you a gospel contrary to the one you received, let him be accursed.*

Galatians 1:8-9 ESV

*Beloved, don't believe every spirit, but test the spirits, whether they are of God, because many false prophets have gone out into the world.*

1 John 4:1 WEB

## Thoughts and Impressions

There appears to be a fair amount of teaching among many believers that God *speaks* to us frequently through our thoughts and impressions. Such thoughts and impressions are usually understood to be given to us by the Holy Spirit. I have leaned toward this viewpoint much of my life, but more recently have had a hard time finding scriptural support for it. I now tend to think this viewpoint is a somewhat distorted way of understanding God giving us knowledge and understanding through the Holy Spirit (as discussed above).

Consider this as a possible explanation of what may often happen: Many believers are living in religious cultures that emphasize hearing God's voice. If God gives them new knowledge and understanding through the Holy Spirit, this will impact their own thoughts and impressions. Since the new knowledge and understanding comes supernaturally (at least in part), they interpret their own thoughts and impressions as God speaking to them.

Perhaps the difference is a matter of semantics more than substance, but I think a misunderstanding in this area can contribute to deception. If we think of our thoughts and impressions as being *spoken* to us directly by the Holy Spirit, when perhaps they aren't, then we are more likely to be led astray.

On the other hand, if we think of our thoughts and

impressions as being associated with our own knowledge and understanding, in part given by the Holy Spirit, then we are more likely to scrutinize those thoughts and impressions more carefully, and we are more likely to avoid deception. We are more likely to consider the possibility that our thoughts and impressions may sometimes originate with spiritual darkness (including our own natural self), rather than spiritual light, and we would be in a better position to be able to reject what is wrong and not be easily deceived.

We should keep in mind that, no matter how much knowledge and understanding we have, we still only *"know in part"* (1 Corinthians 13:9; 13:12).

## Consider Other Possible Sources

As mentioned previously, spiritual communication and spiritual manifestations can have various sources:

- God / good angels
- Satan / evil spirits
- A person's own self (spirit/soul/body)

Dreams and visions illustrate how each of these different sources may be at work. Here are some examples:

- *God came to Abimelech in a dream of the night, and said to him, "Behold, you are a dead man, because of the woman whom you have taken; for she is a man's wife"* (Genesis 20:3 WEB).

- *At Gibeon the LORD appeared to Solomon in a dream by night, and God said, "Ask what I shall give you."* (1 Kings 3:5 ESV).

- Daniel, Zechariah, and Mary all had visions of the angel Gabriel speaking to them (Daniel 8:15-27; Luke 1:8-23; Luke 1:26-38).

- Zechariah spoke of some dreams and visions having their source in idols and diviners: *The idols speak deceitfully, diviners see visions that lie; they tell dreams that are false, they give comfort in vain. Therefore the people wander like sheep oppressed for lack of a shepherd* (Zechariah 10:2 NIV).

- God spoke harshly about some prophets who attributed their dreams to God: *"I have heard what the prophets say who prophesy lies in my name. They say, 'I had a dream! I had a dream!' How long will this continue in the hearts of these lying prophets, who prophesy the delusions of their own minds?"* (Jeremiah 23:25-26 NIV) *"Indeed, I am against those who prophesy false dreams,"* declares the LORD. *"They tell them and lead my people astray with their reckless lies, yet I did not send or appoint them. They do not benefit these people in the least,"* declares the LORD (Jeremiah 23:32 NIV).

- Jude spoke of false teachers being influenced by dreams which are not from God: *Yet in like manner these people also, relying on their dreams, defile the flesh, reject authority, and blaspheme the glorious ones* (Jude 8 ESV).

- Paul warns us: *...even Satan masquerades as an angel of light* (2 Corinthians 11:14 WEB).

- Some dreams which I have had while sleeping were clearly not from God, and I'm pretty sure they weren't just products of my own imagination. I believe some dreams I have had were influenced by evil spirits.

- Other dreams I have had while sleeping seem to be without much purpose, and are likely just the result of my own mind wandering.

Discerning the true source of spiritual things often is not easy. Those who accept all spiritual manifestations as being from God, without question, open themselves up to being deceived.

# Discerning the Difference

Some people say that God speaks to them rather directly every day through their thoughts or impressions, or a voice in their head. How can a person discern whether or not such messages are reliably from God or not? When the occurrence of "God told me..." is rather frequent, as in these cases, there is a rather straight forward way. All such messages clearly attributed to God must be without error all the time, and not contradict clear scriptural principles all the time. Any exception to this standard shows a problem either with the source of the message or with the reception of the message. In either case, if the message received is not 100% reliable, one should not be claiming to be experiencing clear communication from God. Someone claiming "God told me..." when such communication is not reliably from God is surely not on solid ground.

The above way of discernment may be used by both a person claiming to hear from God, and by those who hear a person communicate "God told me...." For people who hear such claims frequently, they may rightly judge whether or not the messages are consistently 100% reliable and consistent with scripture. If not, then the person is clearly not hearing from God clearly.

Along similar lines, is the person who frequently claims to hear from God living a godly life? If they claim to frequently hear from God, but aren't "walking the talk" so to speak, surely we should be cautious regarding what they say God said.

# Learning from History

God appears to relate to each of us somewhat differently, and trying to quantify just how God will communicate with each of us is likely not profitable.

However, it may be profitable to consider the large number

of people who apparently thought they were hearing from God, who apparently were not. History is full of examples of people who claim to be Jesus' followers who apparently believed they had special direction from God about various subjects, which then resulted in ungodly divisions, or led to various wrong teachings or practices.

Many followers of Jesus today reject the belief that God may still speak to us personally, largely because so many deceptions have happened in these areas in the past. So, we need to be careful. We should all keep in mind how limited our present understanding is:

> *For now we see in a mirror, dimly, but then face to face. Now I know in part, but then I will know fully, even as I was also fully known.*      1Corinthians 13:12 WEB

## Growing Up

The way God relates to each of us is partly dependent on our spiritual maturity. Just as parents communicate with their young children differently than with their grown children, so God likely will communicate differently with us as we mature.

Babies and little children need lots of direction from their parents. As they grow and mature, they should need less direction and become more independent, eventually living independent of their parents' continual oversight. The same appears to me to be God's intent for our spiritual lives. Babes in Christ generally lack spiritual maturity and may need lots of supernatural direction from God to help them grow, especially if they lack good fellowship with mature believers. As they grow in maturity, the need for supernatural leading should diminish. I believe God wants people to serve and love him through their own wills and understanding, not continue to be like little children who continually need to be told what to do.

I find the experience of many believers to be similar to this: Early in their lives as followers of Jesus they were more aware of God's guidance and supernatural help. As they matured, those things became less necessary and less frequent.

As we grow in maturity, we should not expect God to continue to relate to us the same as when we were infants in Christ.

## My Experience

I can point to several times in my life when I believe God was clearly involved in guiding me, or helping my understanding about something important, or perhaps just convicting me about something I needed to do or not do. I believe the Holy Spirit was often involved in those things. However, I can't point to any clear direct communication from God in my life. Rather, God seems to speak to me indirectly through scripture, prayer, other people, books, sermons, creation, circumstances, my own spirit's intuition and conscience, and by giving me knowledge and understanding. I think my thoughts and impressions are often *influenced* by the Holy Spirit. However, in my experience, God seems to avoid clear direct communication with me. He seems to prefer that I exercise faith, reason, and discernment rather than simply telling me things directly.

It may be helpful for me to give an example from my own life. Back in my early college days I questioned whether I should stay in school or quit and go off to do some kind of missions work to save the lost (as some people I looked up to seemed to be promoting at that time). I had only truly become a follower of Jesus about a year before, and I wanted clear direction from God regarding this issue. After midterm tests during my second quarter, I packed my backpack and set out for the mountains to petition God for a clear answer. I had no car at the time, and I was hitchhiking my way there, intending to only come back after receiving a clear answer. On the way, a couple of older believers, who were foreign workers on furlough (recently back from Japan, if I recall correctly), saw me hitchhiking and picked me up. They told me they don't usually pick up hitchhikers, but felt impressed by the Holy Spirit to do so in this case. After hearing my story (with more details than shared here), they told me they thought it best for me to stay in school, and why they thought so. They dropped me off many miles short of my intended destination, and I had to decide whether I needed a more direct answer from God or not. After some prayerful consideration, I concluded I had my answer. God had given me the answer I needed through other people and the circumstances associated with meeting those people, not by speaking to me directly.

I've had few experiences like that. Usually I make decisions something like this: I ask God for knowledge and understanding; I spend time in scripture looking for guidance and understanding there; I try to learn more about the issue and various options; and I commit myself to doing what is best before God, regardless of the personal cost. As I gain knowledge and understanding by doing these things, the best path to take usually becomes clear. Is God involved in that? I think so. Would it be accurate for me to say "God told me..."? I don't think so.

## For Further Reflection

- In what ways have you perceived God communicating with you? Are these ways mostly direct or indirect communication?

✱✱✱✱✱✱✱✱✱✱✱

# Chapter 34
# Mishandling Scripture

*Do your best to present yourself to God as one approved, a worker who has no need to be ashamed, rightly handling the word of truth.*                    *2Timothy 2:15 ESV*

*For the time is coming when people will not endure sound teaching, but having itching ears they will accumulate for themselves teachers to suit their own passions, and will turn away from listening to the truth and wander off into myths.*                              *2Timothy 4:3-4 ESV*

---

How do we *rightly handle the word of truth*? How do we avoid *wandering off into myths*? How do we avoid deception when looking at scripture?

Let's consider some important principles.

## Knowledge, Understanding, or Wisdom?

There are at least three ways we can relate to scripture.

First, we can read scripture to simply learn what it says. At this level we are simply acquiring *knowledge* about scripture.

Second, once we know what it says, we should aim to *understand* what it says. We should aim to understand what the authors were trying to communicate within the context and culture it was written in. We should also aim to understand how it applies to us today.

Third, once we understand how it applies to us today, we should put it into practice. *Wisdom* puts scriptural principles into practice.

Recall Jesus' words:

> *"Everyone then who hears these words of mine and does them will be like a wise man who built his house on the*

*rock. And the rain fell, and the floods came, and the winds blew and beat on that house, but it did not fall, because it had been founded on the rock. And everyone who hears these words of mine and does not do them will be like a foolish man who built his house on the sand. And the rain fell, and the floods came, and the winds blew and beat against that house, and it fell, and great was the fall of it."*      *Matthew 7:24-27 ESV*

## God's Viewpoint

When it comes to understanding and applying scripture, the only viewpoint that really matters is God's viewpoint. Paul warned Timothy about our propensity to seek out teachers who will distort the truth and who will tell us what we want to hear. Consider this verse again:

*For the time is coming when people will not endure sound teaching, but having itching ears they will accumulate for themselves teachers to suit their own passions, and will turn away from listening to the truth and wander off into myths.*      *2Timothy 4:3-4 ESV*

This is a huge problem today. Consider the hundreds of thousands of books available on the broad subject of "Religion and Spirituality." It is hard to imagine a religious perspective that is not already supported with multiple books. Clearly, many people are choosing the religious perspective they want to hear, and are *wandering off into myths.* This problem is not limited to unbelievers, but appears to be impacting many believers, as Paul seems to indicate.

Even among people who appear to be strong believers, the degree to which many promote opposing viewpoints shows that many people are clearly not in line with God's viewpoint (since contradictory viewpoints cannot all be correct).

I hope you agree with me that God has the final say regarding the correct understanding of scripture. All our reasonings and beliefs are just *myths* if they don't agree with God, who alone knows and understands all things perfectly.

How can we know God's perspective about scripture? Paul explains that a primary purpose of the Holy Spirit is to help us in this area. Consider these verses:

> *For who knows a person's thoughts except the spirit of that person, which is in him?  So also no one comprehends the thoughts of God except the Spirit of God.  Now we have received not the spirit of the world, but the Spirit who is from God, that we might understand the things freely given us by God.*
>
> *1 Corinthians 2:11-12 ESV*

So, we see that we must depend on the Holy Spirit to help us understand God, to help us understand scripture.

Yet, we aren't to be passive about learning truth, just expecting the Holy Spirit to tell us everything we should know (though at times the Holy Spirit may communicate specific things to us).  In chapter 5 we looked at the many ways we can grow in *knowledge, understanding,* and *wisdom.*  The Holy Spirit plays an important part in those things, as we have discussed, but is not the only factor in play.  Using our own ability to *reason* is also an important factor.

In this chapter we'll look at some ways we can use *reason* to avoid being deceived when we read scripture.  Please do not expect *reason* alone, apart from the help of the Holy Spirit, to protect you from deception.  Rather, humbly look to the Holy Spirit for help as you try to understand scripture and put what you understand into practice.  Our goal should be to align our understanding with God's understanding, and to humbly live our lives based on that right understanding.

# By Example or Teaching?

We ought to make a distinction between what scripture directly teaches and what scripture records as happening. Scripture records a lot of good things that happened, and a lot of bad things that happened. Just because something happened in scripture doesn't mean it should happen in our lives, whether what happened was good or bad. Just because God did something a particular way in the past does not obligate him to do the same today. Just because scripture records that a good person did something does not mean that we should try to do the same. For example, consider these verses:

> *All who believed were together, and had all things in common. They sold their possessions and goods, and distributed them to all, according as anyone had need.*
>
> *Acts 2:44-45 WEB*

Is that how all believers should live today? Some would say "yes," others "no." It's a legitimate question. However, it is important to understand that this passage of scripture is not a teaching passage; it is a history passage, simply recording what happened. The context appears to me to indicate that this was a good thing that happened at that time in that context. However, to conclude that all believers should do the same today, regardless of their circumstances, I think is the wrong way to understand these verses. It appears that believers later had to put limits on those whom they helped financially. Consider these verses:

> *For even when we were with you, we would give you this command: If anyone is not willing to work, let him not eat. For we hear that some among you walk in idleness, not busy at work, but busybodies. Now such persons we command and encourage in the Lord Jesus Christ to do their work quietly and to earn their own living.*
>
> *2Thessalonians 3:10-12 ESV*

> *Give proper recognition to those widows who are really*

*in need. But if a widow has children or grandchildren, these should learn first of all to put their religion into practice by caring for their own family and so repaying their parents and grandparents, for this is pleasing to God.* 1Timothy 5:3-4 NIV

*Anyone who does not provide for their relatives, and especially for their own household, has denied the faith and is worse than an unbeliever. No widow may be put on the list of widows unless she is over sixty, has been faithful to her husband, and is well known for her good deeds, such as bringing up children, showing hospitality, washing the feet of the Lord's people, helping those in trouble and devoting herself to all kinds of good deeds.* 1Timothy 5:8-10 NIV

*If any woman who is a believer has widows in her care, she should continue to help them and not let the church be burdened with them, so that the church can help those widows who are really in need.* 1Timothy 5:16 NIV

These are instruction verses, in which Paul is giving directions about how believers should, or shouldn't, help various people financially. These kinds of verses should carry more weight in how we should live than verses which simply record what happened. Making a distinction between what scripture directly teaches and what scripture records as happening can help us avoid mishandling scripture.

## Is It Applicable?

When scripture is directly teaching something, we ought to determine who the intended audience is, to what degree we are that audience, and to what degree what was taught applies to us. For example, consider this passage of scripture:

*"If any member of the community sins unintentionally and does what is forbidden in any of the LORD's commands, when they realize their guilt and the sin they*

*have committed becomes known, they must bring as*
*their offering for the sin they committed a female goat*
*without defect. They are to lay their hand on the head*
*of the sin offering and slaughter it at the place of the*
*burnt offering. Then the priest is to take some of the*
*blood with his finger and put it on the horns of the altar*
*of burnt offering and pour out the rest of the blood at*
*the base of the altar."* Leviticus 4:27-30 NIV

This is God himself speaking to the people through Moses.
Why don't believers practice animal sacrifices today?
Because we understand that the sacrifices required under the
Mosaic Covenant were a foreshadowing of Jesus' sacrifice
for us. The sacrifice of Jesus is the fulfillment of the
required sacrifices in the Old Testament, as the book of
Hebrews clarifies. The Old Testament sacrificial system
does not apply directly to believers living under the New
Covenant.

Consider another passage from the Old Testament:

*"Will man rob God? Yet you are robbing me. But you*
*say, 'How have we robbed you?' In your tithes and*
*contributions. You are cursed with a curse, for you are*
*robbing me, the whole nation of you. Bring the full tithe*
*into the storehouse, that there may be food in my house.*
*And thereby put me to the test, says the LORD of hosts,*
*if I will not open the windows of heaven for you and*
*pour down for you a blessing until there is no more*
*need."* Malachi 3:8-10 ESV

This is God himself telling the people what to do, through
the prophet Malachi. Is this passage directly applicable to
believers today? Let's consider the context of this passage.

This verse is written to people in the country of Israel, who
were under the Mosaic Covenant, hundreds of years before
Jesus came. The Mosaic Covenant was the law they lived
under, and the tithes that were to be given were essentially

taxes for the purpose of providing for the Levite's who served at the temple, providing food for poor people, and provision for annual feasts. I don't live in the country of Israel, and I am not living under the Mosaic Covenant, but rather under the New Covenant. Under the New Covenant I find this instruction about giving:

> *Each one must give as he has decided in his heart, not reluctantly or under compulsion, for God loves a cheerful giver.*  2Corinthians 9:7 ESV

Those words were written to the believers in Corinth in the first century AD, in reference to a specific offering to help believers near Jerusalem. While those circumstances are not mine, and I can't give to that specific situation, I believe the principle given here is somewhat general in nature and transcends that specific situation. I do encounter similar situations in which I am asked to give to people in need. I believe this verse is an instruction that does apply to me today in those similar situations.

The issue here is not about whether someone should or shouldn't give regularly to their local church, or to a particular ministry or cause, or how much they should give. Rather, the issue here is about proper application of scripture. Using Malachi 3:8-10 (above) to *compel* believers today to give "tithes" appears to me to disregard the context of those verses and appears to me to be a wrong application of scripture.

So, we see that considering whether or not particular verses are intended to apply to us can help us avoid mishandling scripture.

## Context and Culture

Properly understanding the context and culture in which scripture was written is a very important factor in properly understanding scripture. It is also a very difficult task.

Consider some of the barriers to this:

- Thousands of years separate us from what was written.

- Scripture was originally written to people in a different culture in a different time.

- The modern western culture I live in today is very different from a middle-eastern culture two thousand years ago.

- Scripture was originally written mostly in Hebrew and Greek.

- Translations are limited to using words in my language that do not always correlate well with words in the original language.

- We bring our own preconceived ideas and beliefs when we read scripture.

- We tend to hear what we want to hear, rather than truths that may require that we change. Stated another way, we tend to read our own beliefs into scripture.

- Some of the letters in the New Testament were written as part of an ongoing discussion, and those letters show only one side of the discussion. For example, parts of Paul's first letter to the Corinthians were answering questions that the Corinthians had asked, as Paul indicated: ***"Now concerning the things about which you wrote to me..."*** (1 Corinthians 7:1 WEB). We don't have the original letter from the Corinthians to Paul, so we are lacking some context that would be helpful in understanding what Paul wrote.

Even with all these barriers, many believers approach scripture as if none of these barriers exist, as if it is an easy thing to understand scripture clearly and accurately. I find that we tend to think we understand scripture better than we actually do, and are quick to find fault with anyone who understands scripture differently than we do.

As an example of the need to understand context and culture, consider these verses:

> *Women should remain silent in the churches. They are not allowed to speak, but must be in submission, as the law says. If they want to inquire about something, they should ask their own husbands at home; for it is disgraceful for a woman to speak in the church.*
>
> *1Corinthians 14:34-35 NIV*

I think Paul wrote this in response to a specific situation which the Corinthians had written to him about (per 1 Corinthians 7:1). Since we don't have that original letter from the Corinthians to Paul, we are lacking some context which would likely help us understand what Paul intended here.

Should these verses be applied to our gatherings today directly, without considering the context, culture, and what other scriptures say? Should we always forbid every woman present from ever saying anything at any gathering of believers?

At the beginning of the church, women believers were present in their gathering (Acts 1:13-14). Then, this is what happened:

> *They were all filled with the Holy Spirit, and began to speak with other languages, as the Spirit gave them the ability to speak.*
>
> *Acts 2:4 WEB*

This was the fulfillment of a prophecy:

> *"But this is what was uttered through the prophet Joel: 'And in the last days it shall be, God declares, that I will pour out my Spirit on all flesh, and your sons and your daughters shall prophesy, and your young men shall see visions, and your old men shall dream dreams; even on my male servants and female servants in those days I*

*will pour out my Spirit, and they shall prophesy.'"*

This prophecy indicates both *your sons and your daughters shall prophesy.* Did Paul, writing in 1 Corinthians 14:34-35, really mean that it was *disgraceful* for the women present at Pentecost to speak (in Acts 2)? Or are we to believe that the women there didn't speak when they were filled with the Spirit? In what context is it that the *daughters shall prophesy*?

This is a clear example of where understanding the culture and context would be of great help. Unfortunately, some people take verses like these (1 Corinthians 14:34-35), misunderstand them, and apply them in ways God never intended.

Many people believe that the situation which Paul was addressing in Corinth had to do with women speaking inappropriately in a public meeting. Most women of that day apparently had little experience participating in public meetings, and they may have been disrupting the meeting in some way. I think this is likely true to some degree, but I'm not sure that perspective fully resolves this issue. I wish I knew more about the culture and context of those verses, and what question Paul was specifically answering.

As another example of the importance of context, consider this verse:

> *The king's heart is a stream of water in the hand of the LORD; he turns it wherever he will.*   *Proverbs 21:1 ESV*

I have heard this verse quoted regarding present-day rulers, implying that God is in control of whatever they do. However, taking a moment to consider the context and culture of this verse might lead to a different conclusion. Who wrote it? It was a king! King Solomon to be precise. Many believe he was the greatest king in the world in his day. Is he referring to other kings, or to himself? It appears

*358*      *Building on Foundations for Eternal Life*

to me that he is referring to himself, perhaps indicating that he feels the hand of God directing him as he wrote much of the book of Proverbs. Consider another place in scripture where a king appears to refer to himself as "the king." King David wrote this:

> *The king rejoices in your strength, LORD. How great is his joy in the victories you give!*   Psalm 21:1 NIV

In the context of this psalm, King David is clearly referring to himself, not to anyone who happens to be some kind of ruler.

Again, we see that understanding the context and culture of a verse can have a huge impact on how we understand it.

## Scripture or Tradition?

Are your beliefs and actions based on *scripture* or *tradition*? I suspect you may be like me; my beliefs and actions are based on both scripture and tradition. I think that would be the case even if I tried to base my beliefs and actions only on scripture. Tradition has impacted me in ways that are difficult to shed completely.

For clarity, I should note that *reason* and *experience* also influence my beliefs and actions, but that is not our focus here.

A second question is this: Are you able to discern clearly which of your beliefs and actions are based on scripture, and which are based more on tradition? Again, I suspect you may be like me. My answer is something like "I like to think so, but the reality is probably that I am often not clear about that."

As I write this, there has been almost 2000 years of history that has passed since Jesus died, rose, and ascended. There have been around 1900 years that have passed since most of the New Testament was written. A great many religious traditions have come and gone in the last 1900 years that are not clearly supported in scripture. Many of these traditions have been good, and have been appropriate ways to deal with changing cultural conditions. However, some traditions have been detrimental to the church. Some may have started as a good response to a particular situation, but then outlived their usefulness. Others may never have been beneficial, but persisted anyway. Some have been very beneficial, and should still be practiced. Some situations may call for new traditions to be started.

Consider some general categories of things that traditions likely impact:

- Church government and leadership.
- Church buildings and meeting places.
- Meeting formats and practices.
- Religious holidays.
- Church programs and services.
- Worship songs and music styles.
- Church membership practices.
- Church employment practices.
- Giving practices (to people, churches, and charities).
- Parachurch organizations.
- Government policies regarding churches.
- Various doctrines and teachings.

Jesus rebuked the religious people in his day for some of their traditions, which they made more important than God's actual instructions to them. Consider these verses:

*Then Pharisees and scribes came to Jesus from Jerusalem, saying, "Why do your disciples disobey the tradition of the elders? For they don't wash their hands when they eat bread."*

*He answered them, "Why do you also disobey the commandment of God because of your tradition? For God commanded, 'Honor your father and your mother,' and, 'He who speaks evil of father or mother, let him be put to death.' But you say, 'Whoever may tell his father or his mother, "Whatever help you might otherwise have gotten from me is a gift devoted to God," he shall not honor his father or mother.' You have made the commandment of God void because of your tradition. You hypocrites! Well did Isaiah prophesy of you, saying, 'These people draw near to me with their mouth, and honor me with their lips; but their heart is far from me. And in vain do they worship me, teaching as doctrine rules made by men.'"*    Matthew 15:1-9 WEB

Similarly today, we should be careful that our *traditions* are not hindering us from truly following God. We should make a distinction between what is merely tradition, and what is clearly based on scripture. We should be careful to not let traditions hinder our walk with God. On the other hand, many traditions are good and appropriate in today's culture, and should not be opposed just because they are not found in scripture.

## Translation Problems

Many churches today have a "statement of faith" that emphasizes that scripture is inspired by God and is without error in the original writings. The original writings are mostly written in Greek and Hebrew, and, unfortunately, most of us don't know those languages. Most people rely on translations of scripture into their own language when they read scripture. Few claim that translations are fully inspired by God and are without any error. Translation problems contribute to problems in understanding scripture.

All translations are made by imperfect people who have to interpret scripture to some degree when they translate, since no two languages have a direct correlation between sentence structure and word definitions. A literal accurate word-for-word translation is not possible, simply because many words in the original language do not accurately match with a word in the new language.

For an example of a translation problem, let's look at the subject of predestination, which deals with the degree God predetermines or controls whatever happens, and, more specifically, who will be saved or not saved. I understand this to be a secondary issue that believers should not divide over. However, many believers appear to divide over it. It appears to me that translation problems contribute to misunderstandings and division related to this subject.

Here is one verse that has been used to support the belief that God predestines or controls everything, or almost everything:

*"Are not two sparrows sold for a penny? Yet not one of them will fall to the ground apart from the will of your Father."* Matthew 10:29 NIV'84

That is how the 1984 version of the New International Version (NIV) Bible reads. What do I see as a translation problem here? It appears to me that the original verse in the Greek language does not have words that correspond to *"the will of"* in it. It appears that the translators were reading their own beliefs into this verse when they translated it. The NIV translation is not unique in this; some other translations read similarly.

That same verse may be translated more literally like this:

*"Are not two sparrows sold for a penny? And not one of them will fall to the ground apart from your Father."* Matthew 10:29 ESV

I see that the larger context of this section of scripture deals with the care God has for people and his awareness of everything that happens, not that God predestines or controls everything that happens. When the NIV Bible was revised in 2011, the new translation team was apparently aware of this translation problem and modified it to read like this:

*"Are not two sparrows sold for a penny? Yet not one of them will fall to the ground outside your Father's care."*
*Matthew 10:29 NIV*

That's an improvement, in my opinion, but I prefer the more literal rendering of the ESV translation (above), which leaves the meaning of the verse more open to various understandings (by translating that verse more literally *"...apart from your Father"*).

Now let's consider a smaller difference in translation, which can still lead to big differences in understanding and contribute to unnecessary division.

Scripture speaks in several places about a *"book of life"* with names written in it. It is widely understood that those whose names are written in the book of life are saved, and those whose names are not written there are not saved. This seems to be clearly supported by the account of final judgment near the end of Revelation:

*Death and Hades were thrown into the lake of fire. This is the second death, the lake of fire. If anyone was not found written in the book of life, he was cast into the lake of fire.* *Revelation 20:14-15 WEB*

For better or worse, the time frame in which names are written in the book of life has been taken as evidence as to whether individual people are predestined to eternal life or not. If the names of people who are saved were written in the book of life at or before creation, then that may be evidence for predestination. If not, then that may be taken as evidence against predestination. With that background in mind, consider this verse:

*"The beast that you saw was, and is not, and is about to rise from the bottomless pit and go to destruction. And*

*the dwellers on earth whose names have not been written in the book of life from the foundation of the world will marvel to see the beast, because it was and is not and is to come."* Revelation 17:8 ESV

A statement similar to *"written in the book of life from the foundation of the world"* is found in Revelation 13:8.

When were the names written in the book of life? Many understand the phrase *"from the foundation of the world"* to indicate that all the names were written at, or before, the beginning of the world. However, that perspective does not appear to be consistent with these verses:

*For Christ has entered, not into holy places made with hands, which are copies of the true things, but into heaven itself, now to appear in the presence of God on our behalf. Nor was it to offer himself repeatedly, as the high priest enters the holy places every year with blood not his own, for then he would have had to suffer repeatedly since the foundation of the world. But as it is, he has appeared once for all at the end of the ages to put away sin by the sacrifice of himself.*
Hebrews 9:24-26 ESV

In these verses the phrase *"since the foundation of the world"* is derived from the same Greek phrase as *"from the foundation of the world"* in Revelation 17:8. In Hebrews 9:26 the context clearly shows the meaning has the sense of things happening *after* the foundation of the world. The same Greek phrase is also used in Luke 11:50, also in a context that refers to things that happened *after* the foundation of the world.

So, we see how the translation of one minor word can have a big impact on the way many people understand an important secondary issue. We can easily be misled and mishandle scripture if we are unaware of these kinds of translation problems.

As another example, we have previously discussed how some translations indicate in some verses that the Holy Spirit *controls* us (see chapter 32 *"The Holy Spirit,"* under the subheading *"Controlling or Empowering?").* This kind of translation problem can have a profound impact on how people understand God and relate to God.

Consider another example. In my opinion this verse has multiple challenges. Three different translations are shown:

> *We know that whoever is born of God doesn't sin, but he who was born of God keeps himself, and the evil one doesn't touch him.* 1John 5:18 WEB

> *We know that anyone born of God does not continue to sin; the One who was born of God keeps them safe, and the evil one cannot harm them.* 1John 5:18 NIV

> *We know that everyone who has been born of God does not keep on sinning, but he who was born of God protects him, and the evil one does not touch him.* 1John 5:18 ESV

First, consider *"whoever is born of God doesn't sin"* (WEB). That is likely the most word-for-word literal translation of the three, but it fails to communicate the sense of the original language of ongoing sin, rather than an isolated sin. The ESV and NIV overcome that problem some, but at the expense of being less word-for-word.

Second, consider the problem of the second clause. The WEB translation says *"he who was born of God keeps himself,"* which indicates the person who is *born of God* has a responsibility here. The NIV reads *"the One who was born of God keeps them safe,"* where the capitalized **"One"** implies Jesus is the responsible party, and *"them"* implies all who are *born of God* (note that the 2011 NIV translation avoids the use of the word "him" when male gender may not be clearly indicated in the original). The ESV translation is somewhat more ambiguous, perhaps intentionally so. What was the intent of the original author? It's hard to tell, in my opinion. I think it is hard for translators to know also. Obviously, different translation teams interpreted it differently. Whether or not we have a responsibility individually to keep ourselves from sin is an important issue. Based on the rest of scripture, I lean toward the WEB translation as being the preferred way to understand this verse, though we can only keep ourselves from sin with the help of the Holy Spirit.

Third, consider the final clause. The WEB translation reads *"the evil one doesn't touch him,"* which is almost the same as the ESV translation. The NIV translation reads *"the evil one cannot harm them."* Looking up the meaning of the original Greek for the word that correlates with "touch" or "harm" brings us to a variation of the Greek word *"haptomai"* (Strong's G680), which has a sense of "to attach oneself to" (per Strong's Exhaustive Concordance). That seems to make more sense: The evil one cannot *attach himself to* one who is born of God, who keeps himself abiding in Christ, so that person does not keep on sinning. That seems consistent with the rest of scripture (in my opinion), and seems quite a bit different to me than saying the evil one cannot *touch* or *harm* one who is born of God. I see in Revelation 2:10 that the devil can, at times, put believers in prison and possibly have them killed, which seems contrary to how 1 John 5:18 is often translated.

The point here is not whether my understanding of this verse is right or not; the point is that there are translation problems here we should be aware of. We shouldn't be basing important beliefs on single verses with meanings that are not clear. We should be aware of such translation problems so that we are not misled by a particular translation.

How do we discern these kinds of translation problems? Here are some things that should help:

- Understand that translations of scripture are **not**

without error.

- Approach the scriptures humbly, looking to the Holy Spirit for discernment and understanding.

- Look for consistency throughout scripture; compare scripture with scripture (as discussed in the next section). I find that the better I know the whole of scripture, and the better I know God, the easier it is to identify passages affected by translation problems.

- Compare multiple translations when dealing with difficult passages or difficult subjects.

- Some Bible reference books may be helpful in understanding some translation problems.

- Take a neutral attitude regarding things that aren't clear (as discussed in chapter 13 *"A Neutral Attitude"*).

## Compare Scripture with Scripture

If we believe that scripture is inspired by God, and that God is not inconsistent, then we know that scripture is consistent throughout. Different passages of scripture which refer to similar subject matter should be consistent regarding how a subject is properly understood. If there is apparent inconsistency, then that is a good indication that our understanding of scripture regarding that subject is not very good. When there are multiple different passages which are all in agreement on a particular subject, and none in disagreement, then we may have some confidence that our understanding of that subject is correct.

As an example, consider the issue of "eternal security" (a phrase not found in most translations of scripture). The question of whether someone can lose their salvation (once they are saved) seems to divide many believers. It seems to me that there are some pretty strong verses on both sides of this issue, and each side tends to rationalize contrary verses away.  Let's look at some verses on both sides of this issue. These verses are presented in the order they appear in scripture:

*"But when a righteous person turns away from his righteousness and does injustice and does the same abominations that the wicked person does, shall he live? None of the righteous deeds that he has done shall be remembered; for the treachery of which he is guilty and the sin he has committed, for them he shall die."*

*Ezekiel 18:24 ESV*

*"This is the will of my Father who sent me, that of all he has given to me I should lose nothing, but should raise him up at the last day.  This is the will of the one who sent me, that everyone who sees the Son, and believes in him, should have eternal life; and I will raise him up at the last day."*          *John 6:39-40 WEB*

*"My sheep hear my voice, and I know them, and they follow me.  I give eternal life to them.  They will never perish, and no one will snatch them out of my hand.  My Father, who has given them to me, is greater than all. No one is able to snatch them out of my Father's hand. I and the Father are one."*          *John 10:27-30 WEB*

*"Remain in me, and I in you.  As the branch can't bear fruit by itself, unless it remains in the vine, so neither can you, unless you remain in me.  I am the vine.  You are the branches.  He who remains in me, and I in him, the same bears much fruit, for apart from me you can do nothing.  If a man doesn't remain in me, he is thrown out as a branch, and is withered; and they gather them, throw them into the fire, and they are burned."*

*John 15:4-6 WEB*

*For I am convinced that neither death nor life, neither angels nor demons, neither the present nor the future, nor any powers, neither height nor depth, nor anything else in all creation, will be able to separate us from the*

*love of God that is in Christ Jesus our Lord.*
*Romans 8:38-39 NIV*

*But if some of the branches were broken off, and you, being a wild olive, were grafted in among them, and became partaker with them of the root and of the richness of the olive tree; don't boast over the branches. But if you boast, it is not you who support the root, but the root supports you. You will say then, "Branches were broken off, that I might be grafted in." True; by their unbelief they were broken off, and you stand by your faith. Don't be conceited, but fear; for if God didn't spare the natural branches, neither will he spare you. See then the goodness and severity of God. Toward those who fell, severity; but toward you, goodness, if you continue in his goodness; otherwise you also will be cut off.* *Romans 11:17-22 WEB*

*For concerning those who were once enlightened and tasted of the heavenly gift, and were made partakers of the Holy Spirit, and tasted the good word of God, and the powers of the age to come, and then fell away, it is impossible to renew them again to repentance; seeing they crucify the Son of God for themselves again, and put him to open shame.* *Hebrews 6:4-6 WEB*

*For if we go on sinning deliberately after receiving the knowledge of the truth, there no longer remains a sacrifice for sins, but a fearful expectation of judgment, and a fury of fire that will consume the adversaries. Anyone who has set aside the law of Moses dies without mercy on the evidence of two or three witnesses. How much worse punishment, do you think, will be deserved by the one who has trampled underfoot the Son of God, and has profaned the blood of the covenant by which he was sanctified, and has outraged the Spirit of grace?* *Hebrews 10:26-29 ESV*

For those interested, some additional verses to consider are:

Hebrews 13:5, 1 Peter 1:3-5, 1 John 2:19, 2 Peter 3:17-18, and Revelation 3:1-3.

People sometimes use verses like these as "proof texts" to prove their perspective, often looking only at verses that support their viewpoint. Note that the context of each verse should be considered, along with any translation difficulties, to properly understand each verse (I'm not trying to do that here). And we should compare scripture with scripture to avoid misunderstanding and avoid mishandling scripture.

It seems to me that these verses for and against *eternal security* show that this subject is not as simple as many people seem to think. I think we would do well to avoid being divisive about secondary issues like this.

## Reading into Scripture

People often live most of their lives in a particular religious subculture. Without even being aware of it, they adopt that subculture's viewpoint, and read and understand scripture through that religious lens. I still have that problem to some degree, and I think you likely do also.

For example, one area that it seems believers tend to read their own viewpoint into scripture is how they understand the subject of predestination. Verses associated with predestination can often be understood from more than one of these perspectives:

1. A group of people is presently predestined to receive something in the future.

2. Individuals are presently predestined to receive something in the future.

3. A group of people was predestined long ago to receive something they now have today.

4. Individuals were predestined long ago to receive something they now have today.

5. A group of people was predestined long ago to receive something that is still in the future.

6. Individuals were predestined long ago to receive something that is still in the future.

The meaning of a particular verse may be greatly affected by which of those six perspectives it properly fits into. However, it seems to me that few people ever consider those different possible perspectives. People tend to understand such verses from whatever perspective their religious subculture teaches, without ever giving any thought that other viewpoints even exist. It may be okay to not think deeply on these types of topics, but not if you are going to promote division in the body of Christ over these kinds of things.

For example, consider these verses:

*Blessed be the God and Father of our Lord Jesus Christ, who has blessed us in Christ with every spiritual blessing in the heavenly places, even as he chose us in him before the foundation of the world, that we should be holy and blameless before him. In love he predestined us for adoption as sons through Jesus Christ, according to the purpose of his will...*

*Ephesians 1:3-5 ESV*

The phrase "*he chose us in him before the foundation of the world*" is pretty clear when a choice happened (*before the foundation of the world*), but the "*us in him*" is not so clear whether it is referring to specific individuals, or believers as a group. Some may suggest that God chose all people to be holy and blameless through Christ, but those who reject Jesus may not ultimately benefit. It seems to me to at least mean that God chose *before the foundation of the world* that there would be a group of people that would be *holy and blameless*; referring to true believers. Does that mean that God predestined every individual person, before the foundation of the world, to be saved or not saved? Many promote that viewpoint, but that seems to me to be reading into those verses much more than they actually say.

Consider also the phrase *"he predestined us for adoption as sons."* Again we have the question of whether *"us"* refers to believers as a group, or to specific individuals, or possibly to all people. However, the time frames of the predestining and adoption are also not clear just looking at this verse. Paul indicates elsewhere that we are presently waiting to be adopted in the future:

> *Not only so, but ourselves also, who have the first fruits of the Spirit, even we ourselves groan within ourselves, waiting for adoption, the redemption of our body.*
> *Romans 8:23 WEB*

In that sense all believers are presently predestined to future adoption, and that may not have anything to do with God predestining particular individuals long ago. All who follow Jesus are predestined to be adopted, and individuals may become predestined to adoption simply by choosing to follow Jesus.

Consider another passage that is often referenced regarding predestination:

> *For those whom he foreknew he also predestined to be conformed to the image of his Son, in order that he might be the firstborn among many brothers. And those whom he predestined he also called, and those whom he called he also justified, and those whom he justified he also glorified.*
> *Romans 8:29-30 ESV*

Who are those who are *foreknown* and *predestined*? It seems clear that Paul is referring to all true believers here. However, whether these verses are referring to them as a group or as individuals is not clear, in my opinion, but that is not the issue I want to focus on.

The issue I want to look at is the time perspective of these verses. I usually have heard this passage interpreted as though the *"foreknew"* and *"predestined"* happened before creation. However, this passage clearly has a time perspective issue that should be considered. From what perspective in time is Paul writing about all these things happening?

First, let's look at what we are predestined to. It says *"predestined to be conformed to the image of his Son."* All believers should presently be growing in their faith to be more and more like Jesus, but it appears to me that we will only be completely *"conformed to the image of his Son"* in the future, as this verse indicates:

> *Beloved, we are God's children now, and what we will be has not yet appeared; but we know that when he appears we shall be like him, because we shall see him as he is. And everyone who thus hopes in him purifies himself as he is pure.*                    *1John 3:2-3 ESV*

So, from our own present perspective, it looks like Romans 8:29 says we are predestined to something in the future, not something we already have.

Now let's consider the time perspective Paul is writing from. The last part of Romans 8:30 says *"those whom he justified he also glorified."* Note that "glorified" is past tense. I think most believers will agree that, for those of us who are still alive on earth, our *glorification* is still in the future. So Paul appears to be writing either from a present perspective about those who have already left this earth and have already been *glorified*, or from a future eternal perspective in which all of God's people will have already been *glorified*. From either of these perspectives it makes sense to understand the *foreknowing* and *predestining* to be what happens when someone becomes a believer. God *foreknows* us as his children when we become believers, and we become *predestined* to future glory.

So, we see how considering alternate perspectives can result in much different understanding.

Another subject I think many people read their own viewpoint into is Jesus' teaching about marriage, in Matthew 19:3-12. Jesus answered a question from the Pharisees about divorce, and then:

*The disciples said to him, "If such is the case of a man with his wife, it is better not to marry."*

*But he said to them, "Not everyone can receive this saying, but only those to whom it is given. For there are eunuchs who have been so from birth, and there are eunuchs who have been made eunuchs by men, and there are eunuchs who have made themselves eunuchs for the sake of the kingdom of heaven. Let the one who is able to receive this receive it."* Matthew 19:10-12 ESV

Usually I have heard this passage taught such that Jesus agrees with his disciples that it is better **not** to marry; as though that is the only way to understand it (and I formerly thought that's what Jesus meant). However, that viewpoint does not seem to be consistent with what Jesus said. Note that Jesus said *"Not everyone can receive this saying, but only those to whom it is given. For there are eunuchs who have been so from birth..."* It seems to me that eunuchs (those who cannot have a sexual relationship) are said to be the ones who cannot accept the *"saying."* This raises the question as to what *"saying"* Jesus is referring to: the disciples' words saying *"it is better not to marry,"* or his own previous words affirming the normalcy and importance of marriage:

*"Have you not read that he who created them from the beginning made them male and female, and said, 'Therefore a man shall leave his father and his mother and hold fast to his wife, and the two shall become one flesh'? So they are no longer two but one flesh. What therefore God has joined together, let not man*

It doesn't make sense to say that eunuchs can't accept the saying that *"it's better not to marry,"* since eunuchs cannot engage in the normal sexual relationship associated with marriage. So, it appears that the *"saying"* Jesus is referring to is his own previous words (Matthew 19:4-6), which affirm marriage (**not** the disciples' words saying *"it's better not to marry"*). So, I understand that Jesus is saying it is better to marry if people are able to, not that it is better not to marry.

Again, we see how we can read our own viewpoint into scripture, when that viewpoint may not be intended.

## Don't Oversimplify

Consider how complicated natural science has become. The more scientists know about the world, life, and the universe, the more it seems we don't know. I consider that the spiritual world may be just as complicated, or even more complicated. We shouldn't expect there to be easy simple answers to all of our questions about the spiritual realm and the life to come. Yet we long for simple answers, and many people seem to simplify spiritual things to the point that they fall into error.

Considering the field of natural science, scientists are still trying to come up with one unifying theory for everything. However, it seems as though they are still far from that goal. Likewise, theologians have tried to come up with a unifying theory of everything spiritual, often through what is referred to as *systematic theology*. However, in my opinion, they have typically oversimplified things and have fallen short.

For example, the subject of hell and eternal life is an area I think many have oversimplified. There are at least three general views that many people claim scriptural support for:

- Eternal Torment for the Lost
- Limited Torment, Future Destruction

- Eventual Salvation for All

Let's briefly consider each of these views.

**Eternal Torment for the Lost:**  This is sometimes referred to as the traditional view, since it has been the most prevalent view, in recent history at least.  Briefly stated, this view holds that people who die apart from Christ will be condemned eternally to hell, where they will be in torment forever, without end.  This view is typically supported with verses like these:

*"Then he will say also to those on the left hand, 'Depart from me, you cursed, into the eternal fire which is prepared for the devil and his angels...'"*
*Matthew 25:41 WEB*

*"Then he will answer them, saying, 'Most certainly I tell you, because you didn't do it to one of the least of these, you didn't do it to me.' These will go away into eternal punishment, but the righteous into eternal life."*
*Matthew 25:45-46 WEB*

*"And if your eye causes you to sin, tear it out. It is better for you to enter the kingdom of God with one eye than with two eyes to be thrown into hell, 'where their worm does not die and the fire is not quenched.' For everyone will be salted with fire."*  *Mark 9:47-49 ESV*

*The devil who deceived them was thrown into the lake of fire and sulfur, where the beast and the false prophet are also. They will be tormented day and night forever and ever.*  *Revelation 20:10 WEB*

**Limited Torment, Future Destruction:**  This view is different from the traditional view in that it holds that hell is a temporary place of torment.  At the final judgment hell itself will be destroyed, and unbelievers will perish; they will be destroyed and cease to exist when they are cast into the lake of fire (rather than experience conscious torment forever, as appears to be the case for the devil, the beast, and the false prophet, per Revelation 20:10).   This view is typically supported with verses like these:

*A little while, and the wicked will be no more; though you look for them, they will not be found.* Psalm 37:10 NIV

*But the wicked shall perish.   The enemies of Yahweh shall be like the beauty of the fields.   They will vanish— vanish like smoke.* Psalm 37:20 WEB

*For behold, those who are far from you shall perish; you put an end to everyone who is unfaithful to you.* Psalm 73:27 ESV

*A senseless man doesn't know, neither does a fool understand this: though the wicked spring up as the grass, and all the evildoers flourish, they will be destroyed forever.* Psalm 92:6-7 WEB

*For God so loved the world, that he gave his one and only Son, that whoever believes in him should not perish, but have eternal life.* John 3:16 WEB

*...then the Lord knows how to rescue the godly from trials, and to keep the unrighteous under punishment until the day of judgment...* 2Peter 2:9 ESV

*Death and Hades were thrown into the lake of fire. This is the second death, the lake of fire. If anyone was not found written in the book of life, he was cast into the lake of fire.* Revelation 20:14-15 WEB

*"He will wipe away from them every tear from their eyes.   Death will be no more; neither will there be mourning, nor crying, nor pain, any more.   The first things have passed away."* Revelation 21:4 WEB

**Eventual Salvation for All:** This view holds that hell is a place of temporary torment, and that all who go there will eventually repent and receive eternal life.   This view is typically supported with verses like these:

*"Look to me, and be saved, all the ends of the earth; for I am God, and there is no other. I have sworn by myself. The word has gone out of my mouth in righteousness, and will not be revoked, that to me every knee shall bow, every tongue shall take an oath. They will say of me, 'There is righteousness and strength only in Yahweh.'"*
Isaiah 45:22-24 WEB

*For it is written, "'As I live,' says the Lord, 'to me every knee will bow. Every tongue will confess to God.'"*
Romans 14:11 WEB

*Therefore God also highly exalted him, and gave to him the name which is above every name; that at the name of Jesus every knee should bow, of those in heaven, those on earth, and those under the earth, and that every tongue should confess that Jesus Christ is Lord, to the glory of God the Father.* Philippians 2:9-11 WEB

*For to this end we both labor and suffer reproach, because we have set our trust in the living God, who is the Savior of all men, especially of those who believe.*
1Timothy 4:10 WEB

*For the grace of God has appeared, bringing salvation for all people...* Titus 2:11 ESV

*The Lord is not slow concerning his promise, as some count slowness; but is patient with us, not wishing that any should perish, but that all should come to repentance.* 2Peter 3:9 WEB

*And he is the atoning sacrifice for our sins, and not for ours only, but also for the whole world.* 1John 2:2 WEB

I find that all of these diverse verses about hell and eternal life paint a picture that is not as simple as many people try to portray it. Not oversimplifying issues like this can help us avoid mishandling scripture, help us hold a more humble view of our own knowledge and understanding, and help us avoid dividing over secondary issues.

Consider also that some passages may have more than one meaning. For example, a passage may have a direct meaning in line with the specific context in which it was written, while also being prophetic about something that will happen in the future. For example, Psalm 72 may be understood as a prayer by David for Solomon and his kingdom, but it may also be understood as being prophetic about Jesus' future kingdom. I think we oversimplify scripture if we don't recognize multiple levels of meaning that may be present.

In summary, it is easy to mishandle scripture. Mishandling of scripture typically results in spiritual weakness and division among God's people. As we study or teach what scripture says, we should keep in mind Paul's exhortation to Timothy:

*Do your best to present yourself to God as one approved, a worker who has no need to be ashamed, rightly handling the word of truth.* 2Timothy 2:15 ESV

## For Further Reflection

- Have you mishandled the word of truth?

\*\*\*\*\*\*\*\*\*\*\*\*

# Chapter 35
# The Kingdom of God

*"Repent, for the Kingdom of Heaven is at hand!"*
Mathew 3:2, 4:17 WEB

*"But if I by the finger of God cast out demons,*
*then the Kingdom of God has come to you."*
Luke 11:20 WEB

---

What is the primary message and goal of scripture? What is the primary reason that Jesus came? Is the message of scripture primarily about the salvation of people, or something bigger? Consider Jesus' words:

*And when it was day, he departed and went into a desolate place. And the people sought him and came to him, and would have kept him from leaving them, but he said to them, "I must preach the good news of the kingdom of God to the other towns as well; for I was sent for this purpose."* Luke 4:42-43 ESV

What is the *"good news of the kingdom of God"*? What is *"the kingdom of God"*?

Have you noticed how central the Kingdom of God is in the New Testament, and how central the Kingdom was in Jesus teaching? Consider these verses:

*In those days, John the Baptizer came, preaching in the wilderness of Judea, saying, "Repent, for the Kingdom of Heaven is at hand!"* Matthew 3:1-2 WEB

*From that time, Jesus began to preach, and to say, "Repent! For the Kingdom of Heaven is at hand."* Matthew 4:17 WEB

*Now after John was taken into custody, Jesus came into Galilee, preaching the Good News of God's Kingdom, and saying, "The time is fulfilled, and God's Kingdom is*

*at hand! Repent, and believe in the Good News."*
*Mark 1:14-15 WEB*

*He sent them out to preach God's Kingdom and to heal the sick.*
*Luke 9:2 WEB*

*After his suffering, he presented himself to them and gave many convincing proofs that he was alive. He appeared to them over a period of forty days and spoke about the kingdom of God.*
*Acts 1:3 NIV*

*Paul stayed two whole years in his own rented house and received all who were coming to him, preaching God's Kingdom, and teaching the things concerning the Lord Jesus Christ with all boldness, without hindrance.*
*Acts 28:30-31 WEB*

Consider how salvation itself is often spoken about by Jesus in the context of entering God's Kingdom:

*"For I tell you, unless your righteousness exceeds that of the scribes and Pharisees, you will never enter the kingdom of heaven."*
*Matthew 5:20 ESV*

*"Not everyone who says to me, 'Lord, Lord,' will enter into the Kingdom of Heaven; but he who does the will of my Father who is in heaven."*
*Matthew 7:21 WEB*

*And calling to him a child, he put him in the midst of them and said, "Truly, I say to you, unless you turn and become like children, you will never enter the kingdom of heaven."*
*Matthew 18:2-3 ESV*

*"But woe to you, scribes and Pharisees, hypocrites! For you shut the kingdom of heaven in people's faces. For you neither enter yourselves nor allow those who would enter to go in."*
*Matthew 23:13 ESV*

*"And if your eye causes you to sin, tear it out. It is better for you to enter the kingdom of God with one eye than with two eyes to be thrown into hell..."* Mark 9:47 ESV

*"Truly, I say to you, whoever does not receive the*

*kingdom of God like a child shall not enter it."*
Mark 10:15 ESV

*And Jesus looked around and said to his disciples, "How difficult it will be for those who have wealth to enter the kingdom of God!" And the disciples were amazed at his words. But Jesus said to them again, "Children, how difficult it is to enter the kingdom of God! It is easier for a camel to go through the eye of a needle than for a rich person to enter the kingdom of God."*
Mark 10:23-25 ESV

*"Truly, I say to you, whoever does not receive the kingdom of God like a child shall not enter it."*
Luke 18:17 ESV

*Jesus, seeing that he had become sad, said, "How difficult it is for those who have wealth to enter the kingdom of God! For it is easier for a camel to go through the eye of a needle than for a rich person to enter the kingdom of God."*
Luke 18:24-25 ESV

*Jesus answered him, "Truly, truly, I say to you, unless one is born again he cannot see the kingdom of God."*
John 3:3 ESV

*Jesus answered, "Truly, truly, I say to you, unless one is born of water and the Spirit, he cannot enter the kingdom of God."*
John 3:5 ESV

Paul also discusses salvation in the context of the Kingdom of God. Consider these verses:

*Or do you not know that the unrighteous will not inherit the kingdom of God? Do not be deceived: neither the sexually immoral, nor idolaters, nor adulterers, nor men who practice homosexuality, nor thieves, nor the greedy, nor drunkards, nor revilers, nor swindlers will inherit the kingdom of God.*
1 Corinthians 6:9-10 ESV

*Now the works of the flesh are evident: sexual immorality, impurity, sensuality, idolatry, sorcery, enmity, strife, jealousy, fits of anger, rivalries, dissensions, divisions, envy, drunkenness, orgies, and things like these. I warn you, as I warned you before, that those who do such things will not inherit the kingdom of God.* Galatians 5:19-21 ESV

*For you may be sure of this, that everyone who is sexually immoral or impure, or who is covetous (that is, an idolater), has no inheritance in the kingdom of Christ and God.* Ephesians 5:5 ESV

*He has delivered us from the domain of darkness and transferred us to the kingdom of his beloved Son, in whom we have redemption, the forgiveness of sins.* Colossians 1:13-14 ESV

## What Is "the Kingdom of God"?

Before we look at the question *"What is the Kingdom of God?"* a clarification is in needed. In the book of Matthew, the phrase *"Kingdom of heaven"* is common, while in Mark and Luke the phrase *"Kingdom of God"* (or *"God's Kingdom"*) is common. These phrases generally appear to have the same meaning, as may be determined by comparing similar passages. Matthew was apparently writing to a Jewish audience, which often avoided referring to God directly, so that was how Matthew wrote.

So, what Is *"the Kingdom of God"*? While scripture often refers to God's Kingdom, I am not aware of any verses that define it. To answer this question I think we should start with a simple understanding of earthly kingdoms. Please bear with me as I perhaps state the obvious.

A "kingdom" generally refers to a relatively simple form of government with a single person having ultimate authority in all governmental matters. That person is referred to as the "king." A "kingdom" generally has a king, a group of people who are ruled over by the king, and land which they occupy and control. Various people in various positions of authority under the king may help the king rule the kingdom.

Now let's consider how this applies to the meaning of "the Kingdom of God."

As the name "Kingdom of God" implies, God is the king. Since Jesus often refers to the importance of *entering* the Kingdom, it is clear that the Kingdom of God does not include everyone, but only those who have "entered." Based on that, I conclude that the subjects of the Kingdom of God only include those who voluntarily submit to God as their "King" (including angels, people, and every other created being) and meet God's criteria for being in his Kingdom. Likewise, everyone who does not follow God (knowingly or unknowingly) is not part of the Kingdom of God. The Kingdom of God is presently a spiritual kingdom, and physical boundaries do not appear be meaningful. Ultimately, Jesus will return and reign on the earth, and the Kingdom of God will then be a kingdom on Earth, and will be the only kingdom on Earth. Satan's kingdom and other earthly kingdoms will be no more. This transition is discussed in the book of Revelation, and is summarize by this verse:

> *Then the seventh angel blew his trumpet, and there were loud voices in heaven, saying, "The kingdom of the world has become the kingdom of our Lord and of his Christ, and he shall reign forever and ever."*
> *Revelation 11:15 ESV*

However, the kingdom of God is not presently an earthly kingdom. Consider Jesus' words to Pilate:

> *"My Kingdom is not of this world. If my Kingdom were of this world, then my servants would fight, that I wouldn't be delivered to the Jews. But now my Kingdom is not from here."*
> *John 18:36 WEB*

While the Kingdom of God is not *"of this world,"* it is still present in this world. As Jesus clarified:

*Being asked by the Pharisees when the kingdom of God would come, he answered them, "The kingdom of God is not coming in ways that can be observed, nor will they say, 'Look, here it is!' or 'There!' for behold, the kingdom of God is in the midst of you."* Luke 17:20-21 ESV

The kingdom of God is already in our midst. It has a king and subjects, similar to earthly kingdoms. However, it does not have physical boundaries like earthly kingdoms.

## Other Kingdoms and Governments

How does the Kingdom of God relate to other kingdoms and governments? Let's consider both the spiritual realm and the natural realm.

Regarding the spiritual realm, it is important to understand that not everything spiritual is part of God's Kingdom. As with people in the physical realm, not all spiritual beings follow God. As discussed in chapter 10 *"Spirits of Deception,"* the devil is chief among many spirits or angels that live in rebellion toward the Kingdom of God. Consider these verses that refer to the devil and his followers as a separate kingdom:

*"If Satan casts out Satan, he is divided against himself. How then will his kingdom stand?"* Matthew 12:26 WEB

*"If Satan also is divided against himself, how will his kingdom stand? For you say that I cast out demons by Beelzebul."* Luke 11:18 WEB

Now, regarding the natural realm, how does the Kingdom of God relate to natural kingdoms and other forms of human government? This is an area with many differing beliefs among God's people. I'll present my viewpoint here for your prayerful consideration.

Presently, earthly governments, kingdoms, and various organizations are not directly part of either the kingdom of God or the kingdom of Satan, but are influenced by these two spiritual kingdoms to varying degrees, depending on the people associated with them and which spiritual kingdom those people belong to. Some people view all earthly governments as being under the devil's control, partly based on the devil's words to Jesus:

*And the devil took him up and showed him all the kingdoms of the world in a moment of time, and said to him, "To you I will give all this authority and their glory, for it has been delivered to me, and I give it to whom I will. If you, then, will worship me, it will all be yours." And Jesus answered him, "It is written, 'You shall worship the Lord your God, and him only shall you serve.'"* Luke 4:5-8 ESV.

People who hold to that viewpoint apparently believe that the devil was speaking the truth here (they reason that Jesus, in his response, didn't accuse him of lying). However, verses like these have led me to a different conclusion:

*The earth is the LORD's, and everything in it, the world, and all who live in it; for he founded it on the seas and established it on the waters.* Psalm 24:1-2 NIV

*While the words were still in the king's mouth, there fell a voice from heaven, "O King Nebuchadnezzar, to you it is spoken: The kingdom has departed from you, and you shall be driven from among men, and your dwelling shall be with the beasts of the field. And you shall be made to eat grass like an ox, and seven periods of time shall pass over you, until you know that the Most High rules the kingdom of men and gives it to whom he will."* Daniel 4:31-32 ESV

*Then Jesus came to them and said, "All authority in heaven and on earth has been given to me."* Matthew 28:18 NIV

*"You are of your father the devil, and your will is to do your father's desires. He was a murderer from the beginning, and does not stand in the truth, because*

*there is no truth in him. When he lies, he speaks out of his own character, for he is a liar and the father of lies. "*

*John 8:44 ESV*

*Pilate therefore said to him, "Aren't you speaking to me? Don't you know that I have power to release you, and have power to crucify you?"*

*Jesus answered, "You would have no power at all against me, unless it were given to you from above. Therefore he who delivered me to you has greater sin."*

*John 19:10-11 WEB*

*Let every person be subject to the governing authorities. For there is no authority except from God, and those that exist have been instituted by God. Therefore whoever resists the authorities resists what God has appointed, and those who resist will incur judgment. For rulers are not a terror to good conduct, but to bad. Would you have no fear of the one who is in authority? Then do what is good, and you will receive his approval, for he is God's servant for your good. But if you do wrong, be afraid, for he does not bear the sword in vain. For he is the servant of God, an avenger who carries out God's wrath on the wrongdoer.* *Romans 13:1-4 ESV*

*Eat anything sold in the meat market without raising questions of conscience, for, "The earth is the Lord's, and everything in it."* *1Corinthians 10:25-26 NIV*

From these verses it seems clear that God has not yielded total control of the earth and its governments to the devil. The control and influence the devil does have appears to me to be largely accomplished through deception, and is not based on presently having direct authority and power.

Additionally, the book of Revelation shows what will happen in the future as the devil and his associates do temporarily gain significant control over world governments. However, most of what is foretold in Revelation is not the present situation on earth. The devil and his associates today have only limited influence over earthly governments. God's people should not abandon trying to influence governments for good, under the mistaken notion that the devil is in complete control in those realms.

One result of these kinds of misunderstandings is that many believers, who live under a democratic form of government, believe it is wrong to vote in various elections (since they believe it is all controlled by the devil). The result is that unsaved people have more influence in government than they should, and believers have less influence than they should.

In a similar way, many believers take such verses as Daniel 4:32 (above) and reason that since *"the Most High rules the kingdom of men and gives it to whom he will"* that God controls governments and who leads them. These believers also often don't vote, reasoning that they should just trust God regarding the outcome, since God *gives it to whom he will.* Again, the result is that unsaved people have more influence in government than they should, and believers have less influence than they should.

I have a different perspective: Where believers live under some form of democracy, God has *given* the government of that country to the citizens of that country, and the people, including believers, are responsible for electing their leaders and making decisions that are up for a vote. If you live under some form of democracy, and are qualified to vote, what will you do with the governing power you have, which God has entrusted to you? Will you use the power God has given you to promote good in your country, or will you do nothing with it?

Though the context of the following verses primarily has to do with how we use money and wealth, I think the same principle applies to other areas of power and influence:

*"Whoever can be trusted with very little can also be trusted with much, and whoever is dishonest with very little will also be dishonest with much. So if you have not been trustworthy in handling worldly wealth, who will trust you with true riches? And if you have not been trustworthy with someone else's property, who will give you property of your own?"* Luke 16:10-12 NIV

Are you being trustworthy with the resources, power, and influence God has given to you?

## Living Under Existing Governments

Now let's look at a related question: Does the "Kingdom of God" seek to overthrow existing governments and establish itself in their place? Should believers seek to overthrow existing governments?

While the Kingdom of God will eventually supersede all other governments (as explained in the book of Revelation), God does not, generally speaking, call us to oppose legitimate governments today. Consider these verses:

*Let every person be subject to the governing authorities. For there is no authority except from God, and those that exist have been instituted by God. Therefore whoever resists the authorities resists what God has appointed, and those who resist will incur judgment. For rulers are not a terror to good conduct, but to bad. Would you have no fear of the one who is in authority? Then do what is good, and you will receive his approval, for he is God's servant for your good. But if you do wrong, be afraid, for he does not bear the sword in vain. For he is the servant of God, an avenger who carries out God's wrath on the wrongdoer. Therefore one must be in subjection, not only to avoid God's wrath but also for the sake of conscience. For because of this you also pay taxes, for the authorities are ministers of God, attending to this very thing. Pay to all what is owed to them: taxes to whom taxes are owed, revenue to whom revenue is owed, respect to whom respect is owed, honor to whom honor is owed.* Romans 13:1-7 ESV

*Be subject for the Lord's sake to every human institution, whether it be to the emperor as supreme, or to governors as sent by him to punish those who do evil and to praise those who do good. For this is the will of God, that by doing good you should put to silence the ignorance of foolish people. Live as people who are free, not using your freedom as a cover-up for evil, but living as servants of God. Honor everyone. Love the brotherhood. Fear God. Honor the emperor.* 1Peter 2:13-17 ESV

Clearly, these verses do not promote rebellion against human governments. However, sometimes human governments exceed their God-given authority and try to require believers to do things that are clearly contrary to following Jesus, or they may try to prohibit believers from doing things that are necessary in following Jesus. Here are some verse references that give us some guidance in such situations:

- **Exodus 1:15-21:** The Hebrew midwives refused to kill the Hebrew baby boys, in defiance of a government mandate to do so.

- **Exodus 1:22 to 2:10:** Moses' family refused to throw baby Moses into the Nile River, even though the government told them to do so.

- **Joshua 2:1-22 and Hebrews 11:31:** Rahab was commended for hiding the spies, even though this was clearly in defiance of the government she was under.

- **Daniel 3:1-30:** Shadrach, Meshach and Abednego refused to bow down to the image of gold, even though the king clearly required them to do so.

- **Daniel 6:1-28:** Daniel continued praying to God, even

though the king's edict prohibited doing so.

- **1 Kings 18:4, 13:** When Jezebel was killing prophets, Obadiah hid one hundred of them in caves, and supplied them with food and water.

- **Acts 4:1-22:** Peter and John refused to stop talking about Jesus, even though the religious leaders prohibited them from doing so.

- **Acts 5:17-42:** The apostles refused to stop talking about Jesus, even though the religious leaders prohibited them from doing so.

Are you faced with similar circumstances? If so, ask God for wisdom and strength to do what is right, and to deliver you from fear in such circumstances. Only through the power of the Holy Spirit can we remain steadfast through all our trials.

## Entering the Kingdom

All who have salvation through Jesus have already entered into the Kingdom of God, at least in one sense. As Paul wrote:

> *He has delivered us from the domain of darkness and transferred us to the kingdom of his beloved Son, in whom we have redemption, the forgiveness of sins.*
>
> *Colossians 1:13-14 ESV*

We are saved through repentance and faith in Jesus, as discussed in a previous book: *"Foundations for Eternal Life"* (see especially chapter 16 *"What must I Do to be Saved"*). Likewise, we also initially enter the Kingdom of God through repentance and faith in Jesus. Receiving salvation and entering the Kingdom go hand-in-hand.

However, the Kingdom is not yet fully developed, and scripture also speaks of a future entry into God's Kingdom, or a future inheritance of God's Kingdom:

*"When the Son of Man comes in his glory, and all the angels with him, then he will sit on his glorious throne. Before him will be gathered all the nations, and he will separate people one from another as a shepherd separates the sheep from the goats. And he will place the sheep on his right, but the goats on the left. Then the King will say to those on his right, 'Come, you who are blessed by my Father, inherit the kingdom prepared for you from the foundation of the world.'"*

*Matthew 25:31-34 ESV*

*When they had preached the gospel to that city and had made many disciples, they returned to Lystra and to Iconium and to Antioch, strengthening the souls of the disciples, encouraging them to continue in the faith, and saying that through many tribulations we must enter the kingdom of God.*

*Acts 14:21-22 ESV*

*Therefore, since we are receiving a kingdom that cannot be shaken, let us be thankful, and so worship God acceptably with reverence and awe, for our "God is a consuming fire."*

*Hebrews 12:28-29 NIV*

*As you know, we exhorted, comforted, and implored every one of you, as a father does his own children, to the end that you should walk worthily of God, who calls you into his own Kingdom and glory.*

*1Thessalonians 2:11-12 WEB*

*Listen, my beloved brothers. Didn't God choose those who are poor in this world to be rich in faith, and heirs of the Kingdom which he promised to those who love him?*

*James 2:5 WEB*

*Therefore, brothers, be more diligent to make your calling and election sure. For if you do these things, you will never stumble. For thus you will be richly supplied with the entrance into the eternal Kingdom of our Lord and Savior, Jesus Christ.*

*2Peter 1:10-11 WEB*

So, let us rejoice to be part of God's Kingdom today; and let us look forward to an even greater future inheritance in God's Kingdom!

## Living in the Kingdom

How does being part of God's Kingdom affect our lives? Jesus spoke many parables on the topic of what *"the Kingdom of Heaven is like."* Let's start by reviewing what Jesus said on that topic. Here is a list of verses giving the introduction to each parable, and a brief encouragement for each one. If you have time, consider opening scripture and reading each parable in full.

> *He set another parable before them, saying, "The Kingdom of Heaven is like a man who sowed good seed in his field..."*
> Matthew 13:24 WEB

May we not be discouraged by the many weeds growing around us, knowing that they will be separated when the day of harvest comes.

> *He set another parable before them, saying, "The Kingdom of Heaven is like a grain of mustard seed, which a man took, and sowed in his field..."*
> Matthew 13:31 WEB

May the Kingdom grow big in our lives, though it starts out small.

> *He spoke another parable to them. "The Kingdom of Heaven is like yeast, which a woman took, and hid in three measures of meal, until it was all leavened."*
> Matthew 13:33 WEB

May all aspects of our lives be rightly influenced by the Kingdom of God.

> *"Again, the Kingdom of Heaven is like treasure hidden in the field, which a man found, and hid. In his joy, he goes and sells all that he has, and buys that field."*
> Matthew 13:44 WEB

May we rejoice in the great value of the Kingdom, and may we possess it forever.

*"Again, the Kingdom of Heaven is like a man who is a merchant seeking fine pearls..."*　　*Matthew 13:45 WEB*

Again, may we rejoice in the great value of the Kingdom, and may we possess it forever.

*"Again, the Kingdom of Heaven is like a dragnet, that was cast into the sea, and gathered some fish of every kind..."*　　*Matthew 13:47 WEB*

May we be counted among the good fish.

*He said to them, "Therefore, every scribe who has been made a disciple in the Kingdom of Heaven is like a man who is a householder, who brings out of his treasure new and old things."*　　*Matthew 13:52 WEB*

May we understand both new things and old things well.

*"Therefore the Kingdom of Heaven is like a certain king, who wanted to reconcile accounts with his servants."*　　*Matthew 18:23 WEB*

May we forgive others, as God has forgiven us.

*"For the Kingdom of Heaven is like a man who was the master of a household, who went out early in the morning to hire laborers for his vineyard."*
*Matthew 20:1 WEB*

May we be happy to work in the Master's vineyard, and be satisfied to receive the same wages as others who may not have worked as hard or as long.

*"The Kingdom of Heaven is like a certain king, who made a marriage feast for his son..."*　　*Matthew 22:2  WEB*

May we all rejoice at being invited to the marriage feast, and not let the things of this life keep us from being there.

*"Then the Kingdom of Heaven will be like ten virgins,*

*who took their lamps, and went out to meet the bridegroom."*

*Matthew 25:1 WEB*

May we wait patiently for the bridegroom, and have plenty of oil to keep our lamps burning, should he be delayed.

*He also said, "This is what the kingdom of God is like. A man scatters seed on the ground."*

*Mark 4:26 NIV*

May the Kingdom grow in our lives, though we do not know how.

*Again he said, "What shall we say the kingdom of God is like, or what parable shall we use to describe it? It is like a mustard seed..."*

*Mark 4:30-31 NIV*

Again, may the Kingdom grow big in our lives, though it starts out small.

All those parables are helpful in understanding what the Kingdom of God is like, but they aren't very clear regarding how we should live day-to-day in the Kingdom of God. What does our King expect of us? How should we live? To answer those questions, other parts of scripture must be looked at. While answering those questions is beyond the scope of this present book, those questions have already been partly answered in a previous book: *"Foundations for Eternal Life."* That book looks at what scripture says about *"Things We Do," "Things God Does," "Things God and We Do,"* and *"Things We Should NOT Do."* As already mentioned, a free ebook version of that book should be available at

ShalomKoinonia.org

To live rightly in God's Kingdom, it is of utmost importance to understand what God has already done for us in bringing us into his Kingdom. Here is a brief list of some of the benefits of being in the Kingdom of God, of being "in Christ" (these are copied from chapter 52 of *"Foundations for Eternal Life"*):

- Because Jesus shed his blood, our sins are forgiven.
- Because Jesus died, we are set free from sin.
- Because Jesus rose from the dead, we have new life.
- Because Jesus is exalted, the Holy Spirit is poured out.
- We are members of one body, the body of Christ.
- God has given us every spiritual blessing *in Christ*.
- We are no longer condemned.
- We are set free from the law of sin and death.
- We are all sons of God through faith.
- We are God's workmanship, created to do good works.
- We have been brought near to God.

Are these things true of you? If you have genuinely turned to God in repentance, and have faith in the Lord Jesus, then yes, these things are true of you! I encourage you to **read aloud** the following list of the same things, except that each one has been personalized and exclamation marks have been added:

- Because Jesus shed his blood, my sins are forgiven!
- Because Jesus died, I am set free from sin!
- Because Jesus rose from the dead, I have new life!
- Because Jesus is exalted, the Holy Spirit is poured out on me!
- I am a member of one body, the body of Christ!
- God has given me every spiritual blessing *in Christ!*
- I am no longer condemned!
- I am set free from the law of sin and death!
- I am a son of God through faith!
- I am God's workmanship, created to do good works!
- I have been brought near to God!

Perhaps it would be good to read that list **out loud** again! Consider printing that list, posting it where you will see it, and occasionally repeating that list out loud. Knowing who you are *in Christ* is key to walking in wisdom. Keep in mind that all of these things are true of you today, if you are a genuine follower of our Lord Jesus, and are, therefore, part of the Kingdom of God.

Now let's consider some of our future inheritance in the Kingdom of God:

*Then I saw a new heaven and a new earth, for the first heaven and the first earth had passed away, and the sea was no more. And I saw the holy city, new Jerusalem, coming down out of heaven from God, prepared as a bride adorned for her husband. And I heard a loud voice from the throne saying, "Behold, the dwelling place of God is with man. He will dwell with them, and they will be his people, and God himself will be with them as their God. He will wipe away every tear from their eyes, and death shall be no more, neither shall there be mourning, nor crying, nor pain anymore, for the former things have passed away."*

*And he who was seated on the throne said, "Behold, I am making all things new." Also he said, "Write this down, for these words are trustworthy and true." And he said to me, "It is done! I am the Alpha and the Omega, the beginning and the end. To the thirsty I will give from the spring of the water of life without payment. The one who conquers will have this heritage, and I will be his God and he will be my son."*

*Revelation 21:1-7 ESV*

*I did not see a temple in the city, because the Lord God Almighty and the Lamb are its temple. The city does not need the sun or the moon to shine on it, for the glory of God gives it light, and the Lamb is its lamp. The nations will walk by its light, and the kings of the earth will bring their splendor into it. On no day will its gates ever be shut, for there will be no night there. The glory and honor of the nations will be brought into it. Nothing impure will ever enter it, nor will anyone who does what is shameful or deceitful, but only those whose names are written in the Lamb's book of life.*   Revelation 21:22-27 NIV

*No longer will there be any curse. The throne of God and of the Lamb will be in the city, and his servants will serve him. They will see his face, and his name will be on their foreheads. There will be no more night. They will not need the light of a lamp or the light of the sun, for the Lord God will give them light. And they will reign for ever and ever.*   Revelation 22:3-5 NIV

Clearly, our future inheritance in the Kingdom of God is something to long for! I especially like this part:

*"He will wipe away every tear from their eyes, and death shall be no more, neither shall there be mourning, nor crying, nor pain anymore, for the former things have passed away."*   Revelation 21:4 ESV

However, let's not just long for our future inheritance in the Kingdom of God; let's remember that God's Kingdom has already come near to us! We have already been greatly blessed through God's grace!

Recall again some of the benefits of the Kingdom that are already ours: God has given us eternal life, and this life is in his Son Jesus! Our sins have been forgiven! We have been set free from the power of sin! We have been born again! God has poured out his Holy Spirit on us! We are members of one body, the body of Christ! We have been given every spiritual blessing, in Christ!

How great is God's love for us! How marvelous is his grace toward us! How great and marvelous are his works! Therefore, stand firm in the Lord! Let us joyfully follow our King! Let us serve one another in love! Let us rejoice and give thanks to God, through Jesus our Lord, both now and forevermore!

\*\*\*\*\*\*\*\*\*\*\*\*